Homeward Journey

Homeward Journey

Readings in African Studies

Herbert T. Neve
Editor

Africa World Press, Inc.

P.O. Box 1892
Trenton, New Jersey 08607

Africa World Press, Inc.
P.O. Box 1892
Trenton, NJ 08607

Cover Design & Book Design: Jonathan Gullery

Library of Congress Cataloging-in-Publication Data

Homeward journey : Readings in African Studies / edited by Herbert T.
   Neve.
          p.   cm.
     Includes bibliographical references.
     ISBN 0-86543-407-7. -- ISBN 0-86543-408-5 (pbk.)
      1. Africa--History--Juvenile literature.   [1. Africa--History.]
   I. Neve, Herbert T.
   DT20.H65   1993
   960--dc20
                                                          93-28433
                                                            CIP
                                                            AC

dedicated to my
Mother and Father

Both would have been very glad to have seen this book and witnessed its use among the learners of this generation.

Table of Contents

Part I

Introduction to Africa

Definitions

Ancient and Medieval Africa

Part II

The Traditional Way of Life in Africa

Part III

The European Presence in Africa

Part IV

Nationalism, Independence and Nation-Building

ACKNOWLEDGEMENTS I

For permission to reprint copyrighted material, grateful acknowledgement is made to the following sources:

Little, Brown and Company: Excerpt from *The Africans: A Triple Heritage* by Ali A. Mazrui. Copyright © 1986 by Ali A. Mazrui; Copyright © 1986 by Greater Washington Educational Telecommunications Association.

Praeger Publications, an imprint of Greenwood Press: Excerpt from *The Africans, Study Guide* by Colin Turnbull, Toby K. Levine and Colin M. Turnbull, Eds. Copyright © 1986 by Greater Washington Educational Telecommunications, Inc. "The Beginning of the Transatlantic Trade," by Robert I. Rotberg from *The Africans: A Reader,* Ali A. Mazrui and Toby Kleben Levine, Eds. Copyright © 1986 by Greater Washington Educational Telecommunications Association, Inc.

Interact Research Centre: "Traditional African Religion and Christianity" by Vincent Mulago from *African Traditional Religion* by Jacob Olupona, Ed. Published in the United States by the International Religious Foundation and printed by Paragon House. Copyright © 1991 by Interact Research Centre.

Longman Group UK: "The Geography of Africa," "The Maghreb," "The Black Peoples South of the Sahara," "The Changed Situation in the Nineteenth Century," by J. D. Omer-Cooper from *The Making of Modern Africa* Vol I. Copyright 1982 © by Longman Group UK. "Traditional African Art" by J. R. O. Ojo, "African Languages," by Adebesi Afolayan, "Introduction

1550-1888 by Katia M. Mattoso, translated by Arthur Goldhammer, with a forward by Stuart B. Schwartz. Copyright © 1986 by Rutgers, The State University.

AMS Press: Excerpt from *An Account of the Slave Trade on the Coast of Africa* by Alexander Falconbridge, 1977. Public Domain.

The Dorsey Press: "Taken from the Guinea Coast as a Child," by Venture Smith from *Afro-American History – Primary Source*, 2nd edition, 1988, Thomas R. Frazier, Ed. Public Domain.

Atheneum Publishers, an imprint of Macmillan Publishing Company: "Redeeming the African Motherland." by Marcus Garvey from *Philosophy and Opinions of Marcus Garvey* by Amy Jacques Garvey, Ed. Copyright © 1923; Copyright 1925 by Amy Jacques Garvey.

Northwestern University Press: "African Nationalism and Nationhood" by John N. Paden from *The African Experience*, Vol. I, John N. Paden and Edward W. Soja, Eds. Copyright © 1970 Northwestern University Press.

Monthly Review Foundation: Excerpt from *Consciencism* by Kwame Nkrumah. Published by Monthly Review Press. Copyright © 1970 by Monthly Review Press.

The African-American Institute: "The Question of South Africa," by Desmond Tutu from *Africa Report*. Copyright © 1985 by The African-American Institute.

Random House, Inc.: "'No!' He Said," from *Mandela's Earth* by Wole Soyinka. Copyright © 1988 by Wole Soyinka. Excerpt from *Slavery to Freedom* by John Hope Franklin. Copyright © 1947, 1956, 1967, 1974, 1980, 1988 by Alfred A. Knopf, Inc.

Julius K. Nyerere: "The Future of Africa," from *Freedom and Unity* by Julius K. Nyerere. Published by Oxford University Press 1986. Copyright © 1966 by Julius K. Nyerere.

Acknowledgements II

The task of putting these selected reading together began in the spring of 1987 when I was given a term off from my teaching duties by the College of Liberal Arts at Wright State University. I was given my leave to design a new survey course on Africa. That fragile project was launched for the first time in September of that same year. A steady effort was made to improve the selections, the accompanying clarifications, and the overall concept of the course and the accompanying study materials. Now I am confident enough to proceed with the publication of this anthology.

Thanks for the financial and material backing to bring the entire project to this point goes to Lilly Howard, Associate Vice President for Academic Affairs of the University; Perry Moore, Dean of the College of Liberal Arts; and Bill Rickert, Associate Dean and Director of the General Education Program of the College of Liberal Arts.

Professor Barbara Green, my first colleague to collaborate in the teaching of this course, has provided her unwaivering support and encouragement ever since she arrived in the fall of 1987 to take a position in the History Department in the field of African-American Studies. All of us who taught the regional studies courses in the new general education program at that time went through the University sponsored faculty development program in order to prepare for what was to be a distinctly new and different interdisciplinary effort in teaching. Professor Green, in addition to her active participation and outstanding skill in the teaching program, provided invaluable insights and knowledge in the development of this text. She stands at the pinnacle of those to whom I owe a debt of gratitude.

I am deeply grateful to my editor, Mr. Kassahun Checole who saw that this material had the potential for securing a niche in the current market for selling books. His patience, wisdom and evenhandedness in working with me until the end was in sight receives my undying appreciation and gratitude.

Other persons who have helped me with the technical production of this manuscript and without whom this work would not have been completed are Rebecca Steele, Kelly Treat and Win Hammer. Also, for her extreme care, consummate skill and good composure withal in getting the final corrections made in time for publication I am especially indebted to Kelly Treat.

For all else I accept responsibility: and for the faults which those who are concerned will notice as this book enters the stream of paper in print, I will only be too happy to hear about. When the opportunity arrives again the next time, it will be possible for me to do better.

PREFACE

Homeward Journey is a response to a growing need for accessible introductory materials on Africa. An increasing demand that students acquire a global perspective, in general, coupled with the mounting interest in Africa, specifically, calls for the development of study resources which are comprehendible to freshman and sophomore students. *Homeward Journey* is an interdisciplinary work which meets these requisites. The anthology's scope is chronological and topical. It begins with traditional societies and ends with nationalism and independence. Both primary and secondary sources have been selected from the fields of history, geography, anthropology, political science, literature, poetry, art, music and religion. The work is divided into four sections.

Possible definitions of Africa are introduced in section one within a geographical-historical context. As for geography and history, J. D. Omer-Cooper's treatments of African history and geography are set within his extensive knowledge of ethnology and demography. For his unique approach there may be no rival in studies in African history today. Chancellor Williams, in turn, persists with determination and boldness, backed by much research into original sources, to raise essential questions about the ties between ancient Egypt and the rest of Africa. These writers together with Joseph E. Harris and John Hope Franklin provide the student with excellent information on ancient African kingdoms.

In addition to geography and history, the other link to Africa's ancient past is the study of the traditional African sociocultural way of life. Section two focuses on this remarkable phenomenon. Even when the impact of the twin forces of secularization and religion, imported from abroad, are taken into account, the traditional African family precedes all that; and yet today it remains the most vital social institution on the continent.

The specific descriptions of the Ndembu and Gikuyu rituals by Victor Turner and Jomo Kenyatta are like windows to the outside observer looking in on the dynamic processes of social harmonization. John Hope Franklin's description of traditional African society provides an historian's viewpoint based on a more characteristically western type of social analysis. The other readings in this section by both African and non-African writers alike on the diverse cultural expressions are to be viewed from a somewhat synthetic perspective.

The western penetration and domination of Africa is featured in section three. John Hope Franklin's description and analysis of the origins of European traffic in slaves offers excellent insight into Europe's decision to use slave labor to develop the Americas. Katia M. Mattoso's article demonstrates that the African Diaspora's contribution as a result of the trans-Atlantic slave trade extends far beyond the economic realm. Other readings enhance one's understanding of the slave trade and the slave experience.

By the nineteenth century, Europeans' decision to colonize Africa marked the beginning of slavery of another kind. European colonization of Africa between the 1880s and the 1960s in effect was an extension of African slavery. Those features which characterize slavery particularly in the United States and Brazil manifested themselves on a larger, more organized and systematic scale in Africa as European nations supported the rise of their urban-industrial societies by oppressing and exploiting the rich human and material resources of Africa. The course of the impact of this process is described in *Homeward Journey* .

Section four reflects upon the political phenomenon of the extremely rapid and forceful rise of African nationalism, independence and nationhood after World War II. Kwame Nkrumah, Jomo Kenyatta and Julius Nyerere from Ghana, Kenya, and Tanzania, respectively, are among the leaders of the first successful African freedom movements. Born into traditional

African ethnic societies, each of these men assisted in the over-throw of European rule in Africa and led their countries in the achievement of independence and nationhood. The articles by Nkrumah and Nyerere convey some of the awesome sense of the vastness of the change which these individuals symbolize for Africa and its people in the post World War II period. Steve Biko, Desmond Tutu, and Nelson Mandela are representative of the struggle which continues. Marcus Garvey, Oluwole Omoni, John N. Paden, and Basil Davidson help the student to understand the historical, ideological and political dynamic processes of these changes.

Finally, questions for review and discussion, added at the end of each section, are included to clarify central themes and issues and encourage students to develop critical thinking skills. They help them evaluate and respond to what they read within the broad scope of African geographical, social, historical, cultural and political writing.

The methodology is Afrocentric. This refers to a basic principle which has been assumed and asserted by our humen forebears as they interacted with their environments and created their own vibrant and dynamic "worlds" ever since the beginning. It was knowledge by experience that the whole is equal to more than the sum of its parts. Some philosophers today refer to this as "pre-reflective" knowledge. The Afrocentric perspective clearly sees that even when some can allow the place and importance of "lived experience" in their philosophical reflections, it is difficult in the modern technical, scientific and secular orientations to find forms or structures through which the experience is able to find expression.

Afrocentrism is not "nativism;" yet it claims that the traditional social experience of the peoples of Africa today still maintains structures and forms that are more directly capable of giving some meaning to "lived experience" in the sense of the phrase, "The whole is equal to more than...." A corollary to this is the belief that traditional African society is perhaps the only expression of "socio-spirituality" which still exists today as a dynamic social force.

In conclusion, *Homeward Journey* takes students on a comprehensive interdisciplinary journey through Africa from its ancient kingdoms to its place in the Global Village. Students will come away from this volume with a clearer intellectual understanding of the perennial importance of this continent.

present
persistent
enduring

Part I

Introduction to Africa

Africa, the birthplace of humanity, is a vast and diverse continent (30,321,130 square kilometers or 11,682,000 square miles). It is rich in geographical features, climate, history, people and culture. Likewise, examined in a somewhat different light, Africa also is remarkably unified in the same areas as those listed above. And, although these statements may appear to be contradictory, they are not. Both views can be combined to present a perspective of Africa as a whole unit. Indeed, the most widely accepted definition of Africa today, the "Whole Continent" theory is growing in importance as reflected, for example, in the Organization of African Unity (OAU) and in the various attempts to establish both past and present regional cooperation on the continent as well as attempts to establish Africa's future role as a world power.

In order to get close to the richness of Africa, it is vital to study the relationship between Africa's history and geographical features. J.D. Omer-Cooper provides this knowledge in a very brief summary of the geography of the African continent.

Other scholars including Joseph E. Harris, Chancellor Williams and John Hope Franklin contribute selections on ancient and medieval societies and culture that are representative of northern, eastern, western and southern Africa. From the Berbers of northwestern Africa to Egypt and Ethiopia in the east, to Ghana, Mali and Songhay in the west and finally to the southern empires of Monomopata and Angola, one finds evidence of a rich culture and heritage in Mother Africa, hundreds, if not thousands, of years prior to European contact with the continent of Africa and its people.

The level of these ancient and medieval civilizations varied from primitive, nomadic cultures to highly centralized governments, hereditary monarchies with complex bureaucracies and centers of scholarly and commercial pursuits as well as highly skilled and creative artisans. Together these readings present a complete picture of Africa that serve as an introduction to the continent and simultaneously dispel long-standing myths and misconceptions about Africa.

1. Definition of Africa: "Trans-Red Sea Theory"

ALI MAZRUI

Born in Kenya, political scientist Ali Mazrui views Saudi Arabia as part of the continent of Africa. Mazrui asserts that the Red Sea has never constituted either a true natural or cultural barrier between Africa and Arabia. Rather, the Red Sea united the great land mass of Africa with the Arabian peninsula into a single continent. The following selection describes Mazrui's "Trans-Red Sea Theory" and suggests that the problems of cultural, geographical and linguistic identity concerning the Arabian peninsula could partially be solved if scholars accepted his assertions.

Where then is Africa? What is Africa? How sensible are its boundaries? Islands can be very far from Africa and still be part of Africa - provided they are not too near another major land mass. But a peninsula can be arbitrarily dis-Africanized. Madagascar is separated from the African continent by the 500-mile-wide Mozambique channel. Mauritius lies well over 1000 miles from the African coastline. Greater Yemen, on the other hand, is separated from Djibouti by only a stone's throw at the Strait of Bab el Mandeb. Yet Madagascar and Mauritius are politically part of Africa, while Greater Yemen is not. Much of the post-colonial African scholarship has addressed itself to the artificiality of the boundaries of contemporary African states. But little attention has been paid to the artificiality of the boundaries of the African continent itself. Why should north Africa end on the Red Sea when eastern Africa does not end on the Mozambique channel? Why should Tananarive be an African capital when Aden is not?

There have been discussions in Africa as to whether the Sahara Desert is a chasm or a link. Continental Pan-Africanism asserts that the Sahara is a sea of communication rather than a chasm of separation. Yet there are some who would argue that north Africa is not "really Africa." Why? Because it is more like Arabia. But in that case, it would be just as logical to push the boundary of north Africa further east to include Arabia, to refuse to recognize the Red Sea as a chasm, just as the trans-Saharan Pan-Africanist has refused to concede such a role to the Sahara Desert. Why not assert that the African continent ends neither on the southern extremity of the Sahara nor on the western shore of the Red Sea? Should Africa move not only northwards to the Mediterranean but also north-eastward to the Persian Gulf? I am not suggesting that this is within the realms of practical politics or likely geographical redefinition at the moment; rather that we should question Europe's decisions about boundaries of Africa and the identity of Africans.

The most pernicious sea in Africa's history may well be the Red Sea. This thin line of water has been deemed to be more relevant for defining where Africa ends than all the evidence of geology, geography, history and culture. The northeastern boundary of Africa has been defined by a strip of water in the teeth of massive ecological and cultural evidence to the contrary.

The problem goes back several million years when three cracks emerged on the eastern side of Africa. As Colin McEvedy put it:

> One crack broke Arabia away, creating the Gulf of Aden and the Red Sea, and reducing the areas of contact between Africa and Asia to the Isthmus of Suez.

The 'contact' at the Isthmus was definitional. It depended upon looking at the Red Sea as a divide. Three cracks had occurred on the African crust - yet only the one which has resulted in a sea was permitted to "dis-Africanize" what lay beyond the sea. The other two cracks resulted in "rift valleys," straightsided trenches averaging thirty miles across. The eastern and western rifts left the African continent intact but the emergence of a strip of water called the Red Sea had resulted in the physical separation of Africa from Arabia.

The final drama in the separation of the Arabian peninsula from what we now call Africa occurred in the nineteenth century. If the Arabs had been in control of their own destiny they could have been discussing building communications between the two parts of the Arab world. But, in fact, Egypt in the nineteenth century was oriented towards Europe. And so the Suez Canal was built, by a Frenchman, Ferdinand de Lesseps, not in order to facilitate traffic between Africa and Arabia but to make it easier for Europe to trade with the rest of the world. An estimated 120,000 Egyptians lost their lives in the ten years it took to build the Suez Canal (1859-69). A natural cataclysm which had occurred several million years previously and torn off the Arabian peninsula from the rest of Africa was now completed at Suez through its canal. European power and European pre-eminence in map-making decided that Africa ended on the western side of the Red Sea and on the west bank of the Suez Canal, in spite of the similarity of the geology of north-eastern Africa and Arabia on either side of the Red Sea, in spite also of the similarity of language and culture, and the artificiality of a continental boundary based on a man-made canal.

The separation of Arabia from Africa by the Red Sea is not even a geological separation. As Paul Bohannan put it,

> Geologically, the whole of the Arabian peninsula must be considered as unitary with the African continent. The Rift Valley that cuts through the whole begins in Anatolia, in northern Turkey, stretches through what is now the Jordan Valley and the Dead Sea; it then follows down the length of the Red Sea (which is best thought of as an island lake with a small opening into the Indian Ocean), and down through Lake Rudolf.

In spite of the geological unity of Arabia and Africa and the former land link between the two continents at the Suez Isthmus, European geographers classified Arabia as being part of Asia.

What a geological crack had once put asunder, the forces of geography, history and culture have been trying to bind together again ever since. Who are the Amhara of Ethiopia if not a people probably descended from south Arabians? What is Amharic but a Semitic language? What is a Semitic language if not a branch of the Afro-Asian family of languages? Was the Semitic parental language born in Africa and then exported across the Red Sea? Or was it from the Arabian peninsula originally and then descended upon such people as the Amhara? How much of a bridge between Arabia and Africa are the Somali? All these are lingo-cultural questions which raise the issue of whether the geological secession of Arabia several million years ago has been in the process of being neutralized by the intimate cultural integration between Arabia, the Horn and North Africa.

In the linguistic field it is no longer easy to determine where African indigenous languages end and Semitic trends begin. There was a time when both Hamites and Semites were regarded by European scholars such as C. G. Seligman as basically alien to Africa. In due course Hamites were regarded as a fictitious category - and the people represented by the term (such as the Tutsi of Rwanda and Burundi) were accepted as indisputably African. What about the Semites? They have undoubtedly existed in world history. But are they 'Africans' who crossed the Red Sea - like Moses on the run from the Pharaoh? Or are the Semites originally 'Arabians' who penetrated Africa? These problems of identity would be partially solved overnight if the Arabian peninsula was part of Africa.

Excerpt from: Ali Mazrui, *The Africans: A Triple Heritage* (Boston: Little, Brown and Company), pp. 28-32.

2. Definition of Africa: "Whole Continent Concept"

COLIN TURNBULL

While some scholars propose to examine Africa as a divided continent north and south of the Sahara Desert, anthropologist Colin Turnbull insists that Africa is a whole continent with its geography, culture and history intact. Turnbull affirms that there is sufficient cultural unity, despite widespread diversity, to "reasonably generalize" about the whole of Africa. The following excerpt lists the specific cultural features that he believes apply generally throughout the continent of Africa.

There are several vital issues that should be faced squarely in any attempt to understand "Africa" or "Africans." The first question is, Can we reasonably generalize about the whole of Africa? On the whole, the answer to that is yes. In spite of the enormous diversity of outward form there is a high degree of fundamental similarity among indigenous African cultures. Among the many common elements may be found: the importance of cooperation and harmonious community interactions (as contrasted with the rampant individuality of Western culture); the ability to adapt readily to new circumstances, and to assimilate new elements without losing their own fundamental character; the virtually sacred status of family and the land; a sense of unity with the rest of nature, and a belief that the vital force which permeates all things can be manipulated for either good or ill; a belief in the continuous participation of ancestors and the dead in the life of the community; the use of divination to determine the relationship between good or bad behavior and other events, particularly deaths and illnesses; the concept of witchcraft as an explanation for specific events; and an aesthetic approach to all of daily life.

Excerpt from: Toby Levine, Colin Turnbull, et. al. editors, *The Africans, Study Guide* (Westport, CT.: Greenwood Publishing Group, 1980) p. 16.

3. Definition of Africa: "Vital Union — The African Worldview"

VINCENT MULAGO

The following selection by Vincent Mulago, an African theologian, is an excellent description of the importance of the family in Africa. This "vital union" is key to understanding the African Life Cycle and worldview. The family is the last word on the customs, institutions, wisdom, philosophy and religion of Africans. The family is Africa - Africa is the family.

Unity of life and participation.

By unity in life or vital union, we understand a relationship in being and life of each person with descendants, family, brothers, and sisters in the clan, with ancestors, and with God who is the ultimate source of all life: *Nyamuzinda* (the completion of everything) according to the Bashi of Zaire, or *Imana* (source of all happiness) for Ruanda and Burundi; and an analogous ontic relation of each with their patrimony, their land, and all it contains and produces, with all that grows and lives there.

If you wish, vital union is the bond joining together, vertically and horizontally, beings living and dead; it is the life-giving principle in all. It is the result of communion, a participation in the one reality, the one vital principal that unites various beings.

This life, with which Africans are preoccupied, is not simply empirical life but also super-empirical life (life beyond the grave) since, in their view, the two are inseparable and interdependent. Two beliefs underlie veneration of the dead: survival of the individual after death and the interchange of relations between the living and the dead. This double belief, which amounts to an axiom, knows no skeptics.

The life of the individual is understood as participated life. The members of the tribe, the clan, the family know that they live not by a life of their own but by that of the community. They know that, if separated from the community, they would lack the means to survive; above all, they know that their life is a participation in that of ancestors, and that its conservation and enhancement depend continuously on them.

For black Africans, living means existing in the bosom of the community; it means participating in the sacred life - and all life is sacred - of the ancestors; it means a prolongation of the ancestors and preparing one's own prolongation through descendants. There is a true continuation of the family and of the individual after death. The dead form the invisible element in the family, in the clan, in the tribe, and this invisible element is more important. In all ceremonies of any significance, on the occasion of birth, marriage, death, funerals, or investiture, it is the ancestors who preside, and their will yields only to that of the Creator.

Africans believe firmly that there is a living communion or bond of life which makes for solidarity among members of the same family or clan. The fact that we are born into a family, a clan, or a tribe immerses us in a specific current of life, "incorporates" us and molds us to the fashion of that community; it modifies all our being "ontically" and orients us to living and behaving in the manner of that community. So, family, clan, and tribe form wholes in which each member is only a part. The same blood, the same life participated in by all and received from the first ancestor, the founder of the clan, circulates in everyone's veins. For the protection, maintenance, enhancement, and perpetual preservation of this common treasure, it is a duty to work with all our energy, to wage ruthless war against all that is opposed to it, and to support at any price anything that favors it. This is the last word on the customs, institutions, wisdom, philosophy, and religion of Africans.

We have defined vital union, first, as a relation of being or life uniting all the members of one community, and, second, as an analogous ontic relation uniting all its members and all that affects the maintenance or improvement of life, including patrimony and land. This second element also plays its part: all the appurtenances of the ancestors are closely connected with their being; one might refer to these objects that have belonged to the ancestors (spear, drum, diadem, etc.) as instruments of vital union. Life, then, for black Africans, can be understood in two ways: as community in blood, the principal and primordial element, and as community in possessions, a concomitant element making life possible.

Each society, family, clan, tribe, or nation can be considered from the point of view of participation. In fact, the measure of participation in life is the norm of the hierarchy of beings and of social status. An African only counts in their own eyes and in the eyes of society to the extend that they participate in life and transmit life. The logic is quite clear on this point: whoever gives life or any means towards life to another person is to that extent superior to him.

Belief in the enhancement or diminution of beings and in their interaction of beings.

If you ask how a man becomes a chief, it is likely that the answer you get will suggest that it happens by simple default, through the death of all elders who had precedence over him so that he remains the oldest person, or else because he has been designated by his predecessor or by the elders of the clan. However, such response is insufficient and even inexact. "A person becomes chief of the clan...by internal enhancement of vital power, raising the muntu of the patriarch to the level of mediator and channel of power between the ancestors, on the one hand, and the descendants with their patrimony, on the other."

As the Bantu conceive it, then, there is a change that is ontic, a profound transformation, a new form of being. This new form of being modifies, or better, adapts one's intimate being so that it lives and behaves according to the new situation, that is to say, it behaves like the ancestors so as to be a worthy continuation of them. Investiture conferring on the heir the possessions of his ancestors is the rite which is meant to produce this internal modification.

> The king is not a man...
> He is man before his appointment to the throne;
> But once appointed, he is separated from the
> ordinary nobility
> And he acquired a place apart.

Yet, before his designation, before the investiture that consecrates and transforms him, the king is no more than a simple mortal, a man like the others. Now that the finger of God and of his ancestors have pointed him out to assume the government of his people, there is produced in him, precisely by this designation that consecrates the investiture, a total change, a change of heart in the Hebrew sense.

What has happened? All the vital energies, all the blood lineage from the ancestors, all the life which God has placed in them so that he can perpetuate it and make it fruitful, have invaded this man and have so strengthened his being - his *ntu* - that he has become a synthesis of the ancestors and the living expression of the Supreme Being and of His divine munificence.

This can be said also, observing due proportion, of chiefs and of sub-chiefs, extending the consideration as far as simple clan chiefs and fathers of families. Succession is always conceived as an ontic modification, a vital enhancement, the "passing over" of something of the deceased parent to their successors. As there can be an increase in being, so also it can happen that being is violently diminished. As the king is no longer a mere man after his appointment, he can also become a simple mortal again when the ancestors, represented by their descendants - the people - simply on account of the latter's interest and well-being, withdraw their confidence.

To underline the representative character of power, the Bashi have instituted an annual feast, the *omubande*, for renewing the royal investiture. So, just as vital union is a relation in being and life with God, with the ancestors, and with the descendants, a similar ontic relation with the appurtenances that make life possible, similarly vital diminution will be nothing other than the consequence of blocking the flow of the vital current. To bring about a vital impairment of a deceased relative would be to cut off their connection with the living, with the members of their family and of their clan. It is to make sure these connections are never broken that a person strives to live on through descendants. For their part, the living must continue to receive vital influx from ancestors and deceased parents, on pain of seeing their life fade away. Vigor, or life, is the first object of all prayers addressed to ancestors, to deceased parents, and to the spirits of protective heros, and of all prayers invoking the name and intervention of the Supreme Being.

Life is also diminished by any evil spell: sorcerers are universally detested for that. Equally, it is diminished by any violation of the neighbor's rights. Every spiritual or material injury has its repercussion and influence on life. The evil before all others, the greatest of all injustices is to insult the vital honor of someone. It would be such a case "when a less senior person makes a decision independently, disposing of what belongs to the clan, without recognition of the elders." Just as "every service, all help and assistance, counts as a support and enhancement of life for the one who benefits" and as "its value corresponds exactly to the value of the life that is enhanced," so every injustice, however minimal, will be regarded primarily as a slight on the integrity of being, on the intensity of life. Any injustice is regarded, in the first place, as an attack on the life (that is, on the vital force) of the person who is injured; its malice is related to the great respect owed to human life as God's supreme gift...It will not be the extent of damage suffered but rather the importance of the violation of life which will be taken as the basis on which reparation of the damage is calculated."

For Africans, beings always retain their intimate ontic relationship to one another, and the idea of distinct being which happens to be alongside one another but completely independent is quite foreign to their thought. All manifestations of life bring out this element of interaction between beings.

Thus, the black African community forms a vital circuit where the members live in inter-dependence for their mutual advantage. To want to leave this circuit to escape from the influence of members who are vitally superior would amount to no longer wanting to live.

Symbol: the principal means of contact and union.
If the bond uniting the members of a black African community is nothing other than participation, "that is to say, a given solidarity, presenting itself under two inseparable aspects, one personal, the other material," then the principal - often the only - means available to the members of entering into mutual contact and of strengthening union is the symbol. In order to discover the position and role of symbolism in the life and religion of the black African, we must trace the way life manifests itself from birth to death and beyond the grave, pausing at several stages in life, in particular:

> clan initiation
> spirit initiation
> communion in feasting and the blood pact
> rites of purification, confession, and reconciliation
> marriage ceremonies
> rites concerned with death
> investiture rites

From whatever perspective it is considered, symbolism appears as the striving of the human spirit for contact with power, with the invisible world; it breaks out of the limits of "the fragment which is man in the bosom of society and in the midst of the cosmos"; it is a striving for unification. Hence the three elements belonging to the concept of symbol:

Something tangible: a living being as, for example, the king (symbolizing national unity and divine authority), the patriarch (symbolizing the authority of the ancestors over their descendants), the totem (symbol of clanic unity, etc.), words (like the name of the ancestor or the names of powerful personages, animals, materials, etc), actions and gestures (like the imitation of the deeds and gestures of someone).

The role of hierophany, or contact with an invisible power. Man, in quest of means of vital enhancement, comes up against the world, against "things" which in reality are not "things." For in truth there are no "things" there are only channels and reservoirs, which on occasion can contain power. There are two possibilities: either the "things" a man meets which are receptacles to be filled with power, or, on the other hand, the "things" are creatures-creatural. In the first case, there is magic to perform and man appears, somehow, if not as creator of things then at least as creator of powers that confer life. Creatures depend directly on God, and God can at any moment breathe new life into them, provide them with a new potentiality. He makes "things" instruments of his power, he transforms them and creates them anew. So it is that actions, words, or persons can at any time become "powers," either by the competence of the man who by direct force makes it his own power or else by the competence of God the Creator.

So the symbol aims at putting us in contact with invisible powers and forces, by virtue of certain correspondences or resemblances, a relation of connotation or analogy. The mediation of the symbol establishes a current and an exchange of life and vital energies between the being symbolized and the person entering into contact with the being. In this way, the most elementary activity of daily life can be raised to a sublime height when it is discovered "how far it touches on the divine," understanding the "divine" in the sense of all that has power to communicate, to enhance and to influence life in a way that is more than human.

A unifying and effective role. The being symbolized is so present in and so united with its symbol, at least from an operational standpoint, that it becomes possible for it to exercise its actions and influence, as if time and space did not exist. Thus the symbol's action can affect anyone who makes contact with it.

Symbolism appears as a "language" available to all the

members of the community but inaccessible to strangers, a language expressing the relationship of the person using the symbol with Society and with the Cosmos, a language which "on the one hand puts the human person in solidarity with the Cosmos and on the other with the community of which he is part, proclaiming before all members of the community his profound identity." Symbolic experience signifies "not so much myself and the world but rather myself in the world." It abolishes the duality between man and the world and tends toward unification. Everything created is a gift to people from the Creator to ensure their existence, to contribute to the enhancement and safeguarding of their life.

An ethic that flows from ontology. For black Africans, and for the Bantu in particular, we observe that human life, and so man himself, is the criterion of good and evil; the basis of their moral conscience is connected with their philosophy; they attribute good and evil to several sources. Human life, that is, human persons as the center of creation, is the criterion of good and evil. Black African ethics are an anthropocentric and vital ethics. E.N. Mujynaya writes:

> In the world of *ntu*, actions thought favorable to the blossoming of life, capable of conserving and protecting life, of making it flower and increasing the vital potential of the community are, for these reasons, considered good... On the other hand, any act thought prejudicial to the life of the individual or of the community is judged evil, even where it only attacks the material interests of persons, physical or moral.... To understand this attitude, it is necessary to bear in mind that the Bantu consider human life as the most valuable good an that their ideal is not only to live to a good old age protected from anxieties but above all to remain, even after death, a vital force continually reinforced and vivified in and through progeny.... In this *muntu* ideal, it is in relation to life and after-life, that every human act is judged.

The basis of moral conscience relates to the Black African conception of being, which is essentially synthesizing and unifying.

"Being is fundamentally one and all beings that exist are onto-logically bound to one another."

In this organic conception, human being, the human *ntu*, is central:

> Above, and transcendent, is God.... Intermediary between God and man are all the ancestors, deceased members of the family and ancient national heroes, all the ranks of the dis-embodied souls. Below man are all the other beings which, basically, are only means at his disposal to develop his ntu, his being, his life. The Muntu world is very extensive but still unified thanks to the relations and interactions between the ntu. In this sense, one could speak of a global, cosmic philosophy. The bond is the life of Muntu; All the universe, visible and invisible, is summoned to contribute to its main-tenance and enhancement. Everywhere and in all things, there are means of influencing life, and it is important to grasp these and to make their influence beneficent.

> Thus the world appears as a plurality of coordinated forces.

> This order is the essential condition of the integrity of beings. The Bantu add that this order comes from God and must be respected.... Objective morality for black Africans is an onto-logical morality, immanent and intrinsic. Bantu morality holds to the essence of things grasped in their ontology.... We may draw the conclusion that an act or a usage will, in the first place, be qualified as ontologically good by the Bantu and on that ground held to be morally good, and finally, by way of deduction, it will be judged juridically just.... Those are the norms of the good act; obviously the norms for an evil act are parallel to these. Any act or behavior, any human atti-tude or habit which attacks the vital force or growth or the hierarchy of *muntu* is bad. Destroying life is an infringement of the divine plan and the *muntu* knows that such destruc-tion is, above all, an ontological sacrilege; for this precise rea-son, it is immoral and consequently unjust.

So the Bantu ethic is an ethic of participation and communion with others.

While Bantu ethics are anthropocentric, it is no less true

that God is always conceived as the source of life and of all the resources for existence. Even the names used to refer to the Supreme Being are significant in this regard. The proverbs are even more convincing. If good is attributed directly to God, it is different in the case of evil. This comes from people themselves or from the dead or from personified forces of evil. Evil cannot be from God, except as a "medicinal" resource, a means of mercy and goodness.

The Primacy of Religion in the Life of Black Africans

The study of rites and symbols in the life of black African peoples, and of the veneration they offer to their ancestors, and of their attitude to God, leads us to the conclusion that religion permeates the whole life of the black africans - their personal, family, and socio-political life. Religion has the psychological and social function of integration and equilibrium; it enables people to understand and value themselves, to achieve integration, to accept their situations in life, to control their anguish. Thanks to religion, the duality between human beings and their world, visible and invisible, is overcome and unification achieved.

In black Africa, "religion permeates everything. Its guiding influence extends to political, social, and family life. In general, the religious spirit prevails over the political."

The essential characteristic of the religion of blacks and of the Bantu in particular resides in the relation between religion and daily life. "Religion is not an abstract principle," writes A. Kagame, "nor even a collection of such principles, but a leaven which makes these principles work, vitally involved as they are with the religious laws and ceremonies which give external expression to this vitality." With reservations cautioning us against certain expressions, he quotes an impressive passage from Bishop Le Roy:

> "There," comments A. Kagame, "we have a description of a vigorous religion, whose followers blend it with all their activities. What matters is the intention by which nothing is profane. It is only the practitioners of a feeble religion who

categorize their service as variously religious or profane. God cannot have intended that one who cultivates the land should cease to be holy during his work, or that one who works on the water should have to wait for the propitious hour for liturgical celebrations in a church, etc. Each person should ensure by his intention that everything, even his walking and breathing, should become religious activities putting him in constant contact with God." Traditional religion does effectively play its role of reassurance and protection.

Excerpt from: Vincent Mulago, "Africa and Christianity," in *African Traditional Religions in Contemporary Society*, edited by Jacob Olupona (New York: Paragon House, 1991), 120-126.

4. The Geography of Africa

J. D. OMER-COOPER

The following selection is a succinct description of the major geographical features of the continent of Africa. J. D. Omer-Cooper, a historian, asserts that the patterns of geography have had a significant influence on the history of the development of Africa.

In size the African continent with its 30,321,130 square kilometers may be compared with Asia (27,593,900 square kilometers), and the USSR (22,401,000 square kilometers).* This vast land mass straddles the equator, facing the Mediterranean Sea in the north and the Antarctic in the south. Its wide variety of climates and natural conditions has greatly influenced the development of its inhabitants.

One characteristic of Africa is the striking regularity of its coastline, which has relatively few bays and inlets or peninsulas reaching out to the sea. This has meant that the African peoples have not had the same opportunities and incentives for the development of navigation on the sea, whether for long- or short-range trade, as have the peoples of Europe and Asia. Thus, except for the countries bordering the Mediterranean, they have not until comparatively recent times been brought into close and frequent contact with other continents. Until the nineteenth century African development was relatively self-contained, though this does not mean that there were no contacts with other nations, nor that such contacts were unimportant.

The northern part of the continent lies along the Mediterranean Sea and enjoys a climate similar to, though warmer and drier than, that of south Europe. This Mediterranean area is a narrow coastal strip varying in width according to geographical circumstances. It is widest in the north-west corner of the continent, known as the Maghreb (the Arabic word for west) where the modern states of Morocco, Algeria and Tunisia are situated. There the Atlas mountains cause winds from the Mediterranean and the Atlantic to deposit their moisture and the soil has been noted for its fertility from ancient times.

Behind this narrow strip of fertile country with its Mediterranean climate lies the vast desert of the Sahara, greater in extend than the whole of Europe and by far the largest desert in the world. This huge area - which is now almost entirely unin-habited outside the occasional oases which provide welcome islands of green in the almost endless wastes of barren rock and burning sands - was once very different. In remote prehistoric times it enjoyed a reasonable rainfall and supported a consider-able population. Gradually, for reasons which are still not well understood, it dried up and its peoples congregated around the oases or moved further afield. By the time of the ancient Greeks and Romans it was in much the same condition as today. But though the Sahara is such a vast and formidable desert it must not be thought that it separated the northern part of the conti-nent from all contact with the center and south.

On the eastern side of the continent the river Nile, start-ing from two sources, one in the highlands of Ethiopia (the Blue Nile) and the other in the Lake region of East Africa (the White Nile) threads its way across the desert to reach the sea through the many mouths of its delta in Egypt. Every year the rains in Ethiopia and East Africa cause the river to overflow its banks, and as the water subsides it leaves behind a layer of fertile mud which it has brought from the Ethiopian highlands. Along the banks of the Nile there is a narrow cultivable strip containing some of the richest agricultural land in the world. Though it is often no more than a few kilometers wide it can support a dense population and it gave rise to one of the world's most ancient and elaborate civilizations. Navigation is possible along great stretches of the river, and the winding thread of water and the vivid strip of green beside it form one of the strongest links binding the history of the peoples north and south of the Sahara.

In the central and western parts of the Sahara the mountains of Tibesti, Air and the Hoggar capture sufficient rain to make agriculture possible. In other places underground water provides wells and springs to nourish oases. These provide natural staging posts on the caravan routes which from ancient times have criss-crossed the desert, bringing the peoples of West Africa and the Maghreb into contact with each other.

To the south of the Sahara in the west, desert conditions gradually give way to increasing vegetation nourished by the rains brought by warm equatorial winds from the Atlantic. A great belt of savanna which is called the Sudanic belt stretches across the continent. South of the Sudanic belt, along the coast of much of West Africa, stretching inland to varying distances, lies the great West African rain forest which, with a few gaps, meets the dense forests of Zaire (formerly the Belgian Congo) to form one of the largest tropical forests in the world.

Thus the pattern of West Africa geography consists of a fairly regular succession of belts of vegetation, from the Sahara desert, across the grasslands of the savanna belt to the lush forests of the coastal strip. But this pattern is broken by major rivers which have had a significant influence on history, such as the complex Niger-Benue river system which might be described as the Nile of West Africa. Rising in the mountains of the Futa Jallon range in modern Guinea, the river Niger makes a great northward loop almost into the Sahara before turning south into modern Nigeria where it links up with the Benue, another mighty river which rises in the mountains of Cameroon. The combined waters finally find their way to the sea through the maze of creeks and rivers of the Niger delta. In its northward path the Niger runs for part of its course over level ground where it overflows its banks every year when the rains in the Futa Jallon bring down the flood waters to form what is often called the inland delta of the Niger. A relatively dense population can be supported there and it is not surprising that the valley of the Niger should have been the center of some of West Africa's most ancient and powerful kingdoms. Further east, Lake Chad, lying on the fringes of the Sahara and fed by rivers rising in the Cameroon mountains, also modifies the climate and provides agriculture opportunities.

On the eastern side of the continent the highlands of Ethiopia, lying with the triangular projection known as the Horn of Africa, constitute a special environment of their own. They consist largely of volcanic material which breaks down to give a rich soil of almost unlimited depth. It is this soil which washes down the Nile to provide the fertility of Egypt. Abundant rain fall every year and the climate of the cool uplands has been described as the closest to paradise on earth. No wonder the ancient Greeks regarded Ethiopia as the favorite earthly residence of the gods. Between this fertile highland area - a natural center of civilization - and the sea, is the plain of Somalia largely dry and torrid and therefore for the most part suitable only for nomadic herdsmen and incapable of sustaining a large settled population.

Further south again, the African continent consists of a vast plateau rising to its highest point in the Ruwenzori mountains, sometimes described as the spine of Africa. To the west of the Ruwenzori lies the great basin of the Zaire and Kasai rivers system, much of it covered by forest which towards the south gives way to savanna and the Benguella and Shaba (formerly Katanga) plateau where the Zambezi river has its source. East of the Ruwenzori is the region of the Great Lakes: Victoria, Tanganyika, Malawi and many others that are smaller but still large and important. In spite of the presence of the Great Lakes much of this East and Central African plateau is hot and rather dry, covered with a poor tree scrub. There are important exceptions, however. The cool and fertile Kenyan highlands provide excellent farming country. The area between Lakes Victoria, Kyoga and Kivu, the so-called inter-lacustrine region which forms the heart of modern Uganda, benefits from abundant rains which make it a green and fertile land. Here was another natural center for the development of African civilizations. The slopes of Mount Kilimanjaro and the Shire highlands of modern Malawi are other examples.

The southernmost part of the continent constitutes a prolongation of the great African plateau, surrounded by a coastal strip of varying width, the result of age-old erosion of the plateau edge. Like most of the African plateau this is generally rather dry, open savanna country with grass or bush or thorn scrub. Its climate is strongly affected by its southerly latitude and the winter months of June and July can be bitterly cold. On the other hand the southern part of the continent is free from malaria and the tsetse fly which are plagues north of the equator. It is ideal country for cattle-keepers and mixed farmers but cannot support a dense agricultural population.

*According to the *Comparative World Atlas* the size of Africa is 30,321,130 square kilometers and Asia is 44,362,815 square kilometers. Comparative World Atlas (Maplewood, NJ: Hammond Incorporated, 1989) p. 78.

Excerpt from: A. E. Afigbo, E. Ayandele, et. al., editors, *The Making of Modern Africa*, Vol. I, (New York: Longman Group Ltd., 1986), pp. 1-5.

5. The Maghreb and the Berbers

J. D. Omer-Cooper and E. A. Ayandele

The word "Maghreb" means "West" in the Arabic language. The following excerpts by historians E. A. Ayandele and J. D. Omer-Cooper examine the influence of geographical features and cultural character- istics on the development of civilization in northwestern Africa. The Berbers were the major indigenous inhabitants of northwestern Africa. They were fiercely independent. Under the leadership of Queen Dahia Al-Kahina (667-702 A.D.) they courageously resisted the Arab advance led by Hassan al-Numan before they finally succumbed. The majority of the Berbers ultimately intermarried with the Arabs and came under the influence of Arabic culture.

The Maghreb has from very ancient times been the home of many different Berber peoples. Their way of life depended largely on geographical circumstances. Some who lived on the rich lands near the coast or in well-watered parts of the moun- tains were settled agriculturalists; others on the desert fringes or in the Sahara itself lived the life of nomadic pastoralists. The basic pattern was only slightly modified when traders from Phoenicia on the Syrian coast established the city of Carthage in about 750 B.C. An empire was gradually built up along the coastal strip and more intensive methods of agriculture were introduced. Carthage had imperial interests in southern Spain and in Sicily, where it engaged in a long struggle with the Greek city-states. This ultimately brought it into conflict with the rising power of Rome, and after the failure of Hannibal's heroic but futile invasion of Italy (218-203 B.C.) the power of Carthage was destroyed, most of the Maghreb being taken into the Roman empire. A long period of peace and prosperity followed. Agriculture was greatly improved, irrigation works established and desert land brought into cultivation. The Berber peoples increasingly took to settled life and many new cities were founded. To this day the ruins of mighty theatres and other monuments standing in what is now virtually desert land testify to the prosperity of the Roman period. The wealth of the Maghreb cities was not due only to their agriculture, for even at that time caravans were crossing the Sahara to West Africa and bringing back precious cargos of gold and ivory.

Under the Roman empire Christianity spread to the Maghreb, which produced one of the most revered of Christian scholars, St. Augustine of Hippo. But by this time the Roman empire was already in the last stages of decay and excessive taxation and resulting over-farming were wreaking havoc on the Maghreb's agricultural system. As the Roman empire in the west collapsed the Maghreb was overrun in A.D. 429 by Germanic warriors known as the Vandals. Their kingdom in turn was destroyed in A.D. 534 by the forces of the Byzantine empire, which under Justinian was attempting to recapture the lost western provinces. The Byzantine empire, faced with mounting burdens of military expenditure, was oppressive and inefficient. It failed to keep the loyalty of the Berber peoples or to establish itself firmly in the country. In about A.D. 670 Uqba ibn Nafi began the long series of campaigns which culminated in the Arab conquest of the country. The decadent Byzantine administration offered little resistance but the Berbers held out desperately until A.D. 709. Thereafter they joined with their conquerors and participated in the Muslim conquests of Spain and Sicily.

The Arab conquest brought with it a major revolution through the introduction of Islam, which entirely replaced Christianity. Under the new religion the Maghreb went through a long series of political changes. Successive attempts were made to bring the whole area under unified political control together with Muslim Spain, and repeatedly they broke down, giving rise to kingdoms roughly corresponding to the present division into Morocco, Algeria and Tunisia. The city life of the Roman period continued to flourish and the Maghreb enjoyed a high level of cultural development in the early Muslim period.

The most important development between the Arab conquest and the nineteenth century, however, was the migration into the area of nomadic Bedouin Arab peoples generally known as the Banu Hilal and the Banu Sulaym. Their invasion began in the second half of the eleventh century. They infiltrated on to the cultivated land like a swarm of locusts and gradually spread westward from Tunisia to Morocco. The rulers often ignored or even encouraged this invasion for they saw in the newcomers valuable irregular troops who would be pleased to fight under any banner in return for land on which to settle. As the nomads spread out, their demands and the over-grazing of their animals tended to drive the settled cultivators off the land. Much agricultural land reverted to desert conditions. Towns diminished or were abandoned altogether and power shifted nearer to the coast where trade with the outside world still provided a measure of prosperity. All over the fertile lands of the Maghreb agriculture decayed and the intensive techniques of the past gave way to mixed farming of a very poor type. At the same time the coming of the Bedouin peoples brought considerable numbers of true Arabs into the Maghreb where previously they had been a tiny minority. Through intermarriage a high portion of the Berbers were assimilated to the Arabs and the Arabic language became the normal everyday tongue for most of the population, except in mountainous areas such as the Atlas range in Morocco and the Kabylie mountains of Algeria, where the Berbers maintained their old language and culture together with a fierce spirit of independence.

The Berbers

The significance of the divinity that hedged the sultan lies in the fact that it provided him with the spiritual qualifications with which he commanded the obedience of the entire Berber-Arab population of the country in specified circumstances. For politically the Berbers, particularly those of the Sanhaja, Masmuda and Zenata groups living in the *Bilad es Siba* ('the country of disobedience'), were traditionally unsubmissive. They eschewed centralization in any form and would not transfer their loyalty to any unit larger than the clan except when the entire race was threatened by external aggressors. Semi-nomads, these Berbers who lived in the mountainous interior had an intense aversion for the descendants of Arab invaders in the lowlands, for Arab culture and for the Berber agriculturalists living in the *Bilad es Makhzen* (Land of Order) who were law-abiding and tax-paying citizens, and who were prepared to accept the Sultan politically. By contrast, the Berbers of the *Bilad es Siba* (Land of Disorder) had the habit of repudiating the sultan's political claims. They would pray for him in their mosques every Friday and follow him in the holy war; they might allow him to represent them in dealings with foreign powers and sometimes to settle quarrels among them; their chiefs might even accept investiture from him as his officials. But to him they paid neither taxes nor troops, except for services in the holy war. Even the supremacy of the sultan in the *Bilad es Makhzen* was not always complete. It was only in an ineffectual way that the sultan's authority was diffused, administratively, throughout the country. He was the head of the *Makhnes* or Council, which in turn had supervisory control over the caids or tribal chieftains, the sheikhs or village heads and the khalifas, the local administrators.

From the ninth century, when the Idrisids began the welding of the Berber groups into a Moroccan nation, to the period of imposition of French colonial rule, the preoccupation of the various governments was how to bind the various societies together under one ruler in a territory where geography aided particularism, factiousness and sectionalism.

In the circumstances the extent of the power of a sultan depended on his ability and military power. And indeed only three monarchs in Moroccan history before 1800 ever succeeded in welding the various societies into one. No nineteenth-century sultan succeeded in achieving this end. It is not surprising then that Mawlay Suleiman, the occupier of the throne in 1800, was weak, in the face of the political confusion that engulfed the country, a situation worsened by the plague which visited the territory in 1799 and 1800 and which carried away thousands of the inhabitants. Furthermore Suleiman was deprived of the help and loyalty of the *abid al Bukhari*, the army of blacks which had been founded by Mawlay Ismail, ruler from 1672 to 1727, and which had been the prop of Sherifian authority. For in the eighteenth century this army had to be disbanded when it began to interfere with politics. The sultan had to fall back on the unreliable military succor of the loyal chiefdoms of Arab descent whose services were rewarded with grants of land, exemption from taxes and facilities for reaching the highest ranks in government service. It is nothing to wonder at then that the chief feature of Morocco's domestic history through the century was the rebellion of one locality after the other. Sultan Suleiman who ruled from 1792 to 1822 was forced to fight almost without respite against rebellious subjects in every part of his dominion. In 1820 his army was completely defeated by rebels between Meknes and Fez, two of the largest cities in Morocco.

A. E. Afigbo and E. A. Ayandele, et. al., editors, *The Making of Modern Africa*, Volume I (New York: Longman Group, Ltd.: 1976), pp. 10-12, 178-180.

6. Ancient Egypt, Nubia, Kush, and Axum

JOSEPH E. HARRIS

Africans and Their History *from which this excerpt is taken is a landmark reevaluation of the African past and present by the East African expert, Joseph E. Harris, a noted African-American historian. His writings on the early kingdoms and city-states of Egypt, Nubia, Kush, and Axum reveal a rich historical legacy and facilitate the understanding of these diverse and interrelated societies. He provides ample evidence that there were active and effective cultural, social, economic and political ties by the civilization of Egypt with other African civilizations along the Nile River to the south from ancient times.*

Egypt

The beginning of Egyptian history is estimated at 3200 B.C.; there has been positive identification of several dynasties from that period to the conquest of the kingdom by Alexander of Macedonia in 332 B.C., which marks the beginning of the Hellenistic era. Egypt, as noted in the previous chapter, is generally acknowledged as pioneering African agricultural development. Confirmation of this results from the discovery of ancient tools and the location of terraced hills for farming in several places along the Nile Valley, most significantly at Fayum and Merimdeh.

During the early dynasties Egypt frequently raided Nubia for supplies and slaves, and in the process extended its political, economic, and cultural influence. Pharaoh Snefou of the Fourth Dynasty (2680-2258 B.C.), for example, is reported as having said that he returned with 7,000 prisoners and 200,000 cattle from a military expedition in Lower Nubia. If those figures are even half correct, the capture of so many Nubians with a large number of cattle suggests both that Nubia had a prosperous economy and that Egypt relied on it.

By the Sixth Dynasty Nubia seems to have been a very active area for Egyptian expeditions. Nubia was a crossroads area with routes connecting Elephantine, El Fasher in Darfur, Red Sea ports, points around Lake Chad, and regions farther south. Although little is known about the extent to which Nubians and other interior Africans traveled to Egypt and the Red Sea coast, it is clear that inhabitants of an area as active politically and economically as Nubia, which attracted such diverse people as traders, soldiers, and adventurers, must indeed have been very much involved in wide areas extended in all directions. Inner Africa must have dispatched its merchants and emissaries outward; their presence as slaves in the north is established.

Egypt and Nubia shared in the benefits from their relationship: Egypt for the labor, resources, and passageway to the south and west; Nubia for the commerce, skill, and Egypt's links to the Mediterranean Sea. Both areas emerged as viable economic, political, and cultural centers in northeastern Africa with links to other regions of the continent.

Some scholars believe that commercial relations between Egyptians and Greeks were established as early as 3200 B.C., but certainly by the eighteenth century B.C. both commercial and diplomatic relations existed between the two peoples. That this early contact exposed the Greeks to the Africans of a darker hue is revealed by the terms "Aethiopia" and "Aethiopes" which applied to the whole area and its inhabitants south of Egypt. Aethiopes was a general term meaning burnt (dark or black) face, and is comparable with the Arabic Bilad-es-Sudan, meaning land of the blacks. An Ethiopian was thus a person whose skin color was considerably darker than inhabitants in the Greco-Roman world. It would seem, therefore, that at least since the dawn of history Egypt has served as a great magnet attracting people from Asia and Europe to join blacks in the drama of African history. At the same time, Egyptians were themselves active in affairs abroad.

As Egypt expanded its spheres of influence, the political authority of its rulers became more vulnerable. Increasingly, more administrative control was assumed by nobles, and a greater degree of local autonomy was achieved in Upper Nubia. However, Egyptian influence there was great; its achievements in agriculture, technology, writing, engineering, religious ideas and ceremonies, and political organization spread in all directions and affected future developments in Asia and Europe as well as various other parts of Africa.

Kush

The ancient kingdom of Kush is one of the least known of early world powers, in spite of the fact that it was powerful and influential during its time. Of the several classical writers who referred to Kush, Herodotus seems to be the first to mention it by name; others simply called it Ethiopia. Herodotus visited Egypt and traveled as far as Elephantine (modern Aswan), which he regarded as the frontier separating Egypt from Ethiopia. In his description of the world he devoted a chapter to the Nile Valley, discussing mostly geography and myths. About 400 years later Diodorus Siculus wrote of Ethiopia as the source of the Nile. Strabo's geography included a discussion of agriculture and the Meroe army. Pliny the Elder in his Natural History wrote about the Meroe, military campaigns, and geography, but he also listed several towns, most of which no longer exist. There are many other references which indicate that Kush and some of its towns were fairly well known in ancient times. However, none of these sources nor all combined are sufficient to reconstruct Kush's history. By the late third century Kush developed its own language, which is still undeciphered; thus the most important sources about Kush's past remain untapped.

While the origins of the kingdom are not known, it is clear that there was a long period of interaction between the eastern Sudan and Egypt. The area as far upstream as the Fourth Cataract was occupied under the New Kingdom of Egypt (1580-

1100 B.C.). During this period Egyptian influence was strong; there were Egyptian administrators and priests, craftsmen and artists introducing Egyptian techniques and art forms. During the eighth century on the periphery of Egyptianized territory there emerged the state around the capital, Napata, which was the ancestor of Meroe. The origins of Napata are unknown, but there is no reason to think the state did not emerge around local rulers (some have argued that they were Libyans). It is known that it was under Piankhy that the conquest of Egypt was completed by Napata, and he with his successors controlled the country until 654 B.C. when the Assyrians broke Sudanese power, and the Kushites retreated south under King Tanwelanani. It is generally believed that after this defeat the capital of the kingdom was moved to Meroe. No exact date is agreed on other than somewhere in the sixth century B.C. This seems reasonable, especially in view of the fact that in 591 B.C. the Egyptian pharaoh carried out a military campaign that reached Napata, suggesting the need to move the capital for security reasons.

One must also recognize, however, that in spite of the pressure of military events, there was the greater attraction of Meroe in its own right. It was situated in a region of better annual rainfall and could thus produce a greater abundance of food and provide better pastures for cattle. The town was also better located for trade, being on a navigable stretch of the Nile at the end of a caravan route from the Red Sea. The Egyptians and the Romans after them depended on several imports from the Sudan, including gold and ivory. Kushites had already developed the trade route along the Red Sea, bypassing much of the desert and the rough cataracts of the Nile. Moreover, it seems that routes eastward from the Nile had been of importance since early times. There long was considerable interaction between the Horn of Africa and Arabia. Indeed, some of the people of Ethiopia still claim descent from Arabian peoples, and some authorities see an Eastern influence in some of the art and monuments of Meroe and other areas of northeastern Africa. While the earliest document about this commercial contact is the Greek guide for sailors, *The Periplus*, which was written about

2,000 years ago, there is no reason to think that the relationship does not stretch back much farther in time. So indeed, Meroe was more strategically conducive to international trade than was Napata. Its location was also favorable because of the abundance of iron ore and timber for its smelting; thus when the knowledge of iron working was learned, the town became a major producer of iron tools. This obviously made Meroe especially important in the northeast.

There are many large mounds of iron slag (cinders) thought to be the remains of iron smelting. They have been the cause of much speculation about the importance of iron in Meroe's economy. There are six large mounds within the town. It is generally believed that the ore was smelted in furnaces fired by charcoal, the material for which was in abundance in the groves of acacia trees along the Nile. Meroe was therefore fortunate in having the two basic requirements for iron production-the ore and the fuel-and this was probably what made the kingdom powerful for a long time. By the early Christian era iron was fairly common in northeastern Africa, though stone, bronze, and copper continued to be used in many areas.

Since the language of Meroe has not been deciphered, and since there is no great abundance of information otherwise about the kingdom, the description of the people and their life must remain skeletal, being reconstructed mainly from archaeological materials. Admittedly the discovery of palaces, temples, cemeteries and other such things, while important, especially as far as artistic achievements and some history are concerned, tell us little about the life and social organization. But it seems that the main activity of most people of Meroe was some form of agriculture and cattle raising. Some of this activity is shown in artistic reliefs. The tending and milking of cows is shown, for example. Horses were used both for riding and for pulling chariots, and on occasion they were buried with their owners. Strabo reported that millet was one crop, and the discovery of fragments of cloth made from cotton suggests that this plant was grown. This view is strengthened by the presence of spindle whorls (flywheels) and loom weights. Some cloth fragments made from flax show that it too was probably a crop of the area. Elephants and lions, animals rarely seen in Egyptian art, were in evidence. The lion is frequently shown on reliefs as well as in sculpture. The elephant is shown many times and is thought to have been used for the war and ceremony. The elephants used in Ptolemaic and Roman times are believed to have been trained by Meroites.

What about the significance of Meroe in African history? It has been argued that with the fall of the kingdom in the fourth century A.D., many Kushites migrated westward and southward, taking with them their specialized skills and concepts such as state organization, but this remains only speculative with no conclusive evidence to support it. There are objects in some parts of Africa that resemble Egyptian ones and are therefore viewed as of that origin (headrests, musical instruments, ostrich fans), but even if such objects resulted from diffusion, there remains the question of direction. P. L. Shinnie has pointed out that, in the main, the objects of Egyptian appearance are not such as were known to be common in Meroe, and no object of certain Meroe origin has been found away from the Nile to the west.

There is the argument that Kushites carried with them ideas about metal-working techniques. The existence of a long and skilled tradition of bronze working (by the cireperdue method) among the Yoruba and the Bini of Nigeria has raised the question of relationship to Egypt. While this is possible, again there is no evidence to support it. Moreover, there seems to be a gap of about 1,000 years in the established chronology.

On the question of knowledge of iron smelting, there is the same kind of argument: Who was responsible for the dissemination of that knowledge? Meroe is a possible source from which such knowledge could have spread. It was long in contact with areas to the south and west. But so too were areas in North Africa. Carthage was long in contact with areas in the Sudan, and it had begun to work with iron as early as about 500 B.C. and is a possible source. But one should not overlook or minimize the possibility that the people who had the material resources could have developed those techniques themselves.

The kingdom of Kush, however, was indeed an important kingdom in history in its own right. It was urban, materially advanced, literate, and existed in the interior of the continent for about a thousand years, with dynamic relations not only with its immediate neighbors but, through trade, with an international community. In the first century A.D., after the Roman conquest of Egypt, Kush sent ambassadors to Rome, and Emperor Nero sent Roman emissaries to Kush.

This was the high point of Kush. From about 200 A.D. the vital trade routes converging in the kingdom were increasingly invaded by desert nomads and neighboring merchants from Axum.

Axum

The ancient kingdom of Ethiopia evolved around and became known by the name of its capital, Axum. Much of Axum's early history is shrouded in legend. The best known is that of the Queen of Sheba who went from Ethiopia to King Solomon's Jerusalem, where they fell in love and had a son, Menelik. That son thus became the founder of the ruling dynasty-the Lion of Judah-from which the late rule, Emperor Haile Selassie, claimed descent. In addition, Ethiopia's tradition includes a written language, which has provided nearly 2,000 years of historical documentation. Although the identity of the original inhabitants of the area in which the kingdom emerged is not clear, it seems likely that sometime during the first millennium B.C., and Sabaean people of South Arabia, already in commercial contact with the African coast on the Red Sea, settled in the area and intermarried with the indigenous inhabitants. The Sabaeans spoke a Semitic language, Sabaean, and brought their own customs. Out of this culture-sharing emerged the kingdom of Axum, with the port of Adulis becoming a major entrepot where Africans from the interior brought iron, tortoise shells, animals, hides, rhinoceros horn, gold, and slaves to exchange for iron tools, weapons, copper implements, trinkets, cloth, and wine.

Axum thrived on this international trade which involved merchants from regions of the Mediterranean and Red Sea and the Indian Ocean. As a wealthy cosmopolis, Axum included residents from Egypt, the eastern Roman Empire, Persia, and India. Greek was commonly spoken here, and King Zoscales, who reigned about 2,000 years ago, was described as being well versed in Greek literature. But the Axumites also developed their own distinct civilization. They evolved their own language, Ge'ez, with a special script. Unlike Sabaean, it included vowel signs in each letter and was written from left to right. Several stone inscriptions appear in Sabaean, Ge'ez, and Greek. The Axumites became reputable architects and builders in stone, as the famous monolithic stele still seen in Axum reveal. The kingdom also produced bronze, silver, and gold coins.

Axum became a powerful kingdom which extended its control over Africans and Arabians. From the second century A.D. military conquests were made along the Red Sea and the Blue Nile, and during the third century Axum established its authority over peoples on the Arabian coast as far as Aden. It controlled the important trade routes to Meroe, Egypt, Red Sea ports, and had a major influence over the Red Sea trade in general. The kingdom reached its apogee during the fourth century when King Ezana unified Axum, integrated Yemen into the empire, invaded and ultimately destroyed Kush around 330 A.D. Ezana's armies swept as far as the confluence of the Atbara and Nile rivers. This was indeed an epic victory which gave Axum even greater control over caravan routes in northeastern Africa and established the kingdom as an important international power. Indeed, Axum became an ally of Byzantium. Byzantine emperor Justin I sent an emissary to the Axumite king Ella-Atsbeha (Caleb) in 524 and secured the latter's promise to invade Yemen, where Christians were being persecuted. After successfully completing the expedition, the king sent a report to Justin. This close diplomatic cooperation was still in evidence in 531 when Justin's successor, Justinian, sought Axum's support against Persia, but it seems that in this instance Ella-Atsbeha did not have the power to match Persia, which, as one of the great powers in Arabia in the latter part of the sixth century, overran Arabia and gained control over much of the Red Sea trade, including ports which served Axum. Axum was unable to maintain its hegemony in Yemen and was challenged along the Nile by the kingdoms of Nabatia, Makuria (Makurra), and Alodia (Alwa). Finally, Islam's expansion into Egypt in 639, the

Muslim destruction of Adulis in 710, and the establishment of Umayyad control over the Dahlak Islands in 715 signaled a new era for northeastern Africa. From Egypt and the coastal towns on the Red Sea Islam spread along the trade routes to the Ethiopian interior where Ifat, Adal, and other Muslim states appeared at about the same time that Axum was expanding across Shoa and other areas. While the Muslims and Axum maintained a fairly peaceful relationship, the latter was increasingly isolated from the major international centers along the Mediterranean and Red Seas, centers with which she had established long-standing and influential relations.

Axum's decline on the international scene did not signal stagnation at home. The kingdom continued a trend toward unification and the development of its own culture which was manifested largely in the Ethiopian Church, one of the oldest and most significant institutions in Ethiopian history. By the fourth century commercial relations between Axum and the Mediterranean world were well established, the Greek language and literature and Greco-Roman gods were known in the area. In addition, the cultural input from the Red Sea had resulted in a fusion of ideas and cultures which made easier the spread of the Christian faith.

The role of the king was especially important. In pre-Christian Axum, the king offered sacrifices to the gods after each successful expedition and thus became not only the chief military leader, absolute administrator and judge, but the highest priest, and was regarded as possessing divine power, as an inscription of King Ezana shows: "King of kings, the son of the invincible god Ares."

Christianity existed in Axum before it became the official religion. One tradition relates Ethiopia's conversion by St. Matthew who allegedly preached there. There is also the eunuch who was baptized by the apostle Philip, as mentioned in Acts 8:26-40, and who was the treasurer of an Ethiopian queen by the name of Candace. Many Ethiopians believed that he was the first to preach there. Some writers maintain that he was at the court of Meroe, because a certain queen by that name had fought the Romans in Caesar's time. In any case, the spread of

Christianity in Ethiopia began in an unorganized way before it became the official religion.

Foreign Christian traders were in Adulis, the city of Axum, and other trading places, and the Axumite kingdom allowed them to build their own meeting places. It is entirely possible that servants, customers, and neighbors of those traders became familiar with the faith and thus prepared the way for organizing proselytizing. Christianity became the official religion in the fourth century A.D., officially established by Frumentius, a Syrian student of philosophy. He found his way to Axum after encountering an accident at sea. Shortly after his arrival at the capital, the king died and left the kingdom to the queen, who requested Frumentius to help in its administration. This gave him the opportunity to exercise influence over the education of the princess and the construction of prayer houses. It was he who later became the first bishop of Ethiopia and converted King Ezana, who reigned sometime between 320 and 360 and recorded inscriptions of his achievements on slabs of stone. In the first four he showed adherence to pre-Christian beliefs, but the last one showed a change in his beliefs. He no longer attributed his success to Ares, but according to an inscription: "By the power of the Lord of heaven, who in heaven and upon earth is mightier than everything that exists."

With regard to the theology, the Ethiopians accepted the position of the Council of Nicea (325) that Christ is fully God and Man, and that there was never a time when Christ did not exist (a counteraction to Arianism). When the Council of Chalcedon supported the view that Christ is of two natures, divine and human, Egypt and Ethiopia severed their relationships with the Church of Constantinople and Rome, and became leaders of a new group, the monophysites, the Coptic Church of Egypt and the Ethiopian Orthodox Church respectively.

The growth of the church was assisted toward the end of the fifth and early sixth centuries by missionaries, and the support of kings. When the Monophysites were condemned at the Council of Chalcedon in 451 and persecuted by the Byzantine emperors, they received refuge under the Ethiopian Church and helped evangelize in the country. Among these immigrants were the Nile Saints who went to Axum about 502 A.D. and taught in different places. They turned some of the pre-Christian temples into churches, relating themselves thereby to a local institution and thus appealing to the local inhabitants, because they made no major effort to destroy existing houses of worship. Pilgrimages to these places were made by people from different parts of the country.

These religious communities depended on the surrounding villages for supplies and gradually received substantial assistance from various kings. In the sixth century King gabre Maskal presented the monastery of Debra Damo with lands which included many villages. He also gave grants to other communities, setting an example that other kings followed, thereby making these monasteries great land-owning institutions through gifts which were not to be taken away either by the giver or any other ruler. Thus, while this practice limited the resources of the state, it strengthened the church and thus became a source of conflict to the present day.

The monasteries also became centers of learning. During the sixth century the Nine Saints began translating the New Testament and other relevant books into Ge'ez, which became the basis for Ethiopian literature and ecclesiastical expression. Some of the Saints also served as advisers to the kings. The great Ethiopian scholar Yared received his education in one of these church schools. He compiled the Digua, a hymn book which called for the use of such instruments as sistrum and drums to accompany the human voice. In addition to contributing church music, Yared also made important contributions to the development of Ge'ez poetry.

A most impressive cultural achievement occurred during the thirteenth century when the famous rock-hewn monolithic churches were constructed during the reign of King Lalibela. The churches were carved out of solid rock mountains chipped away at the top to a depth of some forty feet. The churches were thus approached by descending a stairway leading to a hewn-out courtyard surrounding the church. The interior of the church was decorated with colorful religious figures. These churches have been called one of the wonders of the world and bear some resemblance in style to the earlier constructed stele at Axum, suggesting a possible continuity in architectural style.

Without a doubt the Ethiopian monarchy and Christian Church reinforced each other and became symbols and bonds of unity and identity for Ethiopians in ancient times, and this whole process was buttressed by the international image of the country provided by the legends of the Queen of Sheba and Prester John and the involvement of the country in world affairs.

By the dawn of the modern era with the persistent expansion of Europeans into Africa, several kingdoms in the northeast had been participants in and contributors to a remarkable history. Attempts to establish a foundation for unity among a great diversity of people in the region, which were unsuccessfully undertaken by Kush, were much more successfully carried out by Axum. Indeed, nation building was in the making.

Nubia

Between the Axumites' conquest of Kush around 330 A.D. and the Arab conquest of Egypt in 639 A.D., there emerged at least three small Nubian kingdoms along the Nile-Nobatia, Makuria, and Alodia. Exactly when they were formed is unknown, but there are references by classical writers to the Nobatae (of Nobatia) invading Egypt and fighting the Roman armies there. Early in the sixth century the Nobatae expanded southward up to the third cataract, probably in the consolidation of their kingdom. Their Merotic heritage met the influence of Byzantine Egypt and could have been Christianized by that contact. By 566 a bishop was appointed in Nobatae, and shortly thereafter Christian churches were built, and Greek was adopted as the language of the church, diplomacy, and official documents.

During the latter part of the sixth century two other kingdoms emerged in Nubia, Makuria with its capital at Dongola, and Alodia with its capital at Soba. Alodia is believed to have sprung from migrations of people south of Meroe. Both Makuria and Alodia converted to Christianity during the sixth century and were influenced by the Byzantine Empire. In 573 Makuria dispatched an emissary to Constantinople where a friendship convention was negotiated with Justin II. Alodia was converted by Egyptian Monophysites. Thus, by 580 many Nubians were Christians and resisted the advance of Islam for about 800 years.

These Nubian kingdoms developed their own culture, only part of which has been reconstructed - thanks to the results of archaeology. Church ruins have been recovered, and the pottery and paintings which adorned them seem to indicate an artistic peak between 800 and 1000 A.D. Inscriptions in Greek, Coptic, and Nubian have been found. Remnants of houses built of sun-dried brick reveal something of their architecture.

Islam made its thrust into Nubia when it besieged Dongola in 651 A.D. This led to a treaty of friendship and trade which lasted for many centuries. An inscription of 1317, however, reveals that Dongola may have been an independent Muslim state; but as late as about 1340 Al Omari wrote that the people of northern Makuria were Christians with a Muslim king. Conversion of the masses to Islam thus seems to have been a slow process in which Nubians retained their own language and customs. Some of them did, however, migrate and settle in southeastern Sudan where they helped to spread the faith. Over the years Nubians developed great military strength. They maintained friendly relations with Egypt, the principal outlet for their trade, which included slaves. This friendship with Egypt later led the Nubians to assist the Fatimid dynasty in its struggle for power.

Thus, in spite of the sparse documentation, enough is known to conclude that Nubia, in the early tradition of Kush, remained a dynamic factor in the history of northeastern Africa. It kept open the north-south channel of communication and cultural diffusion. It helped first to Christianize, later and more effectively to Islamize, much of the Sudan; it also retained much of its own character and carried north inner Africa's presence and influence.

Excerpt from: Joseph E. Harris, *Africans and Their History*, Revised edition, (New York: Mentor - NAL Penguin, Inc., 1987) pp. 39-53.

7. Black Kings and Queens of Egypt

CHANCELLOR WILLIAMS

Egypt's Eighteenth Dynasty is one of the most remarkable royal families in history. Its rulers included Queen Hatshepsut, the first ruler-queen in all humanity, Queen Nefertari, Amenhotep II, Thutmose I and II, Tutankhamen and Ikhnaton. The following excerpt written by the eminent African-American historian, Chancellor Williams, presents an overview of the Eighteenth Dynasty and its impact on Egyptian society. He describes this dynasty as one of the preeminately black dynasties of Egypt. He also addresses directly the issue of racial influences in the changing political climate of Egyptian rule in the course of its lengthy history.

. . . Kamose, the last Theban king in the Seventeenth Dynasty (1645-1567 B.C.), opened a full-scale War of Liberation against the Hebrews and the greatest of the dynasties since the Fourth had now arrived. This was the remarkable Eighteenth Dynasty with a line of kings and queens who became immortal: Ahmose I, Nefertari, Amenhotep II, Thutmose I, Thutmose II, Queen Hatshepsut the Great, Amenhotep III, Ikhnaton, the "Great Reformer," and Tutankhamen. It was called the "New Empire," and so it was in fact. The Hyksos rule was broken and they were "expelled." This however, could only apply to the rulers and their immediate followers. The Hyksos masses were scattered over the country and permanently settled as

"Egyptians." They had become integrated into Egyptian society. Contributing to its development on all fronts, they were not disturbed when their leaders were expelled. There was the usual revival of domestic industry, agriculture and foreign trade, along with the expansions of imperial rule in Palestine and Syria to the Euphrates in Mesopotamia. This expansion of empire and its promise of great wealth from the accompanying expansion of trade meant renewal of the wars against their black brothers holding the economically indispensable South. This time the new and most powerful central government was able to extend its rule farther south than ever; that is, to the Fourth cataract, almost to the Holy City of Napata itself.

For some writers to state the obvious truth that the black rulers of Egypt did not hesitate to wage wars against the black rulers of Southern Ethiopia would have destroyed their biggest myth, that the Egyptians (white Asians or Coloreds) were always the conquering heroes over the blacks in the south. These wars did not always follow a racial pattern.

As would be expected under black rulers, Thebes was again reorganized under the Eighteenth Dynasty and much of its ancient grandeur restored. Temple building in the grand style was resumed. The Eighteenth, like some of the previous African dynasties, was well integrated with "loyal Asians." For there were, it should be needless to say, countless thousands of Asians who were wholeheartedly devoted to the blacks, just as there were thousands of Afro-Asians (Egyptians) as loyal to the black race as any black could possibly be. Therefore, when an overall picture is presented, such as in my discussion of the attitudes of Asians, Afro-Asians and Africans toward each other, one should keep the always big exceptions in mind. Nothing is ever all-white, all-black or, in this case, all half-white. In the case of the half-whites, the record overflows with those who, contrary to the rule, hated the fact of their white blood and stuck to the blacks and their cause all the more tenaciously. These are the kinds of outcomes that reflect the complexities and variations of the human mind, and that make generalizations about a whole people, if anything, ridiculous.

The "Great Eighteenth" had begun under the most favorable circumstances, for one of the great black queens of Egypt, Nefertari, and her equally famous husband, Ahmose I, headed the dynasty. As was the custom, she had been named after some of the distinguished queens of similar name who had preceded her. None of them, however, ranked near Nefertari of the Eighteenth in active participation and leadership in national affairs. She helped her son, Amenhotep, in the great work of national reconstruction. If she did not reach the heights of the greatest black queen of Egypt, Hatshepsut, it was only because the latter was a queen absolute, ruling alone as a king (to emphasize the point she often dressed in royal male attire, including the false beard and wig). But the comparison is hardly fair because each was great in her field of work, and that work was largely predetermined, and the role to be played by each was clear. And that was why, in the end, both Nefertari and Amenhotep I were deified as the founders of one of the world's greatest line of rulers and some of the finest monuments were erected to their memory. Had the people forgotten Ahmose, her husband, who was the true founder?

Queen Hatshepsut, daughter of Thutmose I, was indeed a "man" in many of her aggressive and unyielding characteristics as a ruler. As regent for Thutmose III, she tended to be an absolute ruler and, by expertly relying on her feminine charms, she was able to have her own way without a real check by the Council, something few African kings could do successfully. But it was not all due to "feminine charms," perhaps not at all. For Hatshepsut was, in fact, one of the most brilliant minds that ever ascended the throne of a nation. Her reign was in two parts, one as regent and the other as reigning queen in her own right. There was actually no difference, for Thutmose III was too young to count. Even before becoming legal ruler, therefore, she was actively pushing the things dearest to the hearts of all great African leaders: the expansion of foreign trade, international diplomatic relations, perfection of national defenses, vast public building programs, securing the south and the north through either peace or war and, one of her "pet projects," building a great navy for both commerce and war. Her success on most of these fronts made her one of the giants of the race.

Meanwhile, the next Thutmose was waiting with increasing impatience and frustration to succeed a woman who, to him at least, seemed destined to live forever. The fact that his wife was the Queen's daughter only increased the really morbid hatred of his royal mother-in-law. Consequently, when he finally became King Thutmose III at last, he himself did what Asians and Europeans were to do on a scale so grand that the history of ancient Egypt, as essentially black history, was almost completely obliterated. He undertook to erase her name from all the monuments and temples she had built, destroying all documents bearing her name, and smashing all sculptured likenesses, paintings and, indeed, anything that might indicate that Hatshepsut ever lived. Also, as later Europeans and Asians were to do to all inscriptions reflecting the blacks, Thutmose III had his own name and that of his brother engraved where Hatshepsut's had been chiselled out, thus taking credit for all of her achievements in addition to his own outstanding works. These were many, and need not be detailed since so much of it repeats the works of great leaders already discussed.

Queen Tiy was also one of Egypt's remarkable queens. Amenhotep III and Queen Tiy gave a son to Egypt who was destined to be one of the greats in the black world. This was Amenhotep IV, known to fame as Ikhnaton. He was different from all of his predecessors. He was more preacher than king, and the greatest single spiritual force to appear in the history of blacks. His great religious reform movement aimed at a greater focus on the One and Only Almighty God, Creator of the Universe. The numerous lesser gods had overshadowed the Almighty in involving people by causing them to worship the gods through the endless number of competing cults, all served by a too self-serving priesthood. Such an unheard-of stand by the leader of the nation meant revolution and certain rebellion by the powerful priesthoods all over the land. Yet the new doctrine did not reach the masses and the non-spiritual demands for leadership on pressing earthly fronts put the king in an unhappy situation. One was the continued Asian harassments on the eastern borders. Ikhnaton grew more indifferent as his religious movement declined. After 17 years of heroic efforts, he passed in 1362 B.C., leaving the reins to Tutankhamen. This stepson's efforts to carry on the work of his father had only limited success. The old-time religions still prevailed. Ikhnaton's impact on the nation, however, was everlasting. His proposed reforms had more to do with a shift in emphasis than in faith. But even this seems to have been regarded as a direct threat to the powerful priesthood that, no matter how much divided into numerous cults, could unite in a common cause.

The power of the priesthood rose as the kings of Egypt became more preoccupied with secular affairs than with the religious role as high priest of The Most High. It has been pointed out that the ruler's political influence stemmed not from the constitution but from his close relationship with the gods. The priests themselves had promoted the evolution of an idea of the ruler's role as chief priest and intermediary with the ancestral dead and the gods, to the idea of the ruler's kinship with the gods, thereby becoming divine himself, the son or daughter of a god, and finally, a god himself.

As custodians of the temples, the priests were promoting and making their own positions more powerful and secure by promoting the divine kingship idea. It meant that each king would try to outdo his predecessors in building more bigger and finer temples and colossal burial structures (the pyramids) for the royal saints and the sons and daughters of Amon, Horus, Set, etc.

The priests were in the most strategic positions to acquire great economic and political power for themselves quite naturally and without any particular efforts to do so. They were the first men of learning: scribes, historians, scientists, architects, physicians, artists, mathematicians, astrologers, and especially chemists. Many temples, therefore, were colleges as well as places of worship. The temples were also places through which flowed much of the national revenue. We could go on and on, indicating how and why priests became so politically powerful in Egyptian life that even a great king like Ikhnaton could not overcome their opposition. It was too late for him to escape from the now traditional status of being "divine." One might say it was the price a god has to pay for god-makers.

In 1320 B.C., the Age of the Ramses began. This time, a line of great leaders was not followed by a line of weaklings. This was the Nineteenth Dynasty, 1320-1200 B.C. And while it did not equal the "Glorious Eighteenth," the Ramses kings stamped their periods as one of the most outstanding in the long history of the country. It was only near its end that the usual phenomenon of weakness and decline in the cycle began to set in as general social, economic and political disorganization. The Ramses rule continued through the Twentieth Dynasty, 1200-1085 B.C.

The Twenty-First, Twenty-Second and Twenty-Third periods, 1085-730 B.C., again illustrated, as I had stated before, the fallacy of trying to chronicle African history in Egypt by dynasties. I had pointed out that at various times during the long, long struggles for power we find several different "dynasties" ruling at the same time from their respective capitals in various parts of the country. Every period of weak kings at Memphis or Thebes was a general breakdown during which exactly the same happened over and over again: The Asian Lower Egypt became independent again, and from its capital at Avaris or Sais pushed the expansion of Asian power in Upper Egypt. By 1085 B.C., the Asian population was so vast there that new Asian dynasties were relatively easy to establish almost anywhere north of the First Cataract. During one of these periods, 70 kings in 70 days was reported.

Excerpt from: Chancellor Williams, *The Destruction of Black Civilization*, (Chicago, IL.: Third World Press, 1987), pp. 106-111.

8. Black Civilization South of the First Cataract of the Nile River

CHANCELLOR WILLIAMS

Chancellor Williams in this selection documents the existence and the pervasive influence of the "Black World" in the vast regions of the Nile River from the First Cataract south throughout Kush, Nubia, Meroe and Ethiopia. These centers were powerful and highly developed civilizations distinctive to themselves in contradistinction to Egypt in the north. Joseph Harris in a previous selection (#6) discusses some of this same material more in terms of Egypt's influence on the Black World. Williams turns this around to show how the Black World also influenced Egypt and to a certain extent the rest of Africa as well.

Having lost both upper and lower Egypt, Ethiopia's northern border had been pushed to the First Cataract at Assuan, and Necho II eventually became king of Egypt, beginning the Twenty-Sixth Dynasty, 665-525 B.C. The Egyptian armies were increasingly made up of foreigners and enslaved blacks. It was during this dynasty that the Assyrians were expelled again, this time by nationalistic Egyptians. The blacks' loss of their beloved Memphis, Thebes, and even their Egyptian name now seemed to be final.

Other invasions came. The Persians under Darius the Greek took over, and their domination of Egypt lasted from 525 to 404 B.C., with the assistance of Greek mercenaries. They returned in 343 B.C. to reestablish their rule, but again for only a relatively short duration. Alexander reached Egypt in 332 B.C., on his world conquering rampage. But one of the greatest generals in the ancient world was also the Empress of Ethiopia. This was the formidable black Queen Candace, world famous as a military tactician and field commander. Legend has it that Alexander could not entertain even the possibility of having his world fame and unbroken chain of victories marred by risking a defeat, at last, by a woman. He halted his armies at the borders of Ethiopia and did not invade to meet the waiting black armies with their Queen in personal command. Upon his death, one of his most outstanding generals became Pharaoh as Ptolemy I, thus beginning 300 years of Macedonian-Greek rule. Toward the end of Greek domination, the expansion of the Roman Empire had transferred the real center of power to Rome. Assyria, Persia, Greece, Rome - these empires represent the continuing process of transforming a black civilization into a near-white civilization long before the Christian era.

The Ptolemaic period had been largely one of confusion. The division of power among the Greeks, Macedonians and Egyptians, and intermarriages with the latter, joint rule, etc., made the Ptolemaics, at times, merely nominal rulers. There were times when a native Afro-Asian ruler gained the center of the stage as the star attraction, as in the case of Cleopatra. Upon her death, in 30 B.C., Romans assumed direct control, ruling the country for seven centuries, beginning their reign thirty years before Jesus Christ would be born in the same Palestine where blacks had lived and ruled so long.

After this long period of domination, the arab general Amr-ibn-al-as, entered Alexandria in 642 A.D. with only 4,000 men. The conquest of Egypt by the Muslim armies, which had reached Pelusium two years earlier, was not only to change the character of Egyptian civilization radically, but it was to have a disastrous impact on the dignity and destiny of Africans as a people. The arab conquest had opened the floodgates wider and arabs poured in. Colonization and Islamization progressed. As Egypt became a main center of arab power, this fact found concrete expression in arab-Islamic expansion over North Africa into Spain, and southward into what remained as "The Land of the Blacks."

The New Borderline of the Blacks

We have traced the ancient struggles between Africans, mulattoes and Asians, where the Africans sought not only to resist conquest, but to retake the whole of Egypt. They succeeded at times, but finally lost all of Egypt, as we have seen.

Ethiopia now began at the First Cataract in the north and extended south into present-day Ethiopia. It was now bounded by Upper Egypt, the Red Sea and the Libyan desert. These are rather general geographical designations without any precise meaning, for ancient Ethiopia had no precise southern boundaries. Ancient Ethiopians would say that their land included Egypt and was in fact without boundaries in Africa insofar as non-Africans were concerned. All of the European and Asian doctrines about "unoccupied" regions of Africa at any given period in history are quite meaningless and unacceptable to Africans. For to them, it is just as senseless as it would be to say to a farmer anywhere, "See here now! There are large sections of your land unoccupied and untended. So we'll just come in and take it!"

The Africans' area of great concentration was ancient Nubia between the First and the Sixth Cataracts. It was the land where they had developed the great civilization which they had extended over Egypt. Their work had been appropriated by the invaders as their own.

The geography of Nubia is the geography of much of present-day Sudan and beyond. The Nile flows through its sand and rock deserts with a series of falls and a number of rapids. The country is almost rainless. It is the land of the great Nubian desert. West of the Nile towards the Red Sea was the mining area, rich in gold. It was, even within the concept of these geographical boundaries, the heartland of the black world.

Already pushed by the invaders from the Mediterranean areas in north, northeast and northwest, the Africans were to be further hedged in from the east and southeast as the Asian hordes continued to stream across the Red Sea and the Indian Ocean.

Scraps from Prehistory

The stone age Africans lived about the same as stone age peoples all over the world. They were hunters, fishermen and craftsmen. Archaeologists have dug up some of their tools and other artifacts at Wadi Halfa, Wawa, Sai Island, Wadi Hudi, the Selima oasis, Tangasi, Tagiya and other places. These areas are between the Second and the Fourth Cataracts. Our discussion of specific, concrete evidence of early black civilization up to this point has been confined to the Egyptian north. Most notable among the Neolithic finds in the south were the beautiful, high burnished, black-topped and red pottery bowls, jars, etc. The pottery was artistically decorated in wavy ripples or squares. Their earliest writing was in pictures. So many hundreds of these rock "messages" were found along the Nile through Nubialand that one may well wonder if these prehistoric "historians" had posterity in mind. While many of the pictures portrayed wildlife and other objects of interest in the environment, others went beyond this role of the artist and recorded such historic facts as the conquest of Northern Nubia by the Nubian Pharaoh of the Old Kingdom, Sneferu, in 2730 B.C. This was left a vast waste-land and practically wiped out a civilization that had been developing before Neolithic times.

The "Children of the Sun"

For one thing, the land to the south of Egypt had developed a strong economy that was continuously enriched by a thriving export trade in paper (from papyrus), ivory, gold, ebony, emeralds, copper, incense, ostrich feathers (always greatly in demand), and its famous decorated earthenware. A strong economy also meant a strong Ethiopian army, posing a threat even to an African-ruled Egypt. From the Egyptian viewpoint, the "Land of the Blacks" was a threefold threat. Historically, the blacks who had fled below the First Cataract to escape the various conquests never seemed to accept those conquests as final, and attempted to retake Egypt from time to time.

But it is clear that, having reconquered the Asian-dominated Lower Egypt, the black pharaohs sought integration with the Asians instead of driving them out of the country. The policy of moderation and accommodation was apparently anathema to the "extremist" Ethiopians, proud blacks for whom the prospects of having their children come into the world with a color distinctly different from their own was at once an insult to their watching ancestors, and an offense to the gods themselves.

This attitude might also explain the hostility of the southern blacks toward the Afro-Asian. The latter were not "true" Africans because they were becoming Egyptians, a mixed breed of many races. They were, therefore, traitors in the eyes of "true" Africans whose badge of eternal honor was the blackness of their skin. This was color racism, deeply rooted, for it sprang from religion: They were "Children of the Sun" blessed with blackness by the Sun God himself and thus protected from his fiery rays. They were his children. Their very blackness, therefore, was religious, a blessing and an honor.

The second already stated threat was economic, Egypt's own flourishing export trade, both by sea and caravans, depended heavily on her imports from the south. To cut these off would mean economic panic in an otherwise prosperous land.

The third great fear concerned the mighty Nile River. Suppose the Ethiopians decided to bring Egypt to her knees and starved her to death by diverting the waters of the Nile. Belief in this possibility was ancient and ran deep.

The Egyptian conquest of Nubia, therefore, might remove the military and economic threats, but, insofar as the Nile was concerned, it would settle nothing. Besides, these blacks seemed to be unconquerable. A Sneferu might attempt total extermination of the population, burying every town and village, destroying farms and cattle, leaving the land in utter ruin. Yet, as soon as the armies of destruction withdrew, the surviving Africans would come out from their hiding places and began to rebuild once again.

Like Upper Egypt, this was a land of cities and towns, of temples and pyramids. Africans were the great pyramid builders, the temple builders. They had built the great pyramids of Egypt during their rule. Renewed activity in temple-building came after Nubia was reoccupied by the Eighteenth Dynasty rulers.

All this renewed zeal in building new towns and temples in the south was reconstruction. The Old Kingdom raiders could not destroy all of the temples and other monuments.

The returning Egyptians, therefore, had found many fine temples still in use, others in ruins. All Ethiopian inscriptions on the temples and monuments were erased and Egyptian inscriptions substituted. All outstanding African creations that could not be converted and claimed as the work of Egyptians were destroyed, for now "Egyptian" meant "white" - Asian or European. This was done "to promote national unity." Ethiopian inscriptions, of course, recorded victories over Egypt. The arabs were to carry out the work of eradication in a far more thoroughgoing manner at a later time. All of the south was never completely conquered. The reconquest we are now discussing extended forty or fifty miles below Abu Hamed. History continued to repeat itself. Below the area of conquest the Africans continued to rebuild, reorganizing their fighting forces, and watching an overextended Egypt become weaker and weaker under weak pharaohs who were unable to cope with the interminable struggle for power among the Asians, Egyptians and other incursive groups. In these cycles of consolidation followed by fragmentation into numerous chiefdoms and principalities, Egypt mirrored the results of the human power craze not only in Africa but generally throughout the world. Yet in the long view of her history, Egypt's overall record was one of consolidation and unity that, at times, was not seriously broken for a thousand years.

Napata was a beautiful city that was favored by surroundings that helped to make it so. It was located below the Fourth Cataract above the great curve where the Nile had turned southward and, as through changing its mind, turned north again. An imposing hill, the "Throne of the Sun God," was the site of temples. The city itself was regarded as the "Holy of Holies,"; the capital of what the Egyptians called "The Land of the Gods." But "Napata" referred not only to this central city, but included what today we would call a metropolitan area that covered towns and villages for miles in all directions from the present-day town of Karima. It was to this area that African leaders, including priests of the various cults, retreated when things got too hot in Egypt. Here also, certain African kings preferred to stay even when their positions and power in Egypt were unchallenged. Most of the royal burials in pyramids were at Kurru. The largest pyramid in Ethiopia is that of King Tharqa at Nuri.

After the Syrian-Greek invasion in 590 B.C., the city was again almost completely destroyed. The capital was moved to the other side of the river to Meroe, the historic industrial center.

The blacks apparently had been more concerned with the development of their copper industry than with iron. Iron ore was in an abundance. The earlier failure to exploit it, especially for military weapons, was the reason Assyrians, with their superior iron weapons, were able to sweep the blacks out of Egypt, invading the heartland and destroying the holy city of Napata. The Africans had long since learned the use of iron. They knew all about the smelting process. Why did they allow the Assyrians to get ahead of them? Granting that the ancients kept their military developments secret, as nations try to do today, it was also true that spies, including Africans, were active everywhere. The question is interesting because we are not discussing the period when the African had ultimately surrendered to despair and retrogression, but a period of African power, high civilization and a greatness respected and feared by the ancient world. Even after the onslaught by the Assyrians and their allies, the Africans were to rebuild, from the new capital city of Meroe, a civilization greater than the one just destroyed.

There were many lesser states and countless small chiefdoms in the vast land mass that began where the effective control by Ethiopia ended.

Through all these millenniums of ups and downs, of trials and errors, of great victories and disastrous defeats, through it all the central drive of this once-black land was in the direction of consolidation and progress. Tribes were united into one nation either voluntarily, or that failing, by force. Strong armies were maintained to protect and expand their civilization. The retaking of that part of the homeland that extended north along the Nile to the Mediterranean was at once the deathless dream, the impassioned goal, and the cornerstone of their foreign policy.

These Africans battled the invading Asians decade after decade and century after century until their resistance to conquest and enslavement extended over four thousand years.

From ancient days, therefore, the Africans had, in the very center of the heartland on the continent, a history from which their posterity could learn how unity alone provided the condition for strength and progress, and that each one of a thousand little "independent" chiefdoms were but a standing invitation to the aggressors and the ultimate domination of all. Why did the Africans fail to take this message of salvation as a revealed truth from their own history? What dimmed civilization's light on Barkal Hill and caused an ultimate withdrawal to the bush and the scattering of people hither and yon like hunted beasts? Why did Africans begin to retire from the race with other advancing peoples and fall so far behind that even the memory of former greatness could not inspire a revival because that memory had been almost completely blotted out? I have been detailing some of the answers throughout, and in later chapters we shall explore further answers to questions raised.

We now cross to the west bank of the Nile and journey farther south to the city of Meroe. It is the eighth century B.C., and the move to Meroe was simply a move to what was already the southern capital, only now, instead of having two capital cities in the south, there would be only one.

The Development of Writing

A distinguished line of leaders followed Tanutamon to the throne in 653 B.C., Atlanersa, Senkamanseken, Anlaman, Aspalta, Amtalka and Malenakan - palace, temple, and pyramid builders all. Two of the greatest temples were built by King Aspalta at Meroe: The Sun Temple and the Temple of Amon. The imposing pyramids and rows of huge royal statues added to the majesty and magnificence of Meroe. The royal tombs, as in Egypt, were the repositories of the nation's history. From them archaeologists were able to determine a line of forty-one rulers after the conquest of Lower Nubia. These monuments were not only sources of early African history from within but, of the highest importance, they were elaborately decorated outside with both the first form of writing, hieroglyphics, and the more advanced African inscriptions in their own invented writing.

For the Africans themselves had invented writing, and all attempts to connect this ancient achievement with Egyptian or Asiatic influence have failed. Here the "external influence" school has suffered a major defeat, because the written records found on statues, altars, tombstones, graffiti, etc., were so distinctly African that their native origin could not be successfully disputed. Moreover, the African system of writing was very different from the Egyptian. It was simpler and had vowels, whereas Egyptian had none. There were twenty-three characters or letters in the African alphabet, four vowel signs, seventeen consonants, and two signs of the syllable. New concepts and new or special words could be easily introduced by the old picture system. Clarity and easy reading was assured by measured spacing between words. A system of numerical symbols for mathematics was developed. The African inscriptions on monuments and such records as those found in royal tombs were in a special category. General writing was done on tablets of wood and skins prepared for that purpose. Such things as rocks, walls, vases and broken bits and pieces of earthenware comprised other artifacts where ancient African writing was found.

Again, how and why did all this disappear? How and why was it blotted out or hidden so completely for two thousand years that an ignorant world, which unprecedented research facilities in its universities still believes, teaches and proclaims that the black man had never developed a civilization of his own?

It has been noted that the attractions of Ethiopia, "The Land of the Gods," were great not only because the Egyptians regarded it as the main source of their religion, but also because of its socio-political, economic and strategic importance. When African kings reconquered Egypt and became "Egyptian" pharaohs, they still longed for the motherland to the south, desiring to unite the whole of it with Egypt into one vast empire. They would often retire there, some wanting their final resting place to be in a pyramid below the First Cataract. To the south rested their ancestors whose company they were to join. Here was the capital city of both the black man's world and that of his heaven as well, the holy city of Napata.

During the different periods in which Napata came under a foreign yoke, the capital city of Meroe had to become somewhat holy in its own right, and many of the kings, queens, and other leaders were buried in pyramids there. These were constructed of stone outside of the city proper, sometimes at a visible distance of two or more miles. They were built to stand forever, an attempt that stemmed from the African's actual belief in immortality. This is why their faith included the natural assumption that those who had passed on, their ancestors, were living in the "great beyond," and were, therefore, in the most favorable position to represent the interests of their kinsmen below; or, in short, to serve as mediators between God and man.

The pyramids ringing the city not only added to the physical beauty of the surroundings, but they were also the silent sentinels, the every watchful ancestral presence from which might come either a benediction or a curse.

I am unsparing in my criticism of those African societies which seemed to be governed by fatalism and failed to counterattack against their natural and human enemies. As I read the record, it seemed to me that these groups did not try to meet the awful challenges which confronted them. They gave up too readily and refused to ignore tribal lines or to unite for common survival strategies. They remained scattered here and there, like hunted animals, moving into barbarism and savagery. Such were my strictures and, obviously, I did not give the whole story, even about these groups.

Now, however, and by a glorious contrast, we are in the midst of blacks, the core of all Africa, who met the challenge on all fronts and from every direction; and who fought on and on through the centuries, against the forces of man and nature until they, themselves, were completely overwhelmed.

Three thousand years ago the desert, while slowly moving in on Africa, had not advanced to where it is today. There was more arable land in Ethiopia, although its agriculture did not match that of the rich delta region of Egypt. The blacks were, however, mainly agriculturists like other Africans. Even with their remarkable industrial development, farming went on both sides where the "two Niles" met in their land before continuing as one great river through Egypt to the Mediterranean Sea. Nor should the importance of the Atbara river be overlooked. Even though the surrounding deserts were a problem insofar as agricultural expansion was desired, the more immediate problem was famine from drought. There were years during which no rain fell at all and not a hopeful cloud appeared in the sky.

The Africans met the challenge by constructing a national system of reservoirs. These were strategically located around the capital, at Musawarat, Naga, Hordan, Umm, Usuda, in the Gezira region, at Duanib, Basa, and doubtlessly at other sites not yet excavated.

This master plan to defeat drought and famine by a system of reservoirs was more important than all of the architectural art that found expression in their beautiful statues, temples, palaces, columns and pyramids. The reservoirs were more significant than the monuments, important as these were in hiding the black man's intellectual achievements in the invention of writing deep under the sands.

I rate the reservoirs as the supreme achievement because they reflect the real measure of African man as he met the challenge to survival head-on, with a constructive counter-attack against the adverse forces of earth, sun and sky. The irrigation system, made reasonably effective with their oxen-powered wheels, was a part of this challenge to adverse circumstances.

Piankhi, following Kashta in 720 B.C., began what was quickly to become again one of the greatest world powers of the time. Ethiopia was united with Afro-Asian Egypt under a single imperial rule that extended from the Mediterranean in the north to an undefined boundary in the south. Also unknown was how far its eastern boundary extended southward along the Indian Ocean coastland, how much of Uganda and Abyssinia was included, or how far westward the empire extended. All this is not so important as the point that during this period of triumph, world fame, fear, and an unprecedented prosperity from a flourishing trade with about one-half of the world, African rulers continued to neglect the updating of their military and naval defenses.

Iron was the basis of the technological revolution in warfare. That the Assyrians, Hittites, Persians and other Asiatic nations were equipping their armies with new types of iron weapons, and that these were devastatingly more effective than stone and copper weapons had to be well-known to the Africans. It was not news. As was mentioned before, they not only knew about the use of iron but they had long since developed the iron smelting processes. The trouble was the highly secretive royal monopoly. No secret was more zealously guarded than the smelting of iron. This meant rigidly limited production. Here was fear out-matching both reason and the most elementary common sense. This over-secretiveness which inhibited the expansion of iron production was to contribute mightily to the success of Assyrian arms over them.

Prosperity, too, may have blurred the African's vision. Too much success can be dangerous. In this case so much wealth was piled up from foreign trade, especially in gold, ivory and copper, that the question of iron, if raised, may have been dismissed as "economically unsound." Whatever the reasons were, the fact is that the great iron industries which had developed in this center, spreading over Africa, could have started centuries before.

Even as early as 300 B.C., when iron smelting was employed for more useful purposes than ornaments, the royal monopoly still prevented widespread use. That they knew of the importance of iron is shown by the fact that kings and high priests were often heads of the guild, and the chief iron master would often gain the status of what a prime minister is today. Regardless of the delay, iron smelting and tool-making got underway on a vast scale in Ethiopia at a most crucial period for Africa. Its center was Meroe, and it appears that the biggest iron works were in and around this capital city. This development was at a crucial period because it was the period of increasing migrations from the heartland and the scattering of groups all over Africa. They carried their knowledge of this great technological revolution wherever they went, and they began the use of iron and the development of iron industries wherever they had the opportunity to settle in iron ore areas and remain settled long enough to create a stable society.

This spread of ironworking from the cradle of black civilization is just another example of how other fundamental African institutions spread over the continent, north as well as south, and remained basically unchanged down through the centuries, no matter how numerous were the groups into which the original society became fragmented or how countless were the various languages and dialects that resulted from that segmentation. There were, as a matter of course, many variations and modifications by different survival groups. The most remarkable of the facts was that even those groups that were pushed back into a state of barbarism still held on to some of the basic institutions of the society from which they descended from one to two thousand years before. Neither Christian Europe or Muslim Asia were able to completely destroy those institutions, even in the vast regions over which both had supreme control. And this is why, in a previous discussion, I had suggested a smile of compassion when you read or hear about "Egyptian influence" on this or that black society because, in general, all that could possible be meant is the "influence of early black civilization on subsequent black societies."

The expansion of iron culture, however, was a revolution in technology that ushered in a new age and gave new hope to a despairing people. It meant the use of new instruments of production in agriculture, and the industrial crafts, and, of great importance for a refugee people, for a new kind of military organization and defense. It can be seen, then, that the "Motherland of the Blacks," centered on the Nile around the cataracts, providing her wandering sons and daughters with the instruments of survival, a knowledge that still served them well centuries after the arabs and Turks had overrun that Motherland.

The memory of many things had been lost, however. Who remembered Thebes, Napata, Memphis, Elephantine, Heracleopolis or Nekhab? Indeed, who remembered even Meroe, the most advanced center not only of the African age, but also of writing? And what of the other important towns and cities in Southern Ethiopia (Nubia-Cush), Musawarat, Nuri,

Panopolis, Kerma, Assuan, Soleb, Abu Simbel, Kurusku, Samnah, Philae, Kawa, Dongola, etc? Our constant references to Napata and Meroe might lead those who do not look at the map to think that there were only two important cities in the land.

Forgetting the names of ancient centers of importance was nothing compared to the tragedy of the blacks in almost completely forgetting the very art of writing which they themselves invented! This was one of the most tragic losses, to repeat, that was ever suffered by a whole people. And in view of the anti-black course of subsequent history, the blacks needed their written language and records more than any other people. Just how and why this people discontinued the use of writing has been set forth rather clearly and in some detail in the foregoing pages. However, the matter is of such transcendent importance that I hope some black scholar will devote an entire book detailing this one episode in the long history of Africans. The story would cover the periods of migrations and dispersions when writing was needless if not impossible, to the general loss of the art itself. I say "general loss" again because, of course, some African societies did not completely lose the art of writing even under conditions where its use seemed utterly futile.

The most important fact to keep in mind, however, is that we are considering the early age when relatively few people could write, a small professional class, the scribes. All books, scrolls, inscriptions, letters, etc., were written by them. Therefore, in any society where the scribes were either captured or, for whatever reason, disappeared, the art of writing in that society died. In view of the developments in black Africa, the disappearance of writing is not a mystery at all.

Conquest and domination tended to check migrations and bring a larger measure of iron-ruled stability to the invaded region. An integral part of that iron rule was the introduction of the conquerors' speech and writing, the first step in the process of conquering the soul and minds of the blacks along with their bodies. This was easy because the knowledge-starved "key people" among the blacks eagerly grasped Arabic, French, Portuguese, English, or German as the best route to status in a new civilization. Most of this developed later than the period we have been summarizing, the thousand years in Ethiopia after its last success in retaking Egypt and its defeat and withdrawal with the fall of the Twenty-Fifth Dynasty. Here we speak of the period from the sixth century B.C. to the fourth century of the Christian church in Ethiopia.

Christian Africa

Africa was naturally among the first areas to which Christianity spread. It was next door to Palestine, and from the earliest times there had been the closest relations between the Jews and the blacks, both friendly and hostile. The exchange of pre-Christian religious concepts took place easily and, due to the residence of so many ancient Jewish leaders in Ethiopia - Abraham, Joseph and his brothers, Mary and Jesus. The great Lawgiver, Moses, was not only born in Africa but he was also married to the daughter of an African priest. The pathway for the early Christian church in the "Land of the Blacks" had been made smooth many centuries before.

In a different work I suggested that a major reason why so many later Christian missionaries failed in Africa was because they were bringing refurbished religious doctrines that came from Africa in the first place. The religious belief in sacrifice for the remission of sins was an African belief and practice at least 2,000 years before Abraham. The results of a comparative study of the African, Jewish and Christian religions have amazed many who have undertaken the task. Practically all of the Ten Commandments were embedded in the African Constitution ages before Moses went up to Mt. Sinai in Africa in 491 B.C., a rather late date in African history.

We do not know how much significance should be read into the fact that Christianity began to spread in Ethiopia (Nubia or Cush) only after the destruction of the central Empire with the fall of Meroe. However, the most important development after the Empire passed was not the rise of Christianity, but the rise of the two black states that picked up the mantle and staff of Ethiopia to carry on. These two states were Makuria and Alwa.

Excerpt from: Chancellor Williams, *The Destruction of Black Civilization*, (Chicago: Third World Press, 1987), pp. 118-121.

9. The Black Peoples South of the Sahara

J. D. Omer-Cooper

This excerpt is an account of how most of Africa south of the Sahara came to be inhabited by the existing black populace and how these groups are related. Whereas the West African black peoples turned to agriculture and became sedentary, others further east along the Sudanic belt became nomadic and migratory.

The peoples of Africa south of the Sahara

The black peoples of Negro physical type who now occupy practically the whole of Africa south of the Sahara were once confined to a relatively small part of it. Their early place of origin and the course of their migrations have been much debated but no definite conclusions have been drawn. Nevertheless, it seems fairly certain that at one time they were settled along the Sudanic belt to the south of the Sahara and for a considerable way into the Sahara itself at a time when it was more suitable for human habitation. South of this the whole of the rest of the continent was occupied by other peoples who are now known mainly by discoveries of their stone implements, cave paintings, and occasional skeletons. Throughout most of East, Central and Southern Africa the early inhabitants probably belonged to a people related to the San (or Bushmen) who still survive in parts of Southern Africa. They lived by hunting and gathering wild fruits and tubers. In part of East Africa skeletons and other remains suggest at one time the people there may have been similar to those of North Africa and the lower Nile valley, and in Zaire and parts of the West African forestlands the earliest inhabitants may have been related to the pygmies who still live in the forest of Zaire.

In course of time the peoples of Negro physical type living in the eastern part of the Sudanic belt around the upper Nile valley tended to diverge culturally from the West African group. Their languages developed a very different pattern and their way of life became nomadic and pastoral, based on cattle. They probably also mixed to a considerable extent with the peoples of the Nile valley. The blacks of West Africa, where higher rainfall and the fertile lands of the inland delta of the Niger encouraged a sedentary way of life, became mainly agriculturalists, though there is a major exception in the case of the Fulani, who probably mixed extensively with Berber-speaking groups such as the nomadic Tuareg of the desert. The two main sections of the Negro peoples were never entirely separate; migrations took place in both directions and some of the peoples around Lake Chad, for example, are thought to have come from further east.

The agricultural Negroes of West Africa were naturally able to develop much larger and more dense populations than those who relied exclusively on cattle-keeping. It is probable that they domesticated crops of their own from wild plants, and they also began to grow crops domesticated elsewhere. Then at a period in the remote past which is still unknown, they began to expand very rapidly. This may have been the result of the introduction of techniques for producing and using iron which made it possible to clear the bush more easily, and perhaps also of the introduction of new crops from Asia. Not only did they colonize the great forest areas of West Africa itself but one branch of them spread out of West Africa altogether and gradually spread over almost the whole of the continent south of the Sahara, giving rise to the great family of Bantu-speaking peoples.

These peoples have developed many different ways of life and hundreds of different languages, but they are called by a single name because, although the speakers of one language cannot understand the others, a study of the languages shows that they are related to one another and must have developed from a common origin. Recent research has shown that these Bantu languages are related to the main language group of West Africa and probably developed out of one of its languages.

As the Bantu-speaking peoples advanced they gradually absorbed or expelled the previous inhabitants. In East Africa they came in contact with the cattle-keeping peoples known as the Nilotes and Southern Nilotes. The two groups, Bantu and Nilotes, have commonly been hostile to one another but they have also influenced each other. It may be that it was from contact with the Nilotes that some Bantu-speaking groups acquired the habit of cattle-keeping which they carried with them on their migration to the south. The expansion of the Bantu-speakers over more than half the surface of Africa was a slow and gradual process taking hundreds of years. Though they began to enter Central Africa in the first few centuries A.D., Bantu colonization of Southern Africa was not complete by the nineteenth century. The southern tip of the subcontinent and the area now known as Namibia still provided a home for the earlier peoples who elsewhere had disappeared. Indeed the San and their relatives, the Khoi (or Hottentots), still form a significant element in the population of modern Botswana and Namibia, and it is only comparatively recently that Bantu-speakers began to settle in significant numbers in the neighborhood of Cape Town.

For thousands of years the Bantu-speaking peoples have been engaged in a tremendous enterprise which even to this day is not fully complete. They have had the task of opening up most of sub-Saharan Africa to settled agriculture. They are the true pioneers of Africa. When in addition it is remembered that millions of Africans, including Bantu-speakers, were carried across the sea to the Americas and now form the vast majority of the population of the West Indies as well as a significant part of the population of both the American continents, the scale of their expansion can be realized. Inevitably this colossal colonizing effort absorbed much of their energies.

Excerpt from: J. D. Omer-Cooper, *The Making of Modern Africa*, Vol. I, (New York: Longman, 1986), pp. 13-15.

10. East Africa and Zimbabwe

Joseph E. Harris

The origin and development of East African culture and civilization was a complex process over time. In the following selection Harris alludes to central Tanzania's cave rock-painting art as evidence that the original inhabitants were the present-day Sandawe and Hadza, Khoison language speakers, and early hunters and gatherers. He then goes on to identify the other groups and cultures that contributed to the development of civilization in Tanzania, Zimbabwe and the rest of East Africa. By about 1000 A.D. the Bantus were spread throughout East Africa and were encountered mainly by arabs, traders along the coast. These groups traded and intermarried, producing wealth, power, in a whole new culture and language centered in coastal cities and known as the "Swahili" civilization. Harris also briefly refers to the amazing inland Zimbabwe civilization.

Written accounts of the East African coast date back nearly 2,000 years to the *Periplus of the Erythaean Sea*, a sailor's guide written by an Egyptian Greek merchant. It was probably written during the latter part of the first century A.D., and along with Ptolemy's *Geography*, which for East Africa probably dates from the end of the fourth century A.D., constitute the most informative sources up to the tenth century when al-Masudi, an arab, wrote his very valuable accounts, and the fourteenth century when Ibn Battuta's travel accounts became invaluable sources. There are also chronicles of particular towns written in Arabic or Swahili with Arabic script. The *Kilwa Chronicle*, written about 1530, is the oldest and probably the most reliable. Most of the other town chronicles were written from about the latter part of the eighteenth century. These written sources supplemented by oral traditions, archaeology, linguistics, and anthropology provide the main substance of the history of the East African coast up to modern times.

The precise ethnic identity of the original inhabitants of the eastern coast is unknown, but it is generally agreed that they were probably hunters and gatherers of food. They were probably part of the Khoisan ("click") language family, such as the Sandawe, who live close to the main rock-painting area in central Tanzania, and the Hadza (Tindiga) around Lake Eyasi. Early stone implements have been found at various coastal locations. Subsequent to these early inhabitants, however, the principal components of the present population settled along the coast: the Galla, with linguistic relations with arabs and long contacts across the Red Sea, established settlements in the northern part of the Horn of Africa (Ethiopia and Somalia), and later penetrated into northern Kenya. They remain essentially a nomadic, pastoral people. The Somali also had prolonged contacts with the arabs and settled along the southern shore of the Gulf of Aden. They more readily adopted Islam, probably as early as the tenth century A.D., and intermarried with arabs to a great extent. Their influence has been greatest along the coast, but they also migrated into the interior where communities now reside in Kenya and Ethiopia. The Bantu probably began settling on the coast in small numbers very early, increasing in number by about 500-600 A.D., so that by the end of the first millennium A.D., most of the area had become Bantu-speaking. The great wave of Bantu migrations to East Africa probably originated in present-day Cameroon and moved through Congo (Zaire) and along the Zambezi River to Mozambique and into Tanganyika and Kenya. Today the Bantu represent the largest group of Africans in East Africa.

Some historians have stated that Egyptians, Phoenicians, Persians, arabs, and others may have settled on the coast long before the Christian era. In fact, Herodotus relates an account of the circumnavigation of Africa by Phoenicians, but few historians seem to accept this as fact. It is important to note, however, that East Africa, particularly the area south of the Horn, has been in continuous contact with the whole Indian Ocean complex since the *Periplus* was written, and probably centuries before that. These contacts were facilitated by the monsoon winds which from November through March blow from the northeast and carried dhows from Asia to the East African coast. From May through September the winds reverse themselves, blow from the southwest and so carried the dhows and their crews back to the Arabian peninsula, India, and elsewhere in Asia. This meant that, with the winds blowing from east to west for five months, arabs, Hindus, and other Asians could visit several points on the East African coast, and spend several weeks or months at various places selling their wares and solidifying contacts with local inhabitants. Some of those Asians took up residence, intermarried with the Africans, and thereby provided the genesis of present-day Asian communities in East Africa and the emergence of persons of arab-African descent, the Swahili.

To the early writers this area was known as Azania and to the arabs as the land of the Zenj. The most important pre-Islamic commercial town on the coast seems to have been Rhapta, about which little is known except that it was the center for the export of ivory which arab merchants controlled. Rhapta was probably located on the northern coast of Tanzania. The East African products exported were ivory, gums, shells, cooper, leopard skins, gold, rhinoceros horn, coconut oil, and slaves. From Asia came such items as glass, cloth, spears, hatchets, daggers, awls, lances, beads, and porcelain. The inclusion of the several metal (iron) tools as imports supports the view that iron smelting either was not developed or was underdeveloped. Moreover, near the coast iron ores are very poor.

There is a disputed tradition that following their defeat in Oman by an Umayyad army in the seventh century, two brothers, Suliaman and Said, emigrated from Oman to the land of Zenj. There are also stories of heretic Muslims settling along the coast, and there may indeed be truth in these. Certainly the arabs could easily have started communities. At Merca a colony of Muslim arabs dates from the tenth century and another emerged at Manda near Lamu, and in Zanzibar. Arabs from the area of Bahrein reportedly founded Mogadishu and Brava, probably in the eleventh century.

By the tenth century Muslim settlements had appeared on the islands of Zanzibar and Pemba. Settlements had also emerged in Kilwa, which became the prominent town near the end of the twelfth century. The power of Kilwa is traced to the Shirazi - a derivative of Shiraz, capital of the Persian province of Fars - who very possibly were part of the group of Persian settlement in Mogadishu, Shungways, and other points along the Somali coast. They intermarried with Africans wherever they settled, became Africanized, and established a ruling dynasty at Kilwa and Kisimani Mafia, both of which eventually became very important coastal entrepots. The Shirazi were essentially merchant-rulers who capitalized on the lucrative gold and ivory trade from Sofala, a town south of the Zambezi River on the coast of Mozambique. Kilwa is reported to have gained hegemony over the Sofala trade around the late thirteenth century and probably levied taxes on other merchants trading there. That Kilwa's wealth and influence increased during this period is revealed by the architectural achievements which resulted in the commercial emporium of Husuni Kubwa, Ndogo, and major extensions to the Great Mosque. Stone houses became more common, and valuable Chinese porcelain appeared in larger quantities.

The key items from the coast were gold and ivory which arrived from the interior to Kilwa and Zanzibar, both of which were favorably located near the coast and in the path of the monsoon winds. The source of the gold and ivory was probably Zimbabwe, about which our knowledge is limited. However, archaeology has uncovered some very important evidence which includes impressive ruins of stone structures (probably royal buildings) built between the eleventh and fifteenth centuries. Some of the walls of the buildings are thirty-two feet high, seventeen feet in thickness at the base, and between eleven and fourteen feet at the top. One wall extends about 800 feet in length. The walls were constructed of dry stone mortar, and there is no evidence of the use of scaffolding. Contrary to earlier hypotheses, it is generally agreed that Phoenicians, arabs, and Europeans had not penetrated so deep into the interior so early and could not have constructed those edifices. The general consensus is not only that Africans were the builders of those structures, but that to have done so required a highly developed social and political system to organize and supervise the high labor force, to secure and transport the materials, and to design and construct the buildings - all of which required many years to complete. Moreover, gold and ivory were abundant in the area and no doubt played a significant part in supporting the state through trade with the coast.

During the fifteenth century, in addition to undergoing serious internal dynastic strife, Kilwa was challenged commercially and politically by several other coastal entrepots. Zanzibar exerted its independence and minted its own coins, as did Kilwa. Trade increased at Gedi, where many stone houses were constructed. Pate extended its trading activities, while the rising power of Mombasa became particularly ominous for neighboring towns. It was at this juncture that the Portuguese entered the scene, thereby adding another contending influence which will be considered later. Suffice it here to note that the supremacy of Kilwa was already being undercut prior to the arrival of the Portuguese.

Trends in the interior were affecting coastal developments. This was especially the case among the Yao of northern Mozambique and southern Tanzania. There were active merchants in large areas of the interior and as such responded to coastal developments. As the interior demand for goods from the Orient increased, the Yao pushed farther toward the coast, with which they established commercial links at least by the sixteenth century and probably earlier. Conceivably other people, like the Kamba and Nyamwezi, also had commercial links with the coast. As the merchant states or cities on the coast increased in number, the competition to attract or influence the interior trade increased. Thus, the Portuguese arrived as East Africa was undergoing a commercial expansion stimulated in large measure by Indian Ocean influences which also helped determine East African political trends.

The several city-states along the East African coast were governed by sultans and sheiks with their councils. They periodically established cooperative alliances with a neighbor, but never became unified in an empire or a federation. They were, instead, essentially city-states whose strength rested on their land trade with the interior and their maritime trade overseas. The coast, therefore, was an integral part of a continental and an international mercantile system.

Arabs engaged in trade with East Africans long before the development of Islam, but once the faith appeared, its identity with the Arabic language and culture and its acceptance by ruling and commercial interests in Arabia and North Africa caused arabs and Swahili on the coast to become centers for the propagation of the faith. This was done partly by war but mainly through daily contact and intermarriage with Africans. This led to an identification of East Africans with Islam and Muslim trade, somewhat similar to the West African experience, with this important exception: in West Africa arabs at the outset came to stay, either permanently or for an indeterminate time. While this may have been true of some arabs in East Africa, the attraction and accessibility of Arabia where arabs in East Africa maintained close, direct contacts with relatives, friends, and businesses, and the absence of a strong, centralized force of government to assert an African imperative allowed the continuation of a stronger identity of East African arabs with the wider arab world, and thereby limited their fuller identification with the broader African community.

But much of that was then as evident as the fact of the cosmopolitan character of the East African coast. The Bantu, other Africans, the arabs, Indians, Persians, and possibly some Greeks traded and intermingled in this part of Africa. Such contacts and intermarriages over the centuries led to what is commonly called but more difficult to define as Swahili culture or civilization. It is characterized by Islam, coastal settlement, and the Swahili language, which is basically Bantu with the incorporation of foreign words, mainly Arabic. This was the civilization the Portuguese found when they sailed around the southern tip of Africa near the end of the fifteenth century. To find such a civilization surprised the Portuguese, as their reports reveal in the description of the tall, many-storied buildings, well-laid-out streets, gardens, and parks, and harbors full of ships from the Orient. There was much evidence of luxury and wealth.

Excerpt from: Joseph E. Harris, *Africans and Their History*, (New York: NY.: Mentor - NAL Penguin, Inc., 1987), pp. 67-78.

11. West African Empires of Ancient and Medieval Africa

JOHN HOPE FRANKLIN

That African-American historians consider a knowledge of the African homeland to be important is evidenced by the following excerpt taken from John Hope Franklin's widely used textbook From Slavery to Freedom. *This selection is a descriptive summary of the West African Empires of Ghana, Mali and Songhay. The majority of Africans taken into slavery between 1451 and 1870 came from West Africa. West Africa is the home of the last great African empires to exist prior to European penetration and dominance of that continent.*

Land of Their Fathers

In the last third of the twentieth century, it became a commonplace for African-Americans to speak and write sensitively of the land of their fathers. While some of them could refer to the vast continent of Africa in only the vaguest terms, others could focus quite precisely on the specific areas from which most of their ancestors had come. The emergence of such modern independent states as Ghana, Mali, Chad, Niger, Nigeria, The Gambia, and Upper Volta evoked a deep sense of identification, even though these new countries of the twentieth century had only a slight connection with those nation states of many centuries ago that bore similar names. The connection was there, nevertheless; and the African who left, say, Whydah, for the New World in 1800 may well have had his own roots in one of the

African states of the Middle Ages. Those states where the land of the fathers of the New World slaves as, indeed, they were the land of the fathers of their twentieth-century descendants.

Ghana

When the arabs began to learn of West Africa its civilization was already centuries old. Although the land from the Atlantic to the Nile had enjoyed limited contact with other civilized portions of the world, much of the culture that the arabs found was indigenous to the area. Indeed many well-developed political states had risen and fallen before any lasting contact was established between West Africa and the Near East. These states sprang up in more or less the same general region, from the Mediterranean southward to the Gulf of Guinea and from the Atlantic eastward almost to the Nile. Successively there arose in this region the major states of Ghana, Mali, Songhay, and many lesser states.

The first West African state of which there is any record is Ghana, lying some five hundred miles northwest of its modern namesake. It was also known by its capital, Kumbi Salch. Although its accurately recorded history does not antedate the seventh century, there is evidence that Ghana's political and cultural history extends back perhaps into the very early Christian era. It has been held by some that Ghana was founded and ruled by white men who were probably Berbers from North Africa. This dynasty ruled until about A.D. 700, when the indigenous Soninke people revolted and set up their own dynasty. The earliest observations of Ghana were made when it was a confederacy of a series of settlements extending along the grasslands of the Senegal and the upper Niger. Its boundaries were not well defined, and doubtless they changed with the fortunes of the kingdom. The territory was divided into provinces of which there were several subdivisions, suggesting a rather high degree of political organization. Most of the public offices were hereditary and the tendency was for the stratified social order to become solidified.

The people of Ghana were agricultural, and they enjoyed some prosperity until continuous droughts extended the desert to their principal farmlands. As long as they were able to carry on their farming, gardens and date groves dotted the country-side; and there was an abundance of sheep and cattle in the out-lying areas. They were also a trading people, and their chief town, Kumbi Salch, was an important commercial center during the Middle Ages. By the beginning of the tenth century the Muslim influence from the East was pronounced. Kumbi Salch had a native and an arab section, and the people were gradually adhering to the religion of Islam. The prosperity that came in the wake of arabian infiltration increased the power of Ghana, and its influence was extended in all directions. In the eleventh century, when the king had become a Muslim, Ghana could boast of an army of 200,000 and a lucrative trade across the desert. From the Muslim countries came wheat, fruit, and sugar. From across the desert came caravans laden with textiles, brass, pearls, and salt. Ghana exchanged rubber, ivory, slaves, and gold for these commodities. The king, recognizing the value of this commercial intercourse, imposed a tax on imports and exports and appointed a collector to look after his interests.

Under the negro rulers of the Sisse dynasty, Ghana reached the height of its power. Tribes as far north as Tichit in present Mauritania paid tribute to the king of Ghana; while in the south its influence extended to the gold mines of the Faleme and of the Bambuk. It was the yield from these mines that supplied the coffers of the Sisse with the gold used in trade with Moroccan caravans. In faraway Cairo and Baghdad, Ghana was a subject of discussion among commercial and religious groups.

The reign of Tenkamenin in the eleventh century is an appropriate point at which to observe the kingdom of Ghana. Beginning in 1062 Tenkamenin reigned over a vast empire which, through the taxes and tributes collected by the provincial rulers, made him immensely wealthy. He lived in a fortified castle made beautiful by sculpture, pictures, and windows decorated by the royal artists. The grounds also contained temples in which native gods were worshipped, a prison in which political enemies were incarcerated, and the tombs of the preceding kings. The king, highly esteemed by his subjects, held court in magnificent splendor. His personal attire consisted of robes

made of the most elegant materials available, a turban decorated with jewels, and a gold collar and bracelets.

The king of Ghana personally administered justice to his
subjects in an awe-inspiring spectacle. Taking his seat under a
large open-air pavilion, he welcomed his subjects who desired
some royal favor. Ten armed pages stood behind him, while the
male members of the royal family, magnificently attired, stood
to his right. The governors and imperial officials sat on the
ground before the king. In this setting Tenkamenin sat in judgment of his subjects. After the court was opened with the beating of drums, the king bestowed honors on worthy subjects and
punished those who had incurred his disfavor.

During Tenkamenin's reign the people of Ghana adhered
to a religion based on a belief that every earthly object contained
good or evil spirits that had to be satisfied if the people were to
prosper. The king, naturally, was at the head of the religion. In
1076, however, a fanatical band of Muslims called the
Almoravids invaded Ghana and brought the area under the influence of their religion and trade. They captured the capital and
killed all who would not accept the religion of Islam. The religious strife that ensued was enough to undermine the kingdom
of Ghana. By the end of the eleventh century, Ghana entered a
period of economic decline brought on by a series of droughts
that dried up the important Wagadu and Bagana districts. Under
such trying circumstances it fell easy prey to the waves of conquerors who swept in to destroy the kingdom during the twelfth
and thirteenth centuries.

Mali

As Ghana began to decline another negro kingdom in the
West arose to supplant it and to exceed the heights that Ghana
had reached. Mali, also called Melle and Mandingoland, began
as a strongly organized kingdom about A.D. 1235, but the nucle-
us of its political organization dates back to the beginning of the
seventh century. Until the eleventh century it was relatively
insignificant and its mansas, or kings, had no prestige or influence. In the middle of the eleventh century the king of Mali,
Baramendana Keita, was converted to Islam because he believed

the Muslims responsible for the coming of the much needed rain. In gratitude for this act of Allah, Baramendana made a pilgrimage to Mecca.

The credit for consolidating and strengthening the kingdom of Mali goes to Sundiata Keita. In 1240 he overran the Soso, then leveled the former capital of Ghana. It was a later successor, however, who carried the Mandingoes to new and glorious heights. Variously called Gonga-Musa and Mansa-Musa, this remarkable member of the Keita dynasty ruled from 1307 to 1332. With an empire comprising much of what is now French-speaking West Africa, he could devote his attention to encouraging the industry of his people and displaying the wealth of his kingdom. The people of Mali were predominantly agricultural, but a substantial number were engaged in various crafts and mining. The fabulously rich mines of Bure were now at their disposal and they served to enrich the already well supplied royal coffers.

The best information that the period affords on the level of attainment of these native kingdoms comes from the accounts of the royal pilgrimages to Mecca. The native kings, newly converted to the religion, were as ardent and pious as any arabs of their day. As good Muslims, they looked forward to showing their devotion by making the traditional pilgrimage to Mecca. Such a pilgrimage, moreover, was an excellent opportunity to display the wealth of the kingdom and to attract trade. The historic pilgrimage of Mansa-Musa in 1324 exceeded all visits to Mecca by previous royal personages from the west and was to be matched by few, if any, in the years to come. The entourage was composed of thousands of persons, a large portion of which constituted a military escort. Five hundred servants marched ahead of their king, each bearing a staff of pure gold. Books, baggage men, and royal secretaries were in abundance. To finance the pilgrimage, the king had a caravan of eighty camels to bear his more than twenty-four thousand pounds of gold. Gifts were lavished on the populace, and mosques were built where they were needed. As the camels approached Mecca, their burden was considerably lighter than it was when they departed for the east.

Since any such pilgrimage was a display of wealth and power as well as a holy journey to kiss the black stone of Kaaba, there was no need of proceeding directly to and from Mecca. Mansa-Musa first visited various parts of his kingdom to show his subjects and vassals his tremendous wealth and to demonstrate his benevolence. He then proceeded to Tuat, in the land of the Berbers, and after making a deep impression there he crossed the desert, visited Cairo, and finally went to the holy places of Mecca and Medina. He returned by way of Ghadames, in Tripoli, where he received many honors and from which point he was accompanied to his kingdom by El-Momar, a descendant of the founder of the dynasty of the Almohads. A more significant visitor to return with Mansa-Musa was Ibrahim Es Saheli, or Abu Ishak, a distinguished arabian poet and architect from a Granada family. The two visitors were unimpressed with the modest straw huts that were used in Mali for mosques, whereupon Mansa-Musa engaged his architect friend to supervise the building of pretentious mosques at Timbuktu, Jenne, Gao, and elsewhere. These structures added further splendor to the already well developed kingdom of Mali. For this improvement the king presented Es Saheli with 180 kilograms of gold.

When Mansa-Musa died in 1332, Mali could boast of a political state as powerful and as well organized as any of that period. Traveling in the area a few years later, Ibn Batuta, the celebrated arabian geographer, could report that he was greatly impressed by "the discipline of its officials and provincial governors, the excellent condition of public finance, and the luxury and the rigorous and complicated ceremonial of the royal receptions, and the respect accorded to the decisions of justice and to the authority of the sovereign." In the middle of the fourteenth century Europe was just beginning to feel the effects of her commercial revolution and her states had not yet achieved anything resembling national unity; but Mandingoland, under Mansa-Musa and his successor, Suleiman, enjoyed a flourishing economy with good international trade relations and could point with pride to a stable government extending several hundred miles from the Atlantic to Lake Chad. The people adhered to a state religion that had international connections, and learning flourished in the many schools that had been established. It was not until the fifteenth century that the kingdom showed definite signs of decline and disintegration. The powerful blows of the Songhay and the attacks of the Mossi combined to reduce the power of Mali. The decline did not go on indefinitely, however, and Mali continued to exist for many years as a small, semi-independent state.

Songhay

The negro kingdom that was in a position to dispute the power of Mali by the fifteenth century was Songhay. The latter had experienced a long and checkered career as a kingdom. Beginning in the early eighth century at Gao, near the bend of the Niger, it had remained a small and relatively inconsequential state for many years. In fact, it fell under the powerful influence of Mali, and for a time its rulers were vassals of Mansa-Musa and his successors. Undaunted, the Songhay waited for the first opportunity to throw off the yoke of Mali and to assert their sovereignty. Indeed, Mansa-Musa himself had laid the foundation for the destruction of his own empire. On his return from Mecca in 1325 he visited Gao, which his army had just subdued, and took two sons of the Songhay king as hostages. One of these young men accepted the education given him by Mansa-Musa but remained bitter and planned to escape and return to his people. After careful planning, he succeeded, and in 1355 founded the new and virile dynasty of the Sonnis. Seventeen kings reigned in this dynasty, the last being Sonni Ali, who raised the Songhay to the position of the most powerful kingdom in West Africa.

When Sonni Ali began his rule of the Songhay in 1464 most of West Africa was ripe for conquest. Mandingoland was declining, and the lesser states, though ambitious, had neither the leadership nor the resources necessary to achieve dominance. The hour of the Songhay had arrived. Sonni Ali conceived of a plan to conquer the entire Niger region by building a river navy that would seize control of both banks. By 1469 he had conquered the important town of Timbuktu and then proceeded to capture Jenne and other cities. Finally he attacked the kingdom of Mali, and with its conquest the Songhay kingdom was catapulted into a position of primacy in West Africa. Because of his lack of enthusiasm for the religion of Islam, there was considerable opposition to the rise of Sonni Ali; but he was ruthless with his opponents, who suffered death or exile at his hands. His years were filled with fighting; but when he died of drowning in the Niger in 1492 the kingdom of Songhay had been firmly established as the dominant power of West Africa.

The day of the Sonnis was over, however, and in 1493 the dynasty was overthrown by a powerful general, Askia Mohammed, who became Songhay's most brilliant ruler. From 1493 to 1529 he devoted his energies to strengthening his empire, making his people prosperous, and encouraging learning. He recruited a professional army of slaves and prisoners of war and left his subjects to engage in farming and commerce. Local rulers, four viceroys, and Askia's brother, Omar, as chief lieutenant, maintained peace and administered the empire. In 1494 Omar and the army conquered all of Massina, while in subsequent years most of Mandingoland, the Hausa states, and many other West African kingdoms fell before the power of Songhay. Finally, the empire of the Songhay was extended from the Atlantic to Bornu and from the Berber country in the north to the Mossi and Benin states in the south. It was easily the largest and most powerful state in the history of West Africa.

To be sure, Askia Mohammed was an orthodox Muslim; but one does not get the impression that his pilgrimage to Mecca in 1497 was either for ostentatious display or merely to pay homage to Allah. This shrewd ruler wanted to improve his empire, and he knew that such a journey would prove profitable from many points of view. His retinue was composed primarily of scholars and officers of state, with a military escort numbering only fifteen hundred men. The gold, valued at $900,000, was less than one-fifth of the amount carried by Mansa-Musa almost two centuries earlier. He and his followers conversed with doctors, mathematicians, scientists, and scholars, and they doubtless benefitted from these contacts. They learned much on how to improve the administration of the government, how to codify the laws of Songhay, how to foster industry and trade, and how to raise the intellectual level of the country. Even Askia Mohammed's investiture as caliph of the Sudan may be interpreted as a move to strengthen his country. At a time when Spain and Portugal were disputing the control of the world before Pope Alexander VI and when Portuguese inroads into Africa were increasing steadily, it was a strategic move; for if the Songhay could consolidate all the strength of the Muslim world behind them, they could make a united stand against the Christian Europeans.

Upon his return from the east, Askia Mohammed and his advisers instituted many of the reforms they had studied. He assigned carefully chosen governors, called *fari*, to rule over subdivisions of the empire. He appointed chiefs, or *noi*, to administer provinces and large cities. He reorganized the army on a more efficient basis. The laws of Mohammed and the Koran were the bases for administering justice. In the area of economic life, banking and credit were improved. A uniform system of weights and measures was established, and scales were inspected. Arabians and Negroes were encouraged to trade with other countries. Traders from Europe and Asia visited the markets of Timbuktu and Gao regularly. With government cooperation all of Songhay became prosperous. Alexander Chamberlain has observed: "In personal character, in administrative ability, in devotion to the welfare of his subjects, in open-mindedness towards foreign influences, . . . King Askia . . . was certainly the equal of the average European monarchs of the time and superior to many of them."

It was in the area of education that Askia made his most significant reforms. Everywhere he established and encouraged schools. Gao, Walata, Timbuktu, and Jenne became intellectual centers where the most learned scholars of West Africa were concentrated and where scholars from Asia and Europe came for consultation and study. White scholars like El-Akit and negro scholars like Bagayogo, both jurisconsults, were educated at Timbuktu. By the sixteenth and seventeenth centuries a distinctly Sudanese literature was emerging. At the University of Sankore black and white youths studied grammar, geography, law, literature, and surgery, while in the mosques Askia and his subjects studied the religion of Islam in order to practice and promote it more effectively.

Civil wars, massacres, and unsuccessful military expeditions followed the reign of Askia, who was dethroned by his oldest son. Although there were brief periods of revival, the empire was definitely declining. The Moors viewed the Sudan covetously and began to push down across the desert. With Spanish renegades as their allies, the Moroccans overthrew the Songhay state and began their own brief rule in Timbuktu.

Other States

Among the other states of West Africa was the empire of Wagadugu, commonly known as the Mossi states. It was founded near the middle of the eleventh century by an adventurer named Ubri. Never a large state, it occupied the area south of the bend of the Niger; but its population was always dense, and its people had a fiercely independent spirit. For a time there were actually five states comprising the loose confederation. Cohesion was greatest in time of emergency, and they managed to repel the attacks of Mali and Songhay and remained more or less independent down to the nineteenth century when France incorporated them into its African empire. The governors of the five states constituted the council of state and served as the chief ministers in the imperial organization. Working with them were eleven ministers ruling such departments as the army and finance. Beneath them was a hierarchy of officials, which extended to the most insignificant local functionary.

The strength of the Mossi lay in their efficient political and military system. The emperor was absolute. His subordinates operated with carefully worked out and rigidly defined duties. Each morning the emperor received his ministers of state, who reported on the affairs of the realm. In the evening the ruler dealt with matters concerning public order and criminal justice. The procedures of hearing and decisions bore a striking resemblance to the practice of trial by jury. The emperor made periodic inspection tours through his realm, a procedure that would not have been feasible in a larger country. There was

no standing army, but the political and social system was so organized as to make possible the calling up for military service of
every able-bodied man on the briefest notice. The survival of
the Mossi states in an area that was dominated by powerful
empires such as Mali and Songhay is a testimonial to their effi-
ciency and to their wise leadership.

The Afno, or Hausa, people are said to have had seven
original states, the best known of which were Kano, Zaria, and
Katsina. The Hausa states occupied roughly the area that today
is northern Nigeria. Each kingdom retained its identity, with
Kano emerging into the limelight for a while, then yielding to
Katsina, and so on. There was commerce with the other African
states and across the Sahara. Katsina became a center of learning where law and theology were studied and where the language of the people was refined. It was not until the beginning
of the nineteenth century, when Islam made noticeable inroads,
that the Hausa states began to yield to outside influences.

To the east and west of Lake Chad resided the people of
Kanem and Bornu, respectively. These people were made up of
a large number of tribes that had early been attracted to the region
by the oases and the lake. Some were Berber, while others were
negroid. As an organized state, Bornu-Kanem dates from about
A.D. 1220, but instability characterized the government for the
next two centuries. The copper mines around the lake brought
prosperity to the people, and by the sixteenth century there was
a semblance of order under Idris Alooma (1573-1603). In the seventeenth and eighteenth centuries the Muslims attempted to subdue these people and convert them, but with only slight success.
Complete subjugation by outsiders was not achieved until 1900,
when one portion of Bornu became a protectorate of Britain and
another came under the influence of France.

The absence of substantial physical barriers in some areas
south of the equator made possible the continuous infiltration
of migratory tribes which hampered political stability. The lands
of the Bantu, Bushmen, Hottentots, and Pygmies certainly had
some political organizations, and there is considerable anthropological and archaeological evidence to sustain the view that
in some areas there existed rather advanced cultures. But it is

clear that none of them reached the size or influence of West African states such as Mali and Songhay.

From the mouth of the Niger around to the Cape of Good Hope, there were a number of states that flourished for a time before the sixteenth century. For example, there was the kingdom of the Brama, which lay between Cape Lopez and the mouth of the Congo River, and about which practically nothing is known. The so-called Empire of the Congo, founded in the fourteenth century, dominated the area between Sette Cama in the north and Benguella to the south. Inland it reached as far as the upper Zambezi. With its capital at Banya, modern Sao Salvador, its kings experienced difficulty in maintaining control over the tribes of the Congo valley; and its boundaries shrank steadily in the seventeenth century because of the chaotic situation resulting from Portuguese slavers.

South of the Empire of the Congo was a state near the present city of Mossamedes. Hottentots, Damara, and other tribes in the region constituted the population of the kingdom, whose ruler was called the Mataman. In what is modern southern Africa there was a large homogeneous state inhabited by the Bechuana, Basuto, Zulu, and Hottentot peoples. On the east coast the Matebelle and Makalaka peoples were incorporated in an ancient state that dated from the tenth century. Its instability was caused by frequent incursions by the Wazimba, a cannibalistic people living to the west. The remainder of the eastern coast fell early under the influence of the Muslims and became dependencies of various sultanates founded by the arabs and Persians who gained control of East Africa. In the interior were the kingdoms of the Barotse, the Katanga, and Balubo, extending from the Zambezi to Lake Tanganyika.

The 1591 Moroccan conquest of Songhay had not ended the trans-Saharan trade; the southern terminals had merely shifted eastward to the Hausa states and the Bornu empire. By the early twentieth century, however, when Great Britain, France, and Germany were completing their conquests of West African states, the locus of power in West Africa had long since passed from the savannah kingdoms to forest belt states located along the Gulf of guinea to the south. When the Portuguese first sailed down the West African coast in the fifteenth century, they discovered two substantial states; Benin, located to the west of the Niger delta, and the Kongo kingdom, near the mouth of the Congo River. At Benin, Portuguese sailors bought slaves, beads, and cloth, which they exchanged with Africans further east, along the coast of present-day Ghana, for gold dust. The abundance of certain West African goods so impressed European traders that they named sections of the Guinea coast after these "products" - pepper, ivory, gold, and slaves.

The slave trade, which became the area's dominant form of commerce, played a crucial role as an economic basis for emerging forest belt kingdoms. The Yoruba people to the west of Benin organized themselves into a series of states, the most powerful of which was Oyo. It was the breakup of this empire in the early nineteenth century that created the unsettling conditions of war and disorder that led, in turn, to the delivery of large numbers of Yoruba into the trans-Altantic slave trade. As Oyo declined, Dahomey, a kingdom located within the boundaries of present-day Dahomey, threw off the yoke of its former overlord. Ironically, Dahomey, which owed its seventeenth-century origins to a determination to abstain from the Atlantic slave trade, had by the late eighteenth century become a key West African center for slave exporting. In the nineteenth century this highly centralized state was transformed from a state specializing in the slave trade to one dealing largely in palm oil products. Nonetheless, Europeans used the image of a cruel, barbaric, slaveholding nation as a partial justification for the French invasion and conquest in the 1890s.

Another region to share a similar fate was that of the city-states of the Niger River delta. Ibo traders had made the transition from slaves to palm oil only to be thwarted by British commercial attempts to open up Africa to European commerce. Between 1807 and 1901 Britain and the mighty Ashanti nation of present-day Ghana fought ten wars, culminating in a British conquest of that land.

The states described in this chapter are in no way a complete listing of West African political units. Furthermore, there were other African areas, too, that witnessed the development of impressive states. Some like Egypt, Kush, and Carthage flourished during the pre-Christian era. Others came later. Some areas like Rhodesia and savannah lands south of the Congo basin witnessed different civilizations rising on the sites of their predecessors. Muslim Swahili-speaking city-states located along the Indian Ocean traded with Arabia, India, and Indonesia at a time when European powers were fighting in the Crusades. Ethiopians have a recorded history almost two thousand years old. Other kingdoms are of the more recent origin. The Zulu people, for instance, became a powerful nation only in the nineteenth century. To a greater or lesser degree all had some connection with the inhabiting of the New World with black people.

Excerpt from: John Hope Franklin and Alfred A. Moss, Jr., *Slavery to Freedom*, (Alfred Knopf, 1988), pp. 1-11.

12. The Great Mutota and the Monomopata Empire

CHANCELLOR WILLIAMS

The great stone walls and buildings of the cities of Zimbabwe still stand as a monument to the genius of Emperor Mutota. He designed and built his empire by uniting numerous inland states between the Zambezi and Limpopo Rivers north to south and between the Red Sea and the Kalihari Desert east to west. For most of the 15th century, Zimbabwe was a unified African bulwark against the intrusions of the arabs from their entrepots and settlements on the coast.

The Great Mutota

The year was 1440. The king was Mutota. In just about any other land he would be known to history as Mutota the Great. He and his council were apparently quick to see that even the most advanced states, each standing independently and alone, were doomed unless unified into a single nation with a strong central government. This should be achieved by voluntary association if possible. The divisive influence of the arabs operating in the capitals of the respective states had to be obvious, as they appeared not to feel it necessary to be either as secretive or as subtle as their Portuguese armies. Both the arabs and the Europeans had one thing in common, however. Both had the deeply rooted conviction that they knew the blacks and that their power over them and the continued ability to garner their endless wealth rested squarely on keeping them divided and continuously at each other's throats. No one, except the blacks themselves, needed any argument to show that black unity meant black power and black power meant an end to white domination, from the east or the west.

Mutota and the new leaders saw and understood this very well. They knew where almost all the gold, iron and tin had been going from over 4,000 mines. They knew how all the stratagems used by the blacks to bar the arabs from the interior had failed, and would continue to fail as long as the arabs controlled all overseas trade by controlling the entire seaboard and, having done so unchallenged for so long that they now claimed sovereignty over the whole coastal area. Therefore, Mutota, in 1440, began the campaign to carry out his own "Grand Design," a great plan that aimed at nothing less than uniting blacks in a vast empire that cut across South Africa below the Limpopo River, and covered Rhodesia with an indefinite boundary beyond the Zambezi River in Zambia, and on over Mozambique to the Indian Ocean, sweeping southward again to repossess the entire coastline fronting the new empire.

Now is all of this the same version as given by Abraham and other western historians? Would an arab historian, no matter what the facts might be, present it in this way? Of course not. The western historians, employing their usual club to crush rebellion from the masters' viewpoints, would proclaim "sheer romanticism!" For, see here now, listen: Does not Professor Abraham make it quite clear at the very outset that no black man, king or commoner, could have conceived of such a vast undertaking? What black man, unaided by whites, could have Mutota's great and awe-inspiring vision? Abraham and his school might well thank their God that there were many "white" arabs around to whom such credit could be given. After a review of so many centuries of the ideological stance of writers where blacks are concerned, anger, and outrage should be replaced with amusement. For it has become amusing - to this writer at any rate - to witness the sweating dilemma of these investigators when confronted with any kind of all-black achievements, even in relatively unimportant and routine matters which any human or, any people of any race anywhere would be thought capable of achieving. But where blacks are involved in anything considered outstanding, the whites somehow feel threatened. What is threatened, of course, is the deeply rooted presupposition of the innate inferiority of the blacks. If somewhere in their long history a single record of outstanding achievement by blacks was found by whites and declared at once to be such, rather than "evidently" non-Negroid, if this was ever done the black world has been unable to discover it and, if there is an error here or a misconception, a correction is welcomed.

But, returning to the traditional white line in this case of the Vakaranga king, Abraham and others say that the arabs persuaded him to unify and expand the country north and south and to the Indian Ocean - the arabs who had nothing to gain from a strong and unified black empire and might lose what they had. Professor Abraham says that the arabs "conceived and implanted in the mind of the Rosvi king a desire for empire." The empire was to serve as an "effective umbrella," protecting their operations in the country from the Portuguese. Scholarly reasoning, but logical. Of course, except that there were no Portuguese or Portuguese threats in the area in 1440. They did not arrive until 65 years later.

Meanwhile Mutota moved forward. His first move was to recruit and build up strong, well-trained armies, each under an able general. He displayed the mark of a great executive by his keen insight in the evaluation and selection of men for posts of high responsibility and, in doing so, secured the active support of the Great Council of the realm. It is significant, too, that his leadership strategy included recruiting soldiers from the surrounding states which were not yet a part of the projected empire. Another important move was to secure unity through the voluntary association of as many states as possible before any conquest by force was attempted. The usual African pattern of empire building was followed. All states joining the imperial union were not only assured of autonomy but special rights also, such as membership in the Great Council of the Empire, a privilege denied territories that had to be conquered. With these policies reaffirmed and settled, Mutota's formidable armies began their sweep in the different planned directions and fields of operation. The main drive was northward under the command of the King himself. Within ten years all territory between the Limpopo in South Africa to the Zambezi had been brought under imperial rule. The great undertaking was far from completion when Mutota died in 1450. The objectives had been worked out in detailed specifications of a blueprint for expansion, unification and development of a great empire composed of great states.

Unlike most of the societies we have been studying, the Vakaranga clans had become patrilineal. Therefore, Mutota's son rather than his nephew was the successor to the throne. This was a happy circumstance, since the son, Matope, turned out to be a great statesman-king and general as his late father. He had the greater task because some of the most powerful states in the "blueprint" had yet to be won, and breaking arab control over the seacoasts, the greatest undertaking, had not been achieved. Matope assumed the leadership aggressively, having the good fortune of securing the same loyalty the ablest generals had given to his father, supported by fanatically devoted soldiers. This was no accident, for Matope himself had been a popular young commander during his father's reign. Above all, Changa and Togwa, two of Matope's greatest generals, were his friends. The armies were reorganized, strengthened by the relentless training, and expanded.

This display of both strength and unity among the blacks puzzled the arabs. This was something new, amazing. They had a long history of dealing with blacks, and nothing was better known than the disunity, mutual suspicions and the hostility of one group toward another. How was this spectacle of over thirty different tribal groups forming solid phalanxes of unity under black leaders to be explained? Moreover, the arabs, who had always maintained their own black troops under arab officers, were barred from joining the imperial forces by both Mutota and Matope. All this was seen as a very real threat to the powerful commercial position the arabs had in all the hitherto independent states as well as the equally powerful political influence they enjoyed at the capitals of these states, not to mention their independent status on the coasts.

Matope's campaigns for the unification of many states into one empire were not easy. For although the arabs pledged and proclaimed their undying loyalty to the new Emperor as this mission of empire building advanced, they secretly gave active support to the armies of resisting states. Some of the key states that formed the empire were Mbire, Guniuswa in the southern region; Chidma, Utonga, Barwe, Manyika, Madonda, and Shiringoma formed the eastern southeastern region. It took thirty years of unremitting efforts to complete the Empire of Monomotapa with its long eastern border bathed at last by the Indian Ocean. Every detail of his father's specifications having been carried out in full, a weary Emperor, worn out by the task, retired for the final sleep. The year was 1480.

What would happen now? The great imperial system had been completed. Black unity had been achieved among numerous language groups on one of the widest scales in history, from Zambia down into South Africa. Cities of stone dotted the land, the Zimbabwe cities north and south were the deathless symbols of a people's greatness. The long wars of expansion seem to have stimulated economic development rather than hinder it. The government had gained a more direct control over the mines and mining industries, and this meant more control over the arabs in the interior and on the coast, especially at Sofala, Kilimoni, Sena and Tete on the Zambezi. The agricultural system was actively promoted by the central government and, indeed, just as the vast building operations that produced the amazingly beautiful temples and huge structures such as the Great Zimbabwe were all government sponsored, so were all the other craft industries. Active government sponsorship, promotion and encouragement in all these fields did not necessarily mean government ownership or direct control.

The Emperor Matope also left the country with a great organized religion with a powerful and formally organized priesthood, something unusual in Africa outside of ancient Egypt, Ethiopia, and Abyssinia. The traditional African religion is essentially the same everywhere on the continent, but it is generally unorganized and, therefore, has seldom had an organized priesthood with a single recognized creed or body of prescribed beliefs. Yet just about every African society known believed in one Almighty God, no matter by what name he was called or how many lesser gods there might be. In Monomotapa he was called Mwari -the Vakaranga version and contribution toward national unity.

But would there be unity now that the last of the two great personalities around whom unity revolved had silently stolen away in the shadows of the Great Zimbabwe, gone forever? The question arises whenever a great leader passes; political psychology and mass psychology are crucially combined. Whether a great state survives after the death of the leader who made it great and held its disparate parts together by his charisma alone, would depend upon the good fortune of having a successor of equal greatness, or the miracle of having developed a strong spirit of national community, of oneness, of a loyalty and a sense of belonging to the nation that transcends the tribe.

There were unifying factors which Matope left behind in his great empire. One was the same organized religion led by a highly advanced and literate priesthood. (Religious temples at the Great Zimbabwe was certainly the national center of religion.) The other important factor that should have made unity imperative was the greater prosperity that would flow from economic interdependence and close commercial relations between the constituent states and provinces. The great system of roads and highways, instead of being recaptured by the bush and forests after serving their initial military purpose, could have been converted into permanent national highways, crisscrossing the Empire, and thus serving as the indispensable communication links for administration, trade, travels by the people, and in short, unification. Other factors that should have been a solid foundation for black unity were the similarity of their social institutions and the absolute sameness of their constitutional system.

Yet, with Matope's death the Empire began to break up. Why? Notwithstanding all the forces mentioned above that should have made for unity and stability, the actual fact is that the traditional African political system was fundamentally and structurally anti-empire. The very circumstance of the endless process of segmentation, of forever splintering off to form little independent mini-states, developed a built-in disunity, reinforced by the attending growth of different languages. But self-government or chiefdom was a way of life, not a theory. Chiefs and Elders, as we have seen, were leaders, advisors, and representatives of the people, and not their rulers. The same operating principle prevailed when a group of states united to form a kingdom and kingdoms united to form an empire, but with a disturbing difference: Centralization tended to erode local autonomy, transferring chiefs from the control of their people to the control of the central government. In the case of conquered territories this change was abrupt and painful. And it was one of the principal reasons for later rebellions and the break-up of kingdoms and empires. Therefore, let us say again, to say that arabs and Europeans were solely or even mainly responsible for the destruction of all great African states would be glossing over or attempting to ignore the principal internal factor: disunity. What the whites did, Asians and Europeans, was to appraise this continent-wide disunity and "cash in" on it to the fullest extent possible. They did not have to divide and conquer even, for the blacks were already divided, just as though they were waiting for the foreign conquerors to come. The foreigners' role was to intensify the disunity, to promote the suspicions and hatred that developed from it, and to check any tendency or movement toward unity among the blacks.

Excerpt from: Chancellor Williams, *The Destruction of Black Civilization*, (Chicago: IL.: The Third World Press, 1987), pp. 278-284.

13. Queen Nzinga: The Unconquerable

CHANCELLOR WILLIAMS

The story of Queen Nzinga is that of a remarkable monarch who held off the Portuguese takeover of her country, Angola, for more than forty years beginning in 1623. The following selection recounts the chain of events involving Queen Nzinga and the Portuguese invaders.

Greatness was born out of the savage oppression of the Africans and out of that oppression it grew like a giant. Just why the Portuguese drew so much blood with the lash from already chained and helpless slaves is beyond all human understanding since, if for no other reason, the victims were "articles of commerce" and the source of the very riches slavers sought. Besides, over half of the captured blacks died before reaching their destination. Self-interest, then, should have stayed the murderous hands of the slaves. Nothing did, and that fact was one of the reasons that Queen Nzinga said that the real savages in Africa were the whites. They created the conditions that brought her to the fore.

The Portuguese were so aggressive in their program of dividing the blacks and keeping them fighting among themselves that they overshot the mark, simply went too far. The system of spreading out over the country into the provinces and allying themselves with the various chiefs has been mentioned more than once. But after 1608 the commander-in-chief of the

Portuguese army tightened the noose. This was Bento Cardoso. Under his plan Angola was to be further depopulated by a massive onslaught for slaves through a closely coordinated system in which every chief in the land would be "owned" by a Portuguese and directly responsible to him for a stated quota of slaves. This would bypass the Angolan king (of Ndongo) to whom the provincial chiefs paid their taxes in slaves. This would also mean increased warfare between the chiefdoms in order to meet the increased quotas demanded by raiding into each other's territories. Chiefs failing to secure the required number of slaves were themselves enslaved. Over a hundred chiefs and other notables were sold into slavery in a single year and another hundred murdered by the Portuguese. We may safely assume that the actual number of chiefs enslaved or murdered was greater than that stated above, since the Portuguese, like other nations, generally cut casualty figures for the record. The situation to be considered here however, is the widespread confusion and terror among a hunted and leaderless people. To make matters even worse, if that was possible, the half-savage Jaga, who would join anybody for their favorite game of looting and raping, became allies of Cardoso. The Angolan king, who had been cooperating with the slave traders, now saw himself being ruined on all fronts, losing his people and his profits. He therefore began to resist the Portuguese. The people, even though they knew that their king himself was a slaver, in sheer desperation flocked to support the war of resistance. It paid off. Both the Portuguese and their Jaga allies were checked, and the war dragged on year after year. After Kabasa, the capital city, fell to the Portuguese, their losses had become so heavy that the new governor who had been sent from Lisbon with firm orders to complete the conquest of Angola "once and for all," nevertheless was forced to sue for peace without victory. The Portuguese had suffered a disastrous defeat by the blacks, but the official version, and excuse, was that there was "general illness" in their ranks. Yet the Portuguese insisted on holding Kabasa. The Africans therefore rejected peace proposals as a trick and the war was resumed in a land of famine where food crops and the slave trade itself had come to a standstill. In this desperate state of affairs, the fighting somehow continued, with both sides obviously weakened and in disarray. It was during this period, in 1619, that a new Portuguese commander managed to murder over a hundred chiefs. At this point the Pope intervened, insisting that the wholesale slaughter be ended and peace be pursued. In 1622, a new governor was sent from Lisbon to make peace. Portugal had been appointing "governors of Angola" for over forty years without having control over it.

The peace conference was held at Luanda. The black delegation was headed by the country's ablest and most uncompromising diplomat, Ann Nzinga, not yet queen, but sister of the king - the woman power behind a weak king, and the one responsible for inspiring the people to continue the war of resistance when every hope was gone, unless she herself had become their last hope. But even before the peace conference began, and at the risk of wrecking it, the governor's caucasian arrogance could not be restrained. He had decided on a studied insult at the outset by providing chairs in the conference room only for himself and his councilors, with the idea of forcing the black princess to stand humbly before his noble presence. He remained seated, of course, staring haughtily as she entered the room. She took in the situation at a glance with a contemptuous smile, while her attendants moved with a swiftness that seemed to suggest that they had anticipated this stupid behavior by the Portuguese. They quickly rolled out the beautifully designed royal carpet they had bought before Nzinga, after which one of them went down on all fours and expertly formed himself into a "royal throne" upon which the princess sat easily without being a strain on her devoted follower. Yet she rose at regular intervals, knowing that other attendants were vying for the honor of thus giving to these whites still another defeat. I gather from the different ways this incident is reported that the western mind is unable to grasp its real meaning. Some historians saw it as a cruel and inhuman use of slaves, ignoring the fact that Nzinga's chief claim to fame was that she was the greatest abolitionist of slavery, that she herself had no slaves and, indeed, had not the slightest need for any. One reason might be that she was so much loved and ever blindly followed by her people that it was believed that all would die, to the last man and woman, following her leadership. Such were the men, not slaves, who gladly formed a human couch before the astonished Portuguese for their leader.

She faced the Portuguese governor and spoke as a ruler of the land, and not as a subject of the king of Portugal. She did not recognize the man in the big chair as governor because she did not recognize the existence of a Portuguese "colony of Angola." She only saw before her what her people had been approaching their shores over a hundred years before - pompous white devils bent on the destruction of the nonwhite world. The Ndongo terms for peace were presented as uncompromising demands, and it was clear from the beginning that the Portuguese would have fared better with a man. For before any kind of treaty was signed Portugal had to agree (1) to evacuate Kabasa and all nearby fortifications; (2) the Portuguese were to wage war against the Jaga (a harsh provision since the Jaga had been Portugal's allies in trying to crush Ndongo); (3) all chiefs who had become vassals of the Portuguese king were to be freed and enabled to return to former tributary status at home and, finally, the important concession Nzinga made was to return the Portuguese prisoners-of-war she held. The treaty of 1622 was supposed to end all fighting in the whole west-central region. But the governor, as though to make up for his defeat in the peace negotiations with Nzinga, marched off, almost immediately, to invade Kongo again. The treaty then became dead insofar as its execution was concerned. But Nzingas's brother died the next year and she became Queen of Ndongo. The distressed Portuguese, in order to discredit her, put out the story that she had poisoned him. And while there was not a scintilla of evidence or any basis at all for the concoction, historians have shown their unbiased objectivity by faithfully carrying on the charge for over three hundred years. Yet, if lying is a legitimate aspect of warfare, the Portuguese may have felt justified in trying to destroy such an implacable foe in any way they could. Their greatest trouble was yet to come.

Nzinga became queen in 1623, and went into action at once. Her first major move was to send an ultimatum to the

Portuguese authorities demanding the immediate execution of the terms of the treaty, otherwise war would be declared. While the Portuguese were preparing to meet the Queen's armies, the Dutch fleet appeared as a new threat. The Dutch, themselves great slavers, certainly did not come as liberators of the hard pressed blacks. Their aim was to break the Portuguese monopoly and secure their share of the slave trade and mineral wealth of West and Central Africa. To further these ends, they used the blacks as other white peoples did and still do. No time was lost in forming an alliance with Pedro II, King of Kongo, in his war with the Portuguese. The Dutch had already captured seven Portuguese slave ships at sea, sunk other vessels in the harbors at Luanda and Mpinda, and generally raising hell. All this gave Queen Nzinga more time to prepare for the inevitable. She even reversed her demands for a Portuguese war against the Jaga and formed a military alliance with them herself. Knowing how very unreliable the Jaga were, she sought to make the alliance binding by promising to marry the Jaga chief, Kasanji, and adopting certain desirable Jaga customs.

Nzinga's greatest act, however, probably the one that makes her one of the greatest women in history, was in 1624 when she declared all territory in Angola over which she had control a free country, all slaves reaching it from whatever quarter were forever free. She went further. Since it was clear to her that white power in Africa rested squarely on the use of black troops against black people, she understood the first and only carefully organized effort to undermine and destroy the effective employment and use of the black soldiers by whites - the first and only black leader in history who was ever known to undertake such a task. She had carefully selected groups of her own soldiers to infiltrate the Portuguese black armies, first separating and spreading out individually into Portuguese held territory and allowing themselves to be "induced" by Portuguese recruiting agents to join their forces. The quiet and effective work of Nzinga's agents among the black troops of Portugal was one of the most glorious, yet unsung, pages in African history. For whole companies rebelled and deserted to the colors of the black queen, taking with them the much needed guns and ammunition which she had been unable to secure except by swiftly moving surprise attacks on enemy units. The Queen's armies were further strengthened by the runaway slaves who streamed into the only certain haven for the free on the whole continent of Africa. To the Portuguese, Queen Nzinga had passed the last word in unheard-of audacity when she was able to influence scores of vassal chiefs to rebel against them and join the cause of their own race. This was too much. This woman had to be destroyed. It had come to that.

The Portuguese sent their ultimatum to the Queen from their Luanda stronghold, Portugal's Lisbon in Africa. It demanded the immediate return of all chiefs, soldiers and slaves to Portuguese territory; that is, all who had fled therefrom. Refusal would mean war, the ultimatum concluded. The fact was that a state of war already existed since the Queen's own ultimatum of the previous year. The Portuguese were afraid to move against her stronger forces now, although they continued to give the Dutch threat as the reason for delaying the required all-out attack. Meanwhile, the usual strategy of first instigating factional strife among the blacks was by no means forgotten. It was just that there was so much unity and patriotism in this dominant Angola state, so much fanatical devotion to this "terrible black queen," that internal subversion was almost impossible. They tried to overcome all this by formally declaring that Nzinga was not legally Queen of Ndongo, the throne vacant, and one of their own vassal chiefs, Aidi Kiluanji, was declared king. The Portuguese marshalled all of their forces on land and sea, their special river fleets in particular, to crush Nzinga before the Dutch struck again. But the Queen herself opened the offensive, striking first at the Portuguese puppet king and his forces. The Portuguese captured her principal island stronghold in the Cuanza river in July, 1626, thus dividing her forces, and by a swift encircling movement designed to capture the Queen, cut off her main supporting regiments and forced her not only to retreat but to withdraw from her country. Joy reigned at Luanda and Sao Thome. With Nzinga's flight from Angola it appeared that the black menace was over and victory complete. Aidi Kiluanji was crowned King Philip I of Ndongo.

The solidarity of the blacks remained unbroken, however, and their loyalty to Nzinga remained steadfast. She was "just away a little while," and would soon return. Any child in the most distant bush could tell you that their Queen was "just away on business." So who was this Philip? His name said he was a Portuguese, so he couldn't be King of Ndongo. All Angolan kings and queens were so African that they couldn't be tricked out of their own African names. The Queen herself had dropped "Ann" from her name when she discovered that baptizing a black into Christianity meant surrendering his soul and body not to any Christ, but to the white man. And oral tradition further has it that the people not only rejected "Philip I," but made fun of the very idea that he considered himself to be king. Their blind faith in their Queen and the certainty of her return, according to the same oral record, was not really so blind. Those who understood the coded drum messages spread the news that all guerrilla attacks which occurred throughout the land were attacks which were personally directed by the Queen and that, in fact, she was raising a new army of liberation. Her loyal chiefs and people in Ndongo were to stand by, ready.

The written record, no matter how slanted, supports the oral. For in November, 1627, she crossed the borders back into her country at the head of a strong army, made stronger and stronger as her loyal chiefs and wildly cheering people, including her fanatically devoted freed men, flocked to her standard as she swept forward to recapture the Cuanza stronghold held by Philip I and put him to flight. The Portuguese continued to be amazed at this display of black unity - and under a woman's leadership at that. Black unity was now seen clearly as black power, and that meant an unconquerable people. The Portuguese were resolved to break that unity and the power that developed from it. The revolt against them had become general as Nzinga's victorious forces advanced. The Portuguese retreated to their own strongholds on the coast, giving the Dutch threat as an excuse and not the threat of being annihilated by the Queen's forces.

But as there was in fact no imminent Dutch threat, the Portuguese regrouped and strengthened their forces for an all-out war to destroy Nzinga and this time, not to cease fighting until this was done. They began by giving orders and offering a big reward for her capture, dead or alive. Their slave troops, still the backbone of the Portuguese armed forces, were given the special inducements of land and freedom for her capture. Realizing that such an all-out attempt to capture her meant that countless thousands of her people would die in her defense, she outwitted the Portuguese again by slipping out of the country, instructing her lieutenants to spread the word everywhere that she had fled the country and, mistakenly entering the territory of an enemy, had been killed. To give point to the story, there was general weeping and mourning throughout Ndongo, real weeping and mourning, because the masses believed the story to be true. So did the Portuguese. The only reason for the war having been removed by Providence, the Bishop could celebrate a special mass in celebration of this special blessing, and the Colony of Angola could at last be organized after over fifty years of obstruction. All things now seemed to be happy and going well according to the original grand design.

Then in 1629 the Portuguese stood aghast when Queen Nzinga "burst upon them from the grave" sweeping all opposition before her. She brought in her fierce Jaga allies, apparently willing to do even this to defeat the whites. The Portuguese were completely defeated. She had not only retaken her own country, but had, meanwhile, become Queen of Matamba also, having replaced the weak Queen there. Nzinga was now an empress of two countries. She now redoubled her campaign against slavery and the slave trade by making both Ndongo and Matamba havens for all who could escape from the slaver by rebelling or otherwise. Chiefs engaged in the traffic in nearby states now stood in fear of her wrath. The Portuguese saw "the handwriting on the wall." In order not to lose every foothold in the area, Lisbon suddenly remembered that it had never carried out the treaty signed with Nzinga in 1622, and declared that Portugal's wars against her had been unjust! High level embassies were sent to the Queen in 1639 in efforts to effect a settlement. Nzinga received them, listened to their protestations of eternal friendship, and went ahead with determination in reorganizing both of the kingdoms and undermining colonial rule in areas held by the enemy. That every white man in Africa was an enemy of the blacks was a matter about which there was no room for debate in her mind. Even the holy robes of the priests in Angola not only covered their real mission as agents of empire, but also covered their insatiable lust for the black bodies of their helpless slave girls. She had been forced by the actualities of black-white relations to distrust all whites, along with their tricky treaties.

By 1641 the Dutch had made great progress in reducing the power of Portugal all along the coast, and Nzinga's adamant position made their situation an impossible one to maintain. A despairing governor and council had no choice but to declare war against her once again, a full-scale war. But the situation was now most favorable for the Angolans. Their northern neighbor, Kongi, had become more active in its own war against the Portuguese and, besides, a new and greater king had assumed the leadership. This was Garcia II, who continued the policy of cooperating with the Dutch where and when Kongolese interests were involved. (Some black leaders had learned to use the whites as the whites always used them: when it served their own interests.) The other happy development for Ndongo was that the Dutch invasion of Portuguese-held areas had actually begun in 1641 before any moves could be made against either of the two black states, Kongo and Ndongo.

Nzinga continued her campaign against the Portuguese, winning victories everywhere a battle was joined. With Dutch aid, the great Portuguese stronghold of Masangano fell in 1648. The Dutch, having previously captured Luanda, now found themselves threatened by the steady reinforcements that continued to pour in from Portuguese Brazil. The Dutch withdrew, leaving the blacks in the area, who had helped them to capture and defend this, the most important Portuguese city in Africa, to fend for themselves alone. While the chiefs and their forces did indeed put up a gallant fight, they were massacred in one of the most savage onslaughts on record. The recapture of Luanda by Salvador de Sa, the new governor, and his crushing of black opposition there, led him to initiate new peace efforts with the two kingdoms of Kongo and Nzinga. The Kongolese king refused to answer his letter, but did send a monk to hear the governor's terms. Nzinga also agreed to efforts at negotiations. These gestures by the two African leaders led Salvador de Sa to advise the king of Portugal that all the African states were cowed and their power broken. He knew better, of course, for even the chiefs and their people in his own Portuguese-held territory were still fighting on despite the massacres, and probably because of them.

If the Portuguese had been able to conquer either Kongo or Ndongo-Matamba, no peace offers would have been made. Hadn't they tried it over and over and failed? To be able to conquer both now was out of the question. Again, the old conquest route was invoked: beguiling smiles and protestations of friendship, finding concrete expression in negotiations for peace. The language of diplomacy reached its most brilliant heights of deception in those velvety clauses of proposed treaties which the Africans, if they signed them, would be signing themselves and their people into perpetual bondage. This fact was supposed to be assured by the other fact that the relevant clauses were so ambiguous that they could be interpreted in several different ways - in this case in whatever way the Portuguese chose to interpret them. The very same provisions of the treaties could be read and explained to the blacks in such language that it would appear that the Europeans were not only humbling themselves but also proclaiming the outcome as a glorious victory for the Africans. Of course, no blacks, not even a Nzinga, was supposed to be intelligent enough, sharply intelligent enough, to see through all this. But, stripping away all the glittering verbiage, Nzinga saw at a glance that what it all meant was that she was to be a vassal of the Portuguese king, one paying him a big annual tribute. She would die first. And no one should have known this better than the Portuguese who, at the time of this latest treaty offer, had been at war with her, and repeatedly defeated, for over twenty-eight years. They had met one of the giants of the human race whom they had found impossible to recognize as such because she appeared on the planet not only as a woman but one with black skin. Nzinga, therefore, kept them anxiously waiting for action on the treaty, toying with it for six years, while giving her war-torn land and tired-out people a period for rest and recovery. She was the same queen who had twice fled the country not to save herself but save her people from a slaughter that her flight would prevent. For the same reason she did not want the war resumed again after over forty years of warfare. On the other hand, she would not surrender her country to Portugal and its slave trade. The areas of Angola they still held, including the important islands of Luanda and Sao Thome, belonged to the Angolan people, and some of these areas belonged directed to her own kingdoms of Ndongo and Matamba. Finally, then, in 1656, tired and weary from four decades of relentless struggles, she signed a treaty that was revised and made acceptable to her. Her greatest concession allowed the Portuguese puppet king, Aidi, to head the territory conceded to them.

There were seven more years of a busy life for Queen Nzinga -pushing reconstruction, the resettlement of ex-slaves, and undertaking the development of an economy of free men and women that would be able to succeed without the slave trade. She could not have been unaware that, with the Portuguese still strongly entrenched in the most strategic areas, unless she was succeeded by equally great leaders, all of her labors in defense of the freedom of the blacks would ultimately be in vain. That was the burning question in 1663 as a dull autumn sun lengthened the shadows over the palace grounds where thousands stood in tears: Were there any more Garcias anywhere? Would God send them another Nzinga to hold the line against the truly white devils? The sun slowly went down behind the Angolan trees and darkness spread over the land. Over three hundred years later the blacks of Angola are still fighting the Portuguese, and still waiting for the sunrise.

In the heart-torn state of national mourning the Queen's Council permitted two priests to come in and perform the last rites of the Church. Since the Queen had renounced the Catholic religion many years before her passing, and had banned missions from her country as centers of subversion, this appearance of priests at the royal bedside may be explained either as a once-a-Catholic-always-a-Catholic theory, or as an attempt by Catholic Portugal to give the appearance of final victory on all fronts. In this case it would mean that the most unconquerable of foes, recanting and submissive, had been conquered by their religion in the end. And so it is written in the official documents of Portugal, the written record used by almost all historians of Africa, Nzinga had returned to the Church that had baptized her "Ann." Yet she was one of the very first blacks to see that the Portuguese conquests, the slave trade, and the Church were all inseparably one and the same. The long years of warfare had been equally against all three - the unholy trinity. And she had never surrendered. In 1963, three hundred years after her death, her people, now Catholic themselves, did not believe she had ever returned to the Church.

Excerpt from: Chancellor Williams, *The Destruction of Black Civilization*, (Chicago: IL.: Third World Press, 1987), pp. 260-272.

STUDY QUESTIONS

1. What geological and cultural reasons exist, for including the Arabian peninsula together with Africa as one whole continent?

2. Give the reasons why the Arabian peninsula, according to Ali Mazrui, has not been included as a part of the continent of Africa in recent times.

3. Should the Sahara desert be viewed as a vast chasm which divides the northern part of Africa from the southern part, or should it be seen as a "sea of communication" which joins them together?

4. According to Colin Turnbull, what are the common elements among indigeneous African cultures which unite them?

5. Can you discover ways in which the indigeneous cultures of Africa have a "high degree of fundamental similarity" and also have an "enormous diversity of outward form"?

6. Vincent Mulago coins the phrases "unity in life," and "vital union" synonymously to refer to the single fundamental way in which Africans have come to define themselves. Put this definition in your own words in a few sentences.

7. Define the concept of "power" in the African worldview and how it is transmitted. What is the "moral" order of things in the African worldview which Vincent Mulago describes?

8. Identify the major topographical features of the continent of Africa.

9. What geographical areas have been supportive for the establishment and growth of human civilization throughout Africa? For what reasons have these locations been especially beneficial to human life?

10. What geographical feature of Africa has been the cause for much of its isolation from the rest of the world almost down to the present day? What influence has this had on African civilization?

11. How have the Berbers succeeded in maintaining a measure of independence and freedom from outside control even down to the present day?

12. How does Harris describe the interactions between Egypt, Nubia, Kush Napata and Kush Meroe?

13. What role of importance did the African kingdom of Ethiopia with its capital in the city of Axum play in ancient Africa? How and when was it Christianized?

14. Who were some of the great leaders of the eighteenth dynasty in Egypt and what were some of their accomplishments?

15. What racial observations does Chancellor Williams make about the eighteenth dynasty of Egypt?

16. What evidence does Williams introduce to develop the theory that black civilization south of Egypt played a far more dominant role in ancient African history than most historians are willing to admit? Compare Williams' and Harris' views on the development of civilization south of Egypt.

17. What reasons does Chancellor Williams suggest for the eventual regress of black civilization?

18. Where did the major groups of Africans who inhabit the region south of the Sahara come from, and how did they develop according to current theories?

19. Identify some of the early trading centers along the East Africa coast. What was the Swahili culture? How did it develop?

20. What were the three major empires of ancient and medieval West Africa?

21. Identify the dates, important rulers and special features of the three great empires of ancient and medieval West Africa.

22. Give the names of some of the smaller kingdoms which existed in medieval West Africa and elsewhere south of the Sahara.

23. Where was the Monomopata Empire and how did it come into existence? What, according to Williams was the weakness of this empire that became the reason for its downfall?

24. Who was Queen Nzinga? How did she come to power and how did she unify the Ndongo kingdom against the early efforts of the Portuguese to control Angola?

PART II

The Traditional Way of Life in Africa

Section Two offers insight into aspects of the African Traditional way of life as manifested or revealed in the African Life Cycle. The African Life Cycle or "experience" is characterized by the idea that life is a continuum with several stages including birth, puberty, adulthood, marriage and death. Each stage is marked by ceremonies and rites of passage.

The family as the basis of African society is presented in the selections by John Hope Franklin. The selections by Jomo Kenyatta and Victor Turner both discuss specific aspects of the rites of passage from adolescence to adulthood among the Gikuyu of Kenya and the Bemba and Ndembu of Zambia respectively.

Using the Zulu religious practices, E. Thomas Lawson focuses on the role and significance of religion and spirituality in the African Life Cycle. African religion and spirituality encompasses a worldview that embraces a concept affirming the connectedness of the living, the dead and those yet unborn.

Like African religion and spirituality, the African aesthetic and culture, including art, music and poetry, is linked with everyday life rather than being viewed exclusively apart from it. In some African societies there is no corresponding word to the western term of "art," for artistic expression is central to the

African way of life. Music, art and poetry can have a significance of their own but these art forms more readily become important when they are used in notable social, economic and political events in traditional African society and culture. Since language is so important as a purveyor of culture and knowledge and a key signpost of civilization, a selection on indigenous, creole and foreign is also included in this section on traditional African society.

Part II closes with two poems by contemporary African poets who promote the importance of traditional African culture. The poem, "Congo," by Leopold Senghor praises African motherhood. "Lament of the Drums," by Christopher Okigbo, bemoans the fading of traditional African society as it gives way to European influence.

14. The African Way of Life - Family and Society

JOHN HOPE FRANKLIN

This selection by John Hope Franklin focuses on the traditional African family. He describes the family as the basis of all social, economic and political institutions in traditional African society.

The African Way of Life - Family and Society

It is obviously impossible to make very many generalizations concerning the way of life in a continent so large as Africa, with so many variations in climate, physiography, and population. As in any other area, at any other time, Africa presents variations in degrees of civilization that run the entire gamut from the most simple to remarkably advanced ones. At this point little more can be done than to observe various aspects of the African way of life with a view to understanding more adequately the cultural heritage of these people who have come to claim the concern of Europeans and Americans in recent centuries. If the emphasis here appears to be placed on the way of life in West Africa, it is because there seems to be merit in trying to secure as intimate an understanding as possible of the area in which the bulk of the people lived who later became the black workers of the Americas.

Political Institutions

Wherever we observe the peoples of Africa, we find some form of political organization. They were not all highly organized kingdoms—to be sure, some were simple, isolated family states—but they all seem to indicate the normal capability and desire of establishing governments to solve the problems that every community of people encounters. The family state prevailed in areas where the territory was divided among a number of distinct families and where there was no inclination or desire on the part of these families to merge their resources to organize a stronger state. In such situations the chief of state was extremely powerful, because his political strength was supplemented by the strength that was his by virtue of being head of the family. In some instances, several such states, the constituents of which enjoyed a common ancestry, came together to form a more powerful state known as the clan state. If it became possible to surmount the obstacles of tradition and clannishness, several groups could come together and form what has come to be known as the village state or tribe seat.

Village state flourished all through West Africa. The growth and prosperity of some prompted them to merge, voluntarily or by force, to form small kingdoms, the most popular form of government in Africa. These kingdoms, if they met with a favorable set of circumstances—able leadership, adequate resources, and strong military organization—could grow into federations or even empires, such as those of Mali and Songhay. These various degrees of political organization were attained by Africans in their successive stages of development. Despite the fact that the states existed at different times and at different places, it is remarkable to observe the same essential characteristics that seem to have prevailed in all of them.

The power to govern a state usually resided in a given family and was transmitted by it. Two other families, however, performed important functions in establishing a royal personage on the throne, the electing family and the enthroning family. The electing family could exercise a choice within the royal family. In this way the Africans recognized the stabilizing effect that a royal family might have on the political fortunes of the people.

At the same time, they were practical enough to recognize the fact that the eldest son was not necessarily the ablest or most desirable and felt free to choose their ruler from among any of the male members of the royal family. The new king could exercise no authority until he had been properly invested in office by persons so designated by the enthroning family. These practices had the effect of insuring to the people a more satisfactory monarch than automatic descent of authority might give them.

Each African king of any real importance had a group of ministers and advisers. Indeed, in some states custom imposed on the king the obligation of appointing a given number of advisers and delegating real authority to them. Custom generally conferred each ministerial charge on a certain family. These ministers and other advisers and members of the nobility functioned as a kind of parliament, which in some instances exercised substantial authority. It is interesting to observe that a peculiar African custom served to limit the authority of many kings. If the king did not belong to the family of the first person occupying the ground in his kingdom, he had no rights over the land. Any questions involving the land were settled by the descendants of the first occupants, who could conceivably be an insignificant subject of the king or even a prisoner of war. It seems that most kings were willing to conform to this ancient custom.

It is possible, however, to overemphasize the importance of the central political organization among the Africans. To be sure, the power of the kings, ministers, and subchiefs was considerable; but beneath this semblance of national unity was the strong attachment on the part of the individual to local authority and local loyalties. Each locality had its own "king," and in many matters of a purely local nature this royal personage exercised power that was indisputable. It was this concept of the division of authority—a kind of dichotomy of sovereignty—that kept the great kings sensitive to the possibility of conflict within their realm. Few powerful kings of the great empires and kingdoms ever achieved so much authority as to destroy completely the feeling of local rulers that they enjoyed a degree of sovereignty themselves. Stability could be achieved only through extensive military organization and a carefully organized

central government. That this stability was frequently achieved
is a testimonial to the wisdom, strength, and not infrequent ruth-
lessness of the native kingdoms.

Economic Life ✓

It would be fallacious to assume that Africans were either
primarily nomadic or simply agricultural. There exists in Africa
such a diversity of physical environments that it would be impossible for people to evolve identical ways of life in different parts
of the continent. Essentially agricultural, the peoples of Africa
displayed a remarkable degree of specialization within this
ancient economic pursuit. The African concept of landowner-
ship stemmed from the importance of agriculture in the peoples' way of life. The land was considered so important to the
entire community that it belonged not to individuals but to the
collective community; which was comprised of the first occupants of the soil. One of the most important local dignitaries was
the "master of the ground," who was at the same time the grand
priest of the local religion and the administrator of the soil. The
importance of this official can be clearly seen, it may be recalled,
in the fact that not even the political ruler could make any disposition of land without the consent of the master of the ground.
Individuals or groups of persons could obtain the right to use a
given parcel of land, but such permission did not carry with it
the right of alienation or any other form of disposition. When
the land was not used productively, it reverted to the collective
domain.

Whether the land was held individually or collectively—
and it seems that both practices were prevalent—the tillers of
the soil devoted all their energies to the cultivation of their crops.
Soil was cleared by chopping down trees and burning the under-
brush. The ashes were used to fertilize the ground, which was
in turn prepared for planting by large spades with short handles.
Seeds or sprouts were planted in mounds or embankments that
had been carefully prepared. Frequent weeding was necessary,
especially in new ground, in order to prevent the young plants
from being choked. Millet, wheat, rice, cassava, cotton, fruits,

and vegetables were commonly grown. Dotting the countryside were towers from which watchmen drove away birds and other grain-eating animals. Harvest time was a particularly busy period during which grain was reaped, threshed, milled, and stored, while other fruit and grain were made into fermented drinks, and cotton was manufactured in thread and cloth.

Domestic animals were a part of almost every farm; but in some areas the rural people devoted most of their attention to the grazing of sheep and cattle and the raising of chickens and other fowls. In Northeastern Africa some tribes were known for their great skill in breeding and care of cattle. In the east many villages ascribed so much importance to the raising of cattle that wealth was measured in terms of heads of cattle. The Bantu and Hottentots engaged in farming as well as large-scale cattle raising.

Artisanry was a significant area of economic activity. Even among the so-called backward tribes, there were those who were skilled along various lines. Among many people, there was a remarkable knowledge of basketry, textile weaving, pottery, woodwork, and metallurgy. The pygmies manufactured bark cloth and fiber baskets. The Hottentots devoted much time and attention to making clothing from textiles, skins, and furs. The Ashantis of the Gold Coast wove rugs and carpets and turned and glazed pottery with considerable skill. In many parts of the Sudan there was extensive manufacturing of woodenware, tools, and implements.

The use of iron was developed very early in the economy of Africa. From Ethiopia to the Atlantic, there is much evidence of adroitness in the manufacture and use of iron. Indeed, many careful students of primitive civilizations credit the negroes of Africa with the discovery of iron. The anthropologist Franz Boas insisted that Africans were using iron when European peoples were still in the Stone Age. The simple processes that Africans were found to have used and the early date at which they began to make iron suggest that it was the natives of Africa, and not the Hittites, who first discovered the use of iron. Africa exported iron for many years, and blacksmiths and other workers in iron were found in many parts of Africa. With simple bellows and a charcoal fire, the native blacksmith smelted his ore and forged implements such as knives, saws, and axes. Africans worked also in silver, gold, copper, and bronze. In Benin, bronze and copper implements and art objects testified to the great skill on the part of the smiths, while many artisans, including those of the Yoruba lands, and Mali, devoted their attention to the making of ornamental objects from silver and gold.

The interest of early Africa in the outside world can best be seen in the great attention that was given to commerce. The tendency of tribes to specialize in some phase of economic activity made it necessary that they maintain commercial intercourse with other tribes and with other countries in order to secure the things that they did not produce. Some villages for example, specialized in fishing; others concentrated their talents on metallurgy; while others made weapons, utensils, and so on. In tribes where such specialization was practiced, tradesmen traveled from place to place to barter and to purchase. Upon returning they were laden with goods which they sold to their fellows. Some tradesmen from the West Coast went as far north as the Mediterranean and as far east as Egypt, where they exchanged their goods for the wares of tradesmen from other parts of the world. It is to be recalled that the travels of the kings and emperors did much to stimulate this international traffic. Africa was, therefore, never a series of isolated self-sufficient communities, but an area that had far-flung interests based on agriculture, industry, and commerce. The effect of such contacts on the culture was immeasurable. It can only be said here that these routes of commerce were the highways over which civilization as well as goods traveled and that Africa gave much of her own civilization to others and received a good deal in return.

Social Organization

As among other peoples, the family was the basis of social organization in early Africa. The foundation even of economic and political life in Africa was the family, with its inestimable influence over individual members. Although the eldest male was usually head of the family, there was the widespread practice of tracing relationships through the mother instead of the father. In areas where this matrilineal practice was followed, children belonged solely to the family of the mother, whose eldest brother exercised the paternal rights and assumed all responsibility for the children's lives and actions. In tribes that admitted only female relationship, the chief of the family was the brother of the mother on her mother's side. In tribes that were, on the other hand, patrilineal, the chief was the real father. With either group, those persons forming the family comprised all the living descendants of the same ancestor, female in the matriarchal system and male in the patriarchal system.

In general, the wife was not considered a member of her husband's family. After marriage she continued to be a part of her own family. Since her family continued to manifest a real interest in her welfare, the bride's husband was expected to guarantee good treatment and to pay her family an indemnity, a compensation for taking away a member of the family. This indemnity was not a purchase price, as has frequently been believed. The woman did not legally belong to her husband, but to her own family. Naturally, the amount of the indemnity varied both with tribal practice and the position of the bridegroom. Indeed, in some tribes the tradition was maintained by a mere token payment out of respect for an ancient practice that had once had real significance in intertribal relationships.

Although polygamy existed in virtually every region, it was not universally practiced. The chief of the family would defray the expenses involved in the first marriage of a male member of the family, but if the husband wanted to take a second wife, he would have to meet all the expenses himself. Religion played a part in determining the number of wives a man could have. The native religions did not limit the number. When the Muslims made inroads into the tribes of Africa, they forbade adherents to take more than four wives. Wherever the Christians established a foothold among the natives, they insisted on monogamy altogether. Where polygamy was practiced, it does not appear to have produced many evils. As a matter of fact, the division of household duties in a polygamous family had the effect of reducing the duties and responsibilities of each wife, a highly desirable condition from the point of view of the wives if the husband was without servants or slaves.

The clan, the enlarged family, was composed of all the families that claimed a common ancestor. The clan would develop in the same community or area, but as it became larger and as some families found more attractive opportunities elsewhere it would separate, and one or more families would go to some other area to live. Unless the separation resulted from a violent quarrel or fight, the departing families regarded themselves as still being attached to the clan. Once the unity was broken by separation, however, the clan tended to disintegrate for the reason that cooperation in war, economic activities, and religious life was no longer practicable. Under the strain imposed by separation over the course of time, the traditions and practices of the clan tended to become obscure and unimportant. Consequently, little more than the common name bound members of the same clan together; and new environments and new linguistic influences had the effect of causing the clan names to be changed or modified. In such instances, members of the same clan living in different places would have no way of recognizing each other.

Early in its development, Africa showed signs of social stratification in its many tribes. At the top was the nobility, "the good men," who could prove that they descended from free men. Since they could claim the name of a respected clan, they had a right to the places and positions of respect in the social order. Next was the great mass of workers, who found it difficult or impossible to raise a genealogical tree that would bear careful scrutiny. Although they might carry a perfectly good clan name, they could not prove their right to it and therefore were not able to qualify for a position in the upper class. At the bottom of the social structure were those persons who enjoyed no political or social rights. They were slaves, war captives, disgraced or degraded persons, and those living beyond the pale of the law. It must be added that the social structure had an economic base, and wealth tended to be concentrated in the upper class. Families, moreover, rather than individuals, constituted the several classes. Since families wielded economic power, through their politically important positions or through the domination of certain crafts and other economic pursuits, they had a way of influencing the nature of the social order. Work in itself did not elevate or debase a family, but the particular kind of work did. There was a definite respectability attached to certain types of work, and the graduation toward debasement was equally definite. The working of the soil was the most noble of all pursuits. Following in close order were cattle raising, hunting, fishing, construction, navigation, commerce, gold mining, and the processing of commodities such as soap, oil, and beer. There were variations from tribe to tribe but everywhere there was the tendency to dignify or to degrade families on the basis of the types of work in which they were engaged.

It must not be assumed that persons in the lower levels of the social order enjoyed no privileges or respect. All persons were regarded as necessary to society and were respected for what they contributed. They were accorded numerous privileges because their acknowledged skills earned for them the right to move from one place to another and entrance into groups that otherwise would have been closed to them. Nor is it to be assumed that there was absolute rigidity in the social structure of tribal Africa. As among other peoples, tact, special knowledge, wealth, or good fortune tended to create a fluidity in African society. By taste, a member of a mining family might choose to farm; and although his new occupation did not of itself elevate him from the lower social position of his family, in due time he could gain so much respect and admiration as a farmer that he would be regarded as a legitimate member of the class of noble tillers of the soil. As in almost every society in the world, power and wealth could, in many instances, be substituted for nobility of origin.

Slavery was an important feature of African social and economic life. The institution was widespread and was perhaps as old as African society itself. Slaves were predominantly persons captured in war and could be sold or kept by the persons who captured them. Slaves were usually regarded as the property of the chief of the tribe or head of the family. . . . [and they] became trusted associates of their masters and enjoyed virtual freedom. . . . The child of slaves could not be sold and thus constituted an integral and inalienable part of the family property. Enjoying such security, for it was not uncommon for the children of slaves to be favored with manumission at the hands of their masters.

Excerpt from: John Hope Franklin and Alfred A. Moss, Jr., *From Slavery to Freedom* (New York: Alfred Knopf, 1988) pp. 8-19.

15. The Meaning of Initiation and Circumcision in Gikuyu Society

JOMO KENYATTA

Jomo Kenyatta, the former president of Kenya and leader of the Mau Mau independence movement, has written about the structure and dynamics of the way of life among his own people, the Gikuyu, in his book Facing Mount Kenya. This selection highlights the central importance of the initiation rite and other rites of passage among the Gikuyu and the dynamic meaning and force of rites of passage in the African Life Cycle.

Facing Mount Kenya

In all tribal education the emphasis lies on a particular act of behavior in a concrete situation. While the emphasis lies in the sphere of behavior, it is none the less true that the growing child is acquiring a mass of knowledge all the time. . . .

To turn to our analysis of the Gikuyu system of government. We have seen that the circumcision ceremony was the only qualification which gave a man the recognition of manhood and the full right of citizenship. It is therefore necessary to take the circumcision ceremony as our starting-point. Before a boy goes through this ceremony he is considered as a mere child, and as such has no responsibility in the tribal organization; his parents are responsible for all his actions. If he commits any crime he cannot be prosecuted personally, it is his parents' duty to answer for him. But this liberty ceases immediately he is circumcised, because he is now "full grown," and has assumed the title of a "he-man" (*mondomorome*), and as such he must share the responsibility with the other "he-men" (*arome*). As soon as his circumcision wound heals he joins in the national council of junior warriors, *njama ya anake a mumo*. At this stage his father provides him with necessary weapons, namely, spear, shield, and a sword; then a sheep or a male goat is given to the senior warriors of the district, who receive it in the name of the whole national council of senior warriors. The animal is killed for a ceremony of introducing the young warrior into the general activities and the etiquette of the warrior class.

In former days the ceremony was more elaborate. The weapons of the young warrior were sprinkled with the blood of the ceremonial animal, then the leading warrior shouted a war-cry (*rohio*), his companions stood up brandishing their spears and lifting their shields upwards; and in a ritual tone they chanted in unison the following warrior's resolution (*mweheiwa wa anake*): "We brandish our spears, which is the symbol of our courageous and fighting spirit, never to retreat or abandon our hope, or run away from our comrades. If ever we shall make a decision, nothing will change us; and even if the heaven should hold over us a threat to fall and crush us, we shall take our spears and prop it. And if there seems to be a unity between the heaven and the earth to destroy us, we shall sink the bottom part of our spear on the earth, preventing them from uniting; thus keeping the two entities, the earth and the sky, though together, apart. Our faith and our decision never changing shall act as balance." . . .

Eldership

The third stage in manhood is marriage. When a man has married and has established his own homestead, he is required to join the council of elders (*kiama*); he pays one male goat or sheep and then he is initiated into a first grade of eldership (*kiama kia kamatimo*). The word *matimu*, which means spears, signifies the carriers of spears, which denotes the warriors who have joined *kiama* while still functioning as warriors, and who are carrying spears because they have not yet been given the staff of office. They are not yet elders; they are learners of the *kiama's* procedures. The *kamatimo* act as messengers to the *kiama*, and help to skin animals, to light fires, to bring firewood, to roast meat for the senior elders, and to carry ceremonial articles to and from the *kiama* assemblies. They must not eat kidneys, spleen, or loin, for these are reserved for the senior elders. Any *kamatimo* who dares eat one of these portions from a ceremonial animal is fined a ram, which is killed to purify the offender and at the same time to initiate him into the secret of the higher grade of eldership.

Next to *kamatimo* comes *kiama kia mataathi*, i.e. the council of peace. This stage is reached when a man has a son or daughter old enough to be circumcised. Before the child enters in the circumcision ceremony, the father is called upon by the *kiama kia mataathi* of his village, and asked to prepare himself for a ceremony called *gotonyio kerera*, that is, to be initiated into the core of the tribal tradition and custom. . . .

Religious Sacrificial Council (Kiama Kia Maturanguru)

The last and most honored status in the man's life history is the religious and sacrificial council (*kiama kia maturanguru*). This stage is reached when a man has had practically all his children circumcised, and his wife (or wives) has passed the childbearing age. At this stage the man has passed through all age-grades, has been initiated to them all. Apart from his staff of office, he wears brass rings (*icohe*) in his ears, but he is not yet invested with the power to lead a sacrificial ceremony at the sacred tree (*mogumo mote wa lgongona*). To acquire this privilege he has to pay a ewe. This is taken to the sacred tree where the animal is slaughtered by the elders of the sacrificial council. This ceremony is performed in secrecy and only by the selected few who are fortunate enough to live to that esteemed age. No one outside the members of the sacrificial council is allowed anywhere near the sacred tree when this ceremony is in progress. Half of the animal is eaten by the elders and the other half is burned in the sacrificial fire. The main feature of this ceremony is dedication of the man's life to God (*Ngai*) and to the welfare of the community. What actually happens at the sacred tree with regard to preparation of the ceremony is very hard to say, for the writer has not had the opportunity of attending the ceremony, having not yet reached the required age. But he had the privilege of watching the elders going to and from the sacred tree while herding sheep and goats near the ceremonial grove called *mogumo wa Njathi*.

On coming out from the sacred tree the elders carry bunches of sacred leaves called *maturanguru*. The elders of this grade assume a role of "holy men." They are high priests. All religious and ethical ceremonies are in their hands.

Excerpt from: Jomo Kenyatta, *Facing Mount Kenya: The Tribal Life of the Gikuyu* (London: Secker and Warburg, 1962) pp. 102, 190-191, 193, 196-197.

16. "Growing" Girls into Women and "Making" Boys into Men

VICTOR TURNER

Specific and detailed anthropological studies of selected African groups such as those done by Audrey Richards among the Bemba and by Victor Turner among the Ndembu in Zambia have produced striking results to support the importance of the family in Africa. In this selection, some of the organic dynamism of the rites of passage and symbolic forms used in ritual practices to engender personal transformation in individuals, both male and female, is discussed.

The Forest of Symbols

The passivity of neophytes to their instructors, their malleability, which is increased by submission to ordeal, their reduction to a uniform condition, are signs of the process whereby they are ground down to be fashioned anew and endowed with additional powers to cope with their new station in life. Dr. [Audrey] Richards, in her superb study of Bemba girls' puberty rites, *Chisungu,* has told us that Bemba speak of "growing a girl" when they mean initiating her. This term, "to grow" well expresses how many peoples think of transition rites. We are inclined, as sociologists, to reify our abstractions (it is indeed a device which helps us to understand many kinds of social interconnection) and to talk about persons "moving through structural positions in a hierarchical frame" and the like. Not so the Bemba and the Shilluk of the Sudan who see the status or condition embodied or incarnate, if you like, in the person. To "grow" a girl into a woman is to effect an ontological transformation; it is not merely to convey an unchanging substance from one position to another by a quasi-mechanical force. Howitt saw Kuringals in Australia and I have seen Ndembu in Africa drive away grown-up men before a circumcision ceremony because they had not been initiated. Among Ndembu, men were also chased off because they had only been circumcised at the mission hospital and had not undergone the full bush seclusion according to the orthodox Ndembu rite. These biologically mature men had not been "made men" by the proper ritual procedures. It is the ritual and the esoteric teaching which grows girls and makes men. It is the ritual, too, which among Shilluk makes a prince into a king or, among Luvale, a cultivator into a hunter. . . .

When one examines the masks, costumes, figurines, and such displayed in initiation situations, one is often struck, as I have been when observing Ndembu masks in circumcision and funerary rites, by the way in which certain natural and cultural features are represented as disproportionately large or small. A head, nose, or phallus, a hoe, bow, or meal mortar are represented as huge or tiny by comparison with other features of their context which retain their normal size. (For a good example of this, see "The Man Without Arms" in *Chisungu*, a figurine of a lazy man with an enormous penis but no arms.) Sometimes things retain their customary shapes but are portrayed in unusual colors. What is the point of this exaggeration amounting sometimes to caricature? It seems to me that to enlarge or diminish or discolor in this way is a primordial mode of abstraction. The outstandingly exaggerated feature is made into an object of reflection. Usually it is not a univocal symbol that is thus represented but a multivocal one, a semantic molecule with many components. One example is the Bemba pottery emblem *Coshi wa ng'oma*, "The Nursing Mother," described by Audrey Richards in *Chisungu*. This is a clay figurine, nine inches high, of an exaggeratedly pregnant mother shown carrying four babies at the same time, one at her breast and three at her back. To this figurine is attached a riddling song:

My mother deceived me!
Coshi wa ng'oma!
So you have deceived me;
I have become pregnant again.

Bemba women interpreted this to Richards as follows:

Coshi wa ng'oma was a midwife of legendary fame and is
merely addressed in this song. The girl complains because
her mother told her to wean her first child too soon so that it
died; or alternatively told her that she would take the first
child if her daughter had a second one. But she was tricking
her and now the girl has two babies to look after. The moral
stressed is the duty of refusing intercourse with the husband
before the baby is weaned, i.e., at the second or third year.
This is a common Bemba practice.

In the figurine the exaggerated features are the number of children carried at once by the woman and her enormously dis-
tended belly. Coupled with the son, it encourages the novice to
ponder upon two relationships vital to her, those with her mother and her husband. Unless the novice observes the Bemba
weaning custom, her mother's desire for grandchildren to
increase her matrilineage and her husband's desire for renewed
sexual intercourse will between them actually destroy and not
increase her offspring. Underlying this is the deeper moral that
to abide by tribal custom and not to sin against it either by excess
or defect is to live satisfactorily. Even to please those one loves
may be to invite calamity, if such compliance defies the
immemorial wisdom of the elders embodied in the *mbusa*. This
wisdom is vouched for by the mythical and archetypal midwife
Coshi wa ng'oma.

Excerpt from: Victor Turner, *The Forest of Symbols: Aspects of Ndembu Ritual*
(Cornell University Press, 1967) pp. 101-104.

17. From Kraal to Inkosi: The "Zulu Religious World" as a Total Worldview

E. Thomas Lawson

In this selection, E. Thomas Lawson, an eminent scholar of African religion, describes the religious worldview of one of the major African groups, the Zulu in South Africa. The terms of the language may vary, and some details are not entirely the same, but the basic form and structure and certainly the force and power of Zulu religion can be found in the diverse religious beliefs and practices of other groups throughout Africa.

The Origins of the Zulu People

The origins of the Zulu people are shrouded in the mists of oral tradition. But by using a variety of specialized methods, scholars have been able to penetrate the mists and discover some of the Zulu past. They have concluded that within the last two thousand years there have been a series of migrations of large numbers of people from central Africa into the southern part of the continent. These migrants from the "north" had a linguistic identity, and they are referred to as "Bantu-speaking peoples." This means that although these people spoke many different languages the languages were similar enough in form and structure to deserve a common name, "Bantu." Scholars chose the name Bantu because this word for "people" occurs in

139

a large array of languages spoken by the migrants. These people slowly settled the southeastern area of Africa all the way down to what is now known as the province of Natal in the Republic of South Africa. As their occupation solidified, they began to form special groups. One large group is now known as the Nguni people. The Nguni group consisted of many tribes and clans: the Xhosa, the Fingo, the Tembu, the Pondo, the Swazi, and the Zulu. This process of migration and solidification into special groups, each with a distinct language, was completed by the seventeenth century.

The Zulu at this stage of development were one group of people among many. According to their own traditions, an ancestor named Malandela had two sons named Qwabe and Zulu. These two sons became the chiefs of two clans. Chief Zulu extended his quest for territory until he came to the Mfolosi Valley, an area north of the Thukela River in the present-day province of Natal. There Chief Zulu settled. His clan remained stable and unremarkable until the renowned Zulu chief Shaka emerged as a dynamic leader and warrior. Shaka in a very short time welded many different clans together into one powerful kingdom. He was successful in this endeavor because he developed completely new methods of military conquest, establishing highly disciplined regiments of young men and inventing new ways of deploying them in battle. It is Shaka's prowess as a general that has captivated the imagination of western novelists and filmmakers. Movies about the Zulu warrior continue to be made to this day.

Today there are about four million Zulu in South Africa. They continue to live on a small portion of their original land in the northeast section of Natal. However, many Zulu can be found throughout South Africa working in the mines, as domestic servants, and in those positions in the world of industry and business not reserved for whites. Even under such very difficult conditions some Zulu have been able to attain a high level of education and thus will be found either at the segregated universities provided by the South African government or, in special cases, at one of the English-speaking universities, such as the University of Cape Town or Rhodes University.

Recently, the government of South Africa declared a portion of the province of Natal as the Zulu "homeland," which they named Kwazulu. Supposedly, within this area the Zulu will finally have some political rights. Whether or not this is the case, because this greatly diminished area is not self-sufficient, the Zulu will be forced to continue their dependence of white South Africa, with its system of apartheid. Apartheid is a governmental policy intended to keep the various groups of people living in South Africa separate from each other. Its practical effect is to keep all black people in a position of servitude and without political rights of any kind. The "homeland" is certainly far less in area than the traditional Zulu kingdom. At this moment the Zulu are strongly insisting on their autonomy and freedom, and Zulu leaders have often been some of the most eloquent spokesmen for the rights of all black people in South Africa. In fact, the Zulu chief Albert Luthuli was granted the Nobel Peace Prize for his articulate and peaceful presentation of the case for all the oppressed people of South Africa. And the present Zulu chief, Gatsha Buthelezi, has also acquired a reputation as a spokesman for the rights of Zulu and other black people in South Africa.

While the Zulu people remain in such an oppressed situation it is impossible to speak of an independent kingdom or nation, despite the recently proclaimed Kwazulu. But long before such a proclamation, the buffeting that these people had received from both British and Boer had already destroyed their autonomy.

In 1879 the British invaded the Zulu kingdom established by Shaka and maintained by the succeeding chiefs. Cetshwayo was the last of the Zulu kings or great chiefs. After the British invasion of Zululand he was exiled; the invasion and his exile signaled the end of Zulu territorial and political independence. In 1897 Zululand was ceded to the British colony of Natal. Shortly after this cession, the British and the Afrikaaners engaged in a war disastrous for both. This war created a deep enmity between the two white groups. In 1910 the Union of South Africa was formed as a state within the British Commonwealth. In 1913 the South African government promulgated the Native Land Act, naming a portion of traditional

Zululand as a "native reserve." In fact, by 1906 much of the territory that the Zulu regarded as their own kingdom had already been overrun and was possessed by white Natal settlers of both British and Boer stock. It is the remnants of this native reserve that has now been designated as Kwazulu, the "homeland" of the Zulu people.

The Religious System of the Zulu People

Though I have briefly called attention to the history of the Zulu, I do not intend to discuss the historical development of Zulu religion. There are many good reasons for not engaging in a historical analysis, the most important being lack of information. To study the historical development of a religious tradition means tracing its progress from its inception through its various changes to its present situation. Unfortunately, as with most African religions, such historical documentation is simply not available. We are dealing with an oral culture in which traditions are handed down by word of mouth. Documentation is not, of course, entirely lacking. We do have the diaries of westerners who lived with the Zulu for a period. Some missionaries did make a very serious attempt to record the thought and practice of the Zulu. But such records are too sparse and too unsystematic to give us the kind of information that would permit significant historical analysis.

Rather than getting lost in unclear historical detail, I prefer to look directly at the known patterns of Zulu thought and practice. This way of studying a religion provides a key for opening the doors to at least some of the complex religious world of the Zulu. This approach starts out by viewing Zulu thought and practice as all of a piece. It assumes unity in Zulu life; through the changes brought about in history there is a continuity. Though such an approach acknowledges change, it insists that the Zulu religious system is flexible enough to deal with new situations in terms of its own ideas and practices.

A responsible description of the Zulu religious world must, however, choose some time frame, because, although history is not the focus, it cannot be ignored. It would be whistling in the dark to assert—without evidence—that the Zulu religious world of today is identical with that of five hundred years ago. In the first place, strictly speaking, Zulu identity can only be traced back as far as Chief Zulu, and some argue that it can only be traced back as far as Shaka. I have chosen to describe a system that has been in place for the last hundred and fifty years. Whatever documents we do have are from this period, and they are of sufficiently high quality to give us the kind of information we need. These documents are diaries, reports written by missionaries on the basis of interviews with Zulu, accounts by colonial administrators, and descriptions by various anthropologists and other social scientists. Obviously such documents reflect the biases of those who wrote them, and the information generated depends upon the kinds of questions asked. But they are sufficiently informative to provide us with the materials we need to provide a description of Zulu thought and practice.

Such thought and practice can be understood more clearly when we begin to identify their context. The Zulu people live and act in a religious world. This means that, whether one is talking about the birth of a child, a boy coming of age, the marriage of a young couple, or the death of a person in the family, there will be special places, people, and powers that give them special significance.

One way of getting a clearer view of the Zulu religious world is to pay attention to the places where religious acts take place, the roles assumed by the Zulu in the performance of these acts, the focus of the acts, and the style of action. In what follows, therefore, we shall organize our description of the Zulu religious system according to religious places, religious roles, religious powers, and religious acts.

As one wanders the dusty, red roads of present-day Zululand, one is struck by the simple beauty of the gently contoured green hills stretching to the horizon. These hills have great religious significance for the Zulu, for many of them provide the sites for the *kraal* or Zulu village. Some of these hills will not have *kraals* built on them, and it is such unpopulated hills that provide sites for special rituals the Zulu occasionally perform. But the Zulu *kraal* is the primary locus for ritual action. It is in this religious space that crucial religious performances occur periodically.

The *kraal* is the traditional village. It consists of a circular arrangement of thatched huts, each shaped something like a bee-hive. This circle of huts surrounds a circular cattle enclosure at the very center of the village. This inner circle is also called a *kraal*. So, in effect, you have a *kraal* within a *kraal*, a cattle enclosure within a human enclosure. The village is built on the side of the hill and slopes downward, with the entryways to both the outer circle of huts and the inner circle for the cattle facing toward the bottom of the hill. These entryways invariably face east.

The location of the huts in the circular arrangement is significant, for it indicates both social and ritual relationships of the occupants. The chief hut, on the upper part of the circular arrangement, is the hut of the headman, who is also the priest of the *kraal*. This chief hut is balanced on each side by the huts of the headman's wives, one of whom will be known as the "great wife." Lower down are the huts for the children of the family, for appropriate relatives, and for guests or visitors. Such relatives, guests, or visitors will always have a particular association with this *kraal*, usually a relationship of kinship.

The inner circle is the cattle *kraal*. As with all Bantu-speaking peoples, cattle are of extreme practical and religious importance. It is in the cattle *kraal* that most of the important Zulu religious rituals are performed. In fact some scholars call the cattle enclosure the "temple" of the Zulu people. Although the particular inhabitants of a *kraal* might very well own other types of animals, such as sheep and goats, in the traditional Zulu village such other animals will be kept in separate enclosures— outside the village proper. Only in cases of extreme poverty— a family that owns no cattle at all—will one find sheep or goats in the inner circle. Such a situation is much more likely today than it was in the heyday of the Zulu kingdom.

In each hut in the village will be found the *umsamo*. This is a special place set aside for various objects with ritual significance. In the hut of the headman/priest there will be found a very special *umsamo*. Its particular purpose is to provide a ritual ground for communing with the everpresent family ancestors. Likewise, at the top of the inner cattle enclosure there is a ritual ground for the performance of religious ceremonies directed to the ancestors.

Besides the unoccupied but specially marked hills, then, the *kraal* turns out to be not only a place to live but a place to serve the ancestral powers in the manner that they require. Both places serve as sacred ground for the religious acts that the Zulu regularly perform.

These sacred grounds provide the stage for the many roles assumed by the actors in the Zulu religious drama. What is particularly interesting about these roles is that they identify who the leaders and specialists in the Zulu community are. An examination of them will show how political, social, and religious functions in Zulu society overlap and interact with each other. For example, the headman of the *kraal* leads the rituals for the ancestors, is responsible for decisions that affect the everyday lives of its inhabitants, and maintains the correct relationships between every person in the village.

Of the many roles enacted by the Zulu, eight have a particularly important place in their religious practice. These are those of headman/priest, diviner, herbalist, patient, heaven-herd, supplicant, sorcerer, and witch.

The headman of each Zulu *kraal* is the chief official of the village and also that person most directly responsible for the performance of the ritual acts expected of all Zulu, especially those that address the ancestors. His role is, therefore, political, social, and religious in nature. He is called *umnumzane*. Religiously, he represents the people of the *kraal* to the ancestors and the ancestors of the headman's lineage to the people. This position is of great ritual significance in the religious world of the Zulu because the ancestors are a focal point of their religion. The ancestors have great power, and they act for the good or ill of the villagers. These ancestors require reverence and devotion, and the *umnumzane* ensures that both in attitude and in act the members of the community for which he is responsible perform their religious duty. Whether it be birth, marriage, or death, the headman will be involved in some manner, and it is in the *kraal* that such acts will be performed.

Divination, the ritual acts performed to diagnose the reason for a misfortune or the means to the solution of some human problem, is widespread throughout Africa. As we shall see, it has achieved a highly systematic and intricate character among the Yoruba. Divination is an important activity among the Zulu, and the role of the diviner is widespread in Zulu society.

One needs a special calling from the ancestral spirits in order to become a diviner. Though anyone can become a diviner, this is a vocation in Zulu society that is most often assumed by women. The Zulu regard the ancestors as the ones who do the calling. Such a calling takes a special form. Often it comes in the form of a vision or a dream. Such a visitation is often accompanied by aches, pains, or other bodily disorders. The calling also involves special training under an experienced diviner; divining is not regarded as a casual affair, for identifying the cause of a problem takes great skill.

Diviners find the cause of a problem; herbalists prescribe the cure. Although most Zulu know something about herbs and other kinds of medicines, and many Zulu are experts in the knowledge of and prescription of particular medicines, there are Zulu who are specialists in medicine and who have a wide range of medical knowledge. Such a Zulu specialist is known as an *izinyanga zemithi*, a specialist in medicine, or *izinyanga zokwe-lapha*, a specialist in healing.

Whereas most diviners are women, most herbalists are men. Knowledge of medicine is usually handed down from father to son. But as I have already indicated, there is widespread knowledge of medicine, and particular people in the community will have knowledge of special medicines for special purposes.

One of the most interesting features of Zulu medicine is that it is not a completely traditional system. By this I mean that the *izinyanga* is in constant search for new and more effective medicines, and records show that medicines introduced by westerners have been enthusiastically received and have become part of the medical repertoire. Thus, though it has a strong traditional base, Zulu medicine is a flexible system that has proven to be quite open to new knowledge.

Whereas the roles of headman/priest, diviner, and herbalist are formal and public roles, that of patient, the user of medicine, is an informal and private one. Because of the flexibility of Zulu medicine both with regard to the practitioner and to the materials used, many of the people are self- prescribers. This includes the ability to diagnose and cure one's own illness. Thus the patient may either consult a herbalist, or engage in self-prescription; in either case there is a direct relationship between the patient and the power of medicine. Strictly speaking, mediation on the part of the herbalist is not necessary to tap that power.

The *izinyanga zezulu*, the specialists in matters having to do with the sky—for example, thunderstorms and lightning—have a very important ritual role to play in the Zulu religious drama. These individuals are responsible for "herding" the thunderstorms that frequent Zululand, and they are known, therefore, as "heaven-herds." It should be remembered that cattle are of fundamental importance to the Zulu, and therefore the imagery of cattle and the activities associated with cattle occur quite frequently. (The role of the heaven-herd is always occupied by a Zulu male because of the close association between men and cattle.)

Heaven-herding is a vocation; it is a role to which a man is called in a special way by the God of the Sky: for example, the individual might receive a special sign, perhaps an especially close encounter with a bolt of lightening, that will convince him that the God of the Sky has chosen him for this work. The candidate for the role will then go through a period of apprenticeship with an experienced heaven-herd. Part of his initiation will be having special cuts made on his face by an experienced heaven-herd. This is a special, permanent marking of the face called scarification.

What is special about the role of the heaven-herd is that he will have a ritual relationship with the God of the Sky instead of the ancestors. The weather is under the control of the God of the Sky; it is he who sends the lightning and the wind and the rain. So the job of the heaven-herd is to repel or divert the approaching storm and to mitigate its effects. Just like the *umfaan*, the young lad who herds the cattle to their special grazing spots, the heaven-herd guides the weather for human benefit.

Most of the Zulu religious life centers upon reverence for the ancestors and the ritual obligations associated with these revered predecessors. But occasions do arise when it is thought necessary for special acts to be performed over which the ancestors have no control or into which the ancestors have given no indication that they care to intrude. The Zulu supplicant, that is, anyone who communes directly with the God of the Sky, will know that, in such a situation of dire need, help is possible from the God of the Sky. The God of the Sky is communicated with only in such special situations, when neither the headman/priest nor the diviner nor the herbalist have demonstrated an ability to help. Only then are special acts of supplication to the God of the Sky in order. Such communication with the God of the Sky will take place on those hills known by the Zulu supplicant to be arenas for an encounter with him. It should be noted, then, that what the heaven-herd and the supplicant have in common is a special ritual location—the hills of God, on which to worship him.

Any Zulu can be a sorcerer. In other words, the role of the sorcerer is general; no one person or set of persons is always and consistently a sorcerer. The reason is that sorcery depends upon the situation; a special grievance has to arise for one Zulu to feel that the occasion is ripe for the expression of the grievance. This angered individual, the one with the grievance, will consult with either a diviner or a herbalist. A diviner is the likely consultant if it is the cause of the problem that needs clarification. Of course, if the diviner traffics in medicine then two jobs can be done at the same time. If the aggrieved person is convinced of the cause but requires the means of sorcery, he or she will consult a herbalist with knowledge of those medicines that can have the desired effect.

To engage in sorcery is to have access to medicinal and spiritual power and to use such powers for destructive ends. The intent of the sorcerer is to harm by the straightforward means made available through the knowledge provided by the herbalist and the diviner. And the motive is often revenge. Anyone with a knowledge of medicine can perform sorcery. One simply devises the techniques to use its power (*amandla*) for evil ends.

There is nothing straightforward about the role of the witch in the Zulu religious world. First of all, no one really knows who the witches are. The role of witch is completely private. It is also completely secret. It is important to note this secrecy, because the headman/priest, the heaven-herd, the diviner, and the herbalist are open, traditionally prescribed, and public roles. But the maker of witchcraft is that unknown individual, almost always considered to be a woman, who misuses valid and good power for invalid and evil ends. Witchcraft is a threat to public order, an unbearable strain on traditional social organization, a challenge to revered tradition. Witches derive their power from, and base their operations in, a shadowy world that is neither that of the ancestors nor that of the God of the Sky. And their purpose is the destruction of what is good, especially those processes that create and enhance life. The *abathakati*, then, is the specialist in evil, the one who twists the system with its centers of power for destructive purposes.

Failure to show due reverence for the ancestors may result in sickness and suffering; the consequences of witchcraft are destruction and death. Such destruction and death comes neither from the God of the Sky nor from the ancestors nor from medicine. Nor does it come even from sorcery, which is the straightforward expression of anger due to justifiable grievances. It comes from the twisted use of power for evil ends.

Any woman can become a witch; she becomes one through the experience of possession. It is possible, however, for a Zulu to be a witch without even knowing it. This cannot be said of any other role in Zulu society. Witches are regarded as having superhuman properties; they can fly at night, can become invisible, and can act on others at a distance. Witches also have a relationship to special kinds of snakes, and the presence of a snake of a certain kind is a clue to the operation of witchcraft.

Understanding the nature and function of these eight roles advances our knowledge of the world view of the Zulu and leads us to questions about the centers of power around which they revolve. We now have two locations for the Zulu religious drama, the *kraal* and specially designated unoccupied hills. We have the roles played by those enacting the drama: the headman/priest, the diviner, the herbalist, the heaven-herd, the supplicant, the patient, the sorcerer, and the witch. What is the drama about? It is about the use and misuse of power, *amandla*. But what is power for the Zulu, and how is such power expressed?

Power is that which is capable of bringing about a change in a situation, an alteration of a status, a variation in a condition. For the Zulu there are three legitimate elements that are capable of exerting power in this sense. These sources of power are the ancestors, the God of the Sky, and medicine. As we have already seen in our discussion of witchcraft, there is also evil power. Evil power is the misuse of power for destructive ends. Legitimate power sustains life in an orderly, customary fashion. When judgment is necessary it follows from the acknowledged structure of the Zulu religious world. Illegitimate power destroys life. It introduces disorder, disrupts human relationships, unleashes vengeance, and destroys the equilibrium that characterizes the intricate balances of everyday Zulu life.

The role of ritual is to maintain and enhance the relationships the Zulu have to the powers of life. The following sections describe the Zulu conceptions of each of these powers in more detail.

The ancestral spirits variously known as the *amalozi*, *amakhosi*, or *amathonga*, are of fundamental significance for the Zulu. They are the departed souls of the deceased. Although they are regarded as having gone to abide in the earth, they continue to have a relationship with those still living in the *kraal*. They are regarded as positive, constructive, and creative presences. They are also capable of meeting out punishment when they have been wronged or ignored. Veneration is their due. Failure to show proper respect to them invites misfortune, proper veneration ensures benefit. The *amalozi*, therefore, are powers for either good or ill. When such power is judgmental it is not regarded as destructive, for its purpose is to maintain traditional relationships. For an ancestor to bring misfortune on a living member of the *kraal* is viewed as a legitimate expression of wrath attributable to the failure of one or more living members of the *kraal* to do their duty.

The Zulu make a distinction among ancestors. Zulu society is patrilineal, that is, authority and inheritance proceed through the male line from father to son. The important ancestors for a *kraal* are male ancestors, particularly the former headman/priest. Of course the great chiefs of the Zulu nation are also very important ancestors, and there will be occasions when they are addressed by praise songs and appealed to for help.

The ancestors are regarded as living in or under the earth. They are also identified with the earth. But they have a particular association with two places in the *kraal*, the *umsamo* and the cattle *kraal*, especially that place in the cattle *kraal* where the important religious rituals are performed. They are constantly watching over the activities of their descendants.

The Zulu word for the sky is *izulu*. It is clear, therefore, that the Zulu have a religious relationship to the sky as well as to the earth, the abode of the ancestors. In fact, the Zulu trace their ancestry to an act of creation by the God of the Sky. The God of the Sky, Inkosi Yezulu (literally, "chief of the sky"), also has a special name Umvelingqangi, which means "that which appeared first." It also implies "the first of twins." Presumably the other twin is the earth. The God of the Sky is male, father; the earth is female, mother. Upon death the ancestors return to mother. Only in special circumstances do people go to be with Umvelingqangi.

The God of the Sky and the earth are regarded as having brought forth Abantu ("the people"). But the view of the origin of Abantu is a complicated one. First, the Zulu do believe that the Amazulu (the Zulu people) come from the God of the Sky; the God of the Sky sent down through a hole in the dome of the sky a male still attached to an umbilical cord. Then a reed was used to cut the umbilical cord. Second, the Zulu also say that humankind came from the breaking off of reeds. These two accounts might reflect two traditions, now merged, or they might reflect a distinction between the origins of the Zulu and the origins of all people, or it might indicate that the creation of the first man by the God of the Sky is a later story. Some scholars argue that it is a later story developed under the influence of the Christian missionaries.

The ancestors are usually referred to as a group, the *amakasi*, whereas the singular, Inkosi, refers to the God of the

Sky. Yet the ancestors are clearly referred to as people of the earth. It is probable that the God of the Sky is not a later addition but has been present for a long time in the religious system of the Zulu. But the role of the High God has been misunderstood and misinterpreted. Clearly, in the earliest accounts recorded by travelers and missionaries, he appears but is confused with Unkulunkulu, the first man, who also had a creator-like role in establishing the first people.

The God of the Sky has praise names associated with him. Praise names (*isibongo*) and the highly stylized poetry associated with praise names are of fundamental importance in Zulu life. All important personages in the history of the Zulu people have praise names associated with them, and praise poems are sung at important occasions. The fact of *Umvelingqangi* having praise names is important proof of his traditional and continuing importance in the Zulu religious world.

Praise is important in Zulu social relations, and the ceremonial use of praise names is one very important method the Zulu use to recapitulate their history. In fact there are transcriptions of the *isibongo* of all the Zulu kings back to King Zulu himself. These praise poems are an important source of historical information and clearly reflect the Zulu attitudes toward their past leaders. They also express reverence and respect for all sources of power, whether these be ancestors or the High God.

As we have already indicated, it is unusual for a Zulu to approach the God of the Sky; it is the ancestors who are most frequently addressed. But there do arise conditions of dire need, both for individuals and for groups—for example, a severe drought—and on such occasions, when neither medicine nor the ancestors have been effective in alleviating a bad situation, the Zulu will address the God of the Sky, as supplicants. Then the Zulu will take to the hills, there to commune with *Umvelingqangi* in isolation from the world of the *kra*al and the ancestors occupying it.

The God of the Sky has a special relationship with thunder and lightning. Storms are his direct acts. Should a person be killed by lightning, he or she is regarded as having been taken by *Umvelingqangi*. Such people do not become ancestors. They do not reside under the earth, are not present in any of their usual locations; in fact, they are to be buried as close as possible to where they were taken, and they are not ever to be talked about. They are "with the God of the Sky." Because of this, no mourning for them is encouraged or permitted. Whereas the ancestors have gone down, the people killed by lightning have gone up.

The third type of power acknowledged by the Zulu is the power of medicine. The power of medicine is neither the power of the ancestors nor the power of the God of the Sky; it has its own power. One might almost say that medicine represents a system of its own. The God of the Sky, the ancestors, and medicine can each act for the good or ill of people. All are capable of bringing about change in a situation, alteration of a status, variation of a condition.

All three powers are capable of treating illness, but it is the particular nature of medicine to maintain or restore health, although it can be misused in acts of sorcery. The point to remember is that medicine does not depend upon either the power of *Umvelingqangi* or the ancestors for its efficacy. It stands on its own, and its *amandla* can be added to by new knowledge.

Evil power is negative and destructive. It is not an independent, autonomous power as are the God of the Sky, the ancestors, and medicine; it derives its influence from these three positive elements in the Zulu religious world. The three positive elements maintain and enhance and ensure normal, traditional relationships. *Abathakatha* is the misuse of positive power for destructive ends. As such it is a serious and constant threat to the social fabric. Those who manipulate this evil power tamper with established objects, actions, and roles. When the three other sources of power are expressed, legitimate action occurs even if its consequences entail pain, suffering, and death, for in such instances there has been failure to perform an appropriate obligation. To use witchcraft is to participate in the shadowy world of evil and to go outside the bounds of all that is good and right and prescribed. Whereas the practitioners of medicine are known and public, the practitioners of evil are hidden from view. Whereas the sorcerer will misuse the *amandla* of medicine for bad ends, the witch will twist the entire fabric of the system for destructive purposes and introduce death into the world.

We now know who the practitioners of the various religious roles are, and we know the various expressions of power in the Zulu religious world. The question is, How does the system work? How do those who assume the roles that they do in the Zulu religious world relate themselves to the sources of power?

First I will summarize with a diagram what we have seen thus far. This diagram uses a set of interlocking triangles to represent the relationships that hold in Zulu religion between the ritual roles and sources of power. The base of each triangle symbolizes the observable, ritual aspect of Zulu religion. The apex of each triangle indicates the power each role is designed to tap.

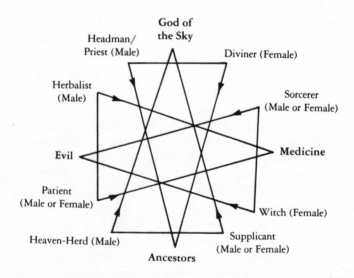

Figure 2

There are four triangles, which represent the four powers (the God of the Sky, the ancestors, medicine, and evil) and the four sets of roles that can be discerned in Zulu religion. The four triangles are interlocked to emphasize the interconnectedness of the various roles with each other and with the sources of power.

In the case of the God of the Sky, it is the heaven-herd and the supplicant who perform the ritual actions necessary to provide the power available from that source. In the case of the ancestors, it is the headman/priest and the diviner who are responsible for the rites that establish and maintain the right relationship with these sources of power. In the case of medicine, it is the herbalist and the patient who have the knowledge and perform the deeds necessary to derive the healing and the protection available from this source. In the case of evil, it is the sorcerer and the witch who have the knowledge and intent to distort and twist the power generally available from the other sources for destructive ends.

Such a diagram describes graphically roles and relationships that the Zulu believe to be important, real, and effective; it permits us to organize the information available from the observers of Zulu life as well as from the Zulu themselves and to ask further questions.

I now propose to show how particular events in Zulu life can be seen as expressing the Zulu religious system in action. We shall see how the various roles in the religious system function in the everyday life of the Zulu, especially in those important events understood as stages on life's way.

Consider the following situation: the headman of a particular Zulu *kraal* has died in the prime of life of an unexpected illness. How will the religious system come into play? Who will do what?

If the members of the Zulu *kraal* still follow the traditional Zulu ways, there are a number of rituals that will be performed. First, the body of the deceased headman will be prepared. This will involve the ritual washing of his face, the shaving of his head (the hair will be retained and buried with him), and the manipulation of his body into a sitting position with his knees drawn up to his chin. Then the body will be bound in oxhide or, if it is not available, in a blanket and placed against one of the poles supporting the hut, where it will then be shielded from view by a covering of some sort. These actions will be performed under the supervision of the new headman/priest, the first son of the deceased leader.

After these initial acts a grave will be dug near the main hut of the *kraal* by the first son. The burial will occur at night. In recent times this aspect of the ritual has not always been adhered to except in the case of especially distinguished figures. The less frequent adherence is due to the influence of Christianity which usually performs burials during the day. When the body is placed in the grave near the main hut, it is positioned so that the head of the body faces the hut. During these activities there will have been the sounds of wailing and lamenting; the actual funeral procession takes place in complete silence.

For a month after the burial, the behavior required of everyone in the *kraal* is quite specific. There can be no work. There is quiet and inactivity. No sexual activity is permitted during this month-long period of mourning.

The event of death in a Zulu *kraal* is regarded as a time of great danger for everyone. This means that everyone must be protected from the powers that have caused the death. In the situation we are discussing, the death is untimely. Such deaths will either be regarded by the members of the *kraal* as punishment from the ancestors for failure to perform some obligation to them or for having offended them in some way or may be regarded as having been caused by an act of either sorcery or witchcraft. The point is that, although there may have already developed some suspicion among the mourners about the possible cause, no one knows yet exactly why the death has occurred. It is important, therefore, for the people to find out why. It is also important for the survivors to avoid further problems. Two of the roles we have described will therefore come into play; that of the diviner and that of the herbalist or specialist in medicine. It will be the diviner's obligation to identify the cause of the untimely death and the herbalist's to provide the medicines that will protect the villagers. The diviner's activities will stretch over a considerable period; those of the herbalist are more immediate.

Immediately after the headman has been buried, the people of the *kraal* will begin taking medicines as a protective device. As we have already found, medicine has its own power and is not reducible to the other powers in the Zulu religious world. Either the herbalist will prescribe the appropriate medicines to take or, because knowledge of medicine is quite widespread in the Zulu community, there will be self-prescription. This act of taking medicine is so important that no one from the affected *kraal* is permitted to leave it or to communicate with people in other *kraals* until the medical treatment has occurred. Some of the medicine will be placed on the *umsamo*, and some of it will also be used to treat the cattle.

Having taken the medicines that will provide the strength and protection necessary in such a dangerous situation, the people will then perform other important ritual acts. There will be a ritual washing in the closest stream, the ritual slaughter of an animal such as a goat, and the purification of the hut of the deceased headman. The slaughter of the goat is not regarded as a sacrifice to the ancestors but as yet another form of medicine to protect the survivors from danger. The goat, in fact, is called *imbuzi yamakhubalo*, "the goat of medicine."

The general period of mourning lasts for a month, but this period does not apply to the widow of the deceased headman, for whom the period of mourning is a year. The month-long period of mourning for all but the closest relatives comes to an end with the *ihlambo* ceremony. *Ihlambo* means "the washing of spears" of all the men associated with the *kraal*. In actual practice the ritual is more complicated than the washing of the spears, for both the men and the women of the village are expected to perform those acts that signal the end of the period of mourning. In practice, the men ritually wash their spears and the women ritually wash their hoes. They are "washed," however, not with water but with action. The men wash their spears by going on a hunt and the women, by hoeing in the fields. After these religious acts have been performed, the implements are regarded as having been cleaned, and the people are free to return to their normal patterns of living. But one more ritual has to be accomplished during the *ihlambo;* the praises of the departed headman must be sung, an animal must be sacrificed, and there must be a final taking of medicine.

Now the widow of the headman is alone in the continuation of mourning for the rest of the year. To symbolize her mourning, she will wear a grass headband (*aintambo*), refrain from sexual relations, and live a life of great circumspection. At the end of the year-long period of mourning, she will be ritually purified with the appropriate medicines and then be ready either for marriage to one of the brothers of the deceased or for the journey back to her parents' *kraal.*

And now the kraal is ready for the final ritual, the *ukubuyisa idlozi,* "the bringing home of the ancestor." All this time the deceased headman has been in an "in-between" state, neither here nor there. He is now ready to be joined with the other ancestors by being brought home, for the ancestors though living in an "underworld" also live right in the *kraal.* The deceased headman must, therefore, be brought back to his rightful place among the living, there to continue to exert his influence collectively with the *amakhosi,* the group of ancestors. His presence in the umsamo, in the doorways, in the cattle *kraal,* and in the hearts and minds of the people needs to be ensured. Failure to perform the *ukubuyisa idlozi* would create danger for all members of the *kraal.* It clearly would be treated by the ancestors as an insult.

The *ukubuyisa* is a festive occasion involving joy, feasting, and fellowship. A special ox is sacrificed, and other animals are also killed. Special portions of the ox are placed on the *umsamo;* other portions are ritually burned; and the rest remains in the hut of the deceased headman. The following day all of the ox is eaten; none of it can be left over or removed from the *kraal.* The other meat and food prepared can be removed or given as gifts to members of other *kraals.* The ancestor may be guided to the *umsamo* from the grave site by the new headman/priest, the chief son of the former headman/priest, by making marks with twigs. At the *umsamo* the *idlozi* (ancestor) may be called upon to return to his rightful place. This will be the first time that the ancestor is addressed and praised along with the other ancestors. For it is now right and good to show him reverence and respect and to treat him as a source of power for good or ill. And now the chief son is ready to assume completely the role of headman/priest.

It should be clear from the description of the death of the headman/priest and the actions performed by the members of the *kraal* that key elements of the religious system are at work. Special places have provided the ritual ground for religious actions, special roles have come into play, and special powers have been acknowledged. The *kraal* provides the scene for the burial rites and the burial plot. And within the *kraal* the *umsamo* assumes special importance as one place where the ancestors are communicated with. There are also special roles at work, those of the headman/priest, the diviner, and the herbalist. And special powers are acknowledged, the power of evil that has caused the death because of the activities of witchcraft, the power of medicine that prevents the danger from spreading, the power of the ancestors who maintain the people and situation in balance and who receive the deceased into their world. This description has given us the occasion to examine some of the details of a rite of passage, in this case from the everyday world to the world of the ancestors. It also provides the opportunity to discuss other rites of passage practiced by the Zulu, under the rubric of the stages on life's way.

Excerpt from: E. Thomas Lawson, *Religions of Africa* (New York: Harper and Row, 1984) pp. 15-33.

18. Traditional African Art

J. R. O. Ojo

This selection is a historical description of art from traditional African societies throughout the continent from ancient to recent times. J. R. O. Ojo emphasizes the uniqueness, authenticity and originality of African art.

In this section, we shall discuss briefly the art of selected periods, peoples and areas. We shall divide our case studies into two groups: ancient and recent. In the first group, we shall examine rock art, Nok terra-cottas, Ife, Igbo-Ukwu and Benin bronzes, as well as a group of bronzes from Jebba and Tada. In the second group, we shall discuss Ekpu figures from Oron, Igbo Mbari houses and Ikenga carvings, Yoruba masquerade headpieces, and Lega artifacts from Central Africa.

Our division into ancient and recent is in some respects arbitrary. Paintings and engravings on rock surfaces have been executed in comparatively recent times in some parts of Southern Africa. In Nigeria, Benin art is unique in that, unlike Igbo Ukwu and Ife, production has continued till the present day. Tada bronzes are still used in annual ceremonies connected with the culture hero of the Nupe people. In the case of recent art, there is evidence that art objects in this category were produced and used alongside objects which have survived from antiquity. It must be noted, however, that what we refer to as ancient art is made in non-perishable materials which, unlike some of the ephemeral materials used for 'recent' art, have survived the ravages of time.

Ancient Art

African Rock Art

Paintings and engravings on rock surfaces are found in North Africa, especially in the Saharan region, the Libyan Desert, the Nile Valley, in the Sudan, West and Central Africa, and East and South Africa. Rock shelters in the mountainous areas of the Sahara contain pictures of elephants, lions, antelopes and birds as well as human beings armed with bows and arrows. Some of the animals depicted are now extinct, thus reflecting climatic changes which have taken place in the Sahara.

The Tassili region, 2000 square miles of high mountains and dried-up river beds, is very rich in rock art. Several thousand years ago, when the Sahara was humid, the area was covered with forest and traversed by rivers. There were giraffes, elephants, antelopes, rhinoceroses, goats and bulls on the plateau. The inhabitants decorated their rock shelters with representations of the animals they hunted, their ceremonies, their gods and everyday happenings. These scenes of family groups, hunts, battles and ceremonies serve as testimony to the artistic genius of the African.

Attempts have been made to date these pictures. It is suggested that the Tassili was occupied by the sixth millennium B.C., and that artistic creativity started soon after. On the basis of actual pictures, we are given four periods. Pictures of the earliest period show hunters of buffaloes, elephants, rhinoceroses (one of which is 26½ feet long), giraffes and ostriches. In one of the hunting scenes, one human being is represented as 11 feet high. The hunters use clubs, throwing sticks, axes, bows and arrows. The next period is known as the cattle period. Dated about 4000 B.C., it may have overlapped with the hunter period. The third period, dating from about 1200 B.C., is the horse period, the pictures showing horse-drawn chariots, riders and horses and (presumably after about 700 B.C.) camels together. The fourth and most recent period shows camels, horses and other animals which are still to be found in the Sahara today. These are antelopes, oryx, gazelles, ostriches and goats. An examination of weapons has also been used to indicate time dimension in Saharan rock art. Those depicted are stone axes, throwing sticks, bows and arrows, javelins, swords and firearms.

In Ethiopia, apart from the representation of elephants and lions, rock art reflects the pastoral origins of the present-day inhabitants. In Tanzania, modern rock art exists side by side with older examples showing human figures with hunting gear and figures wearing elaborate ornaments.

Examples of rock art abound in Zambia, Mozambique, Zimbabwe, South Africa, Swaziland, Lesotho, Botswana and Namibia. A site may contain one or as many as over a hundred pictures. These may contain single figures or animals; animals and figures may be combined in compositions which depict recognizable activities. The subject matter is everyday life—walking, running, hunting, dancing, feasting and fighting. It is difficult to date these works. Archaeological deposits found in association with some examples have been dated to 7000 years ago, but using the subject matter of the pictures, scenes of combat with Zulus have been dated to about A.D. 1800. There are also scenes of Europeans with rifles and horses.

Dated to between 900 B.C. and A.D. 200 (some place the earliest point at 500 B.C.), Nok art is regarded by some scholars as the precursor of Ife art. It is not the intention here to argue about the merits and demerits of this suggestion. It must be pointed out that the corpus of Ife art includes not only terra cottas, but also bronzes, stone carvings and beads. In postulating relationships on iconographical grounds between art forms, one must exercise great caution, especially where considerable distances of time and space are involved. Resemblances of form must be accompanied by a corresponding resemblance in the meaning of form in order to buttress any theory that contacts have taken place.

Nok Art

Terra-cotta (or baked clay) figures associated with the Nok culture were found during tin-mining activities in the plateau region around Jos in northern Nigeria: The first object came from the town of Nok, but other terra cottas have been found in various places on the River Kaduna, and at Katsina Ala, south of the River Benue. These represent at present the western-most and easternmost limits of the Nok culture. Similar terra cottas have also been found around Zaria to the north and Abuja to the south. The finds include naturalistic and non-naturalistic figures and heads, some with elongated ears. Found in association with them are stone and iron axes similar to those depicted on the figures. There are also ornaments and pottery. From Zaria, the northern marginal area of Nok culture, come surface finds of heads, torso, hands and feet in association with potsherds.

Ife Art

As indicated above, the corpus of Ife art consists of bronzes, terra cottas, stone carvings and beads. Among other things, there are also bead-making crucibles, fragments of metal-smelting furnaces, and potsherd pavements (pavements paved with broken pottery, the pieces stuck in the ground with the edges up). Just as the high degree of naturalism of the art objects has attracted scholars, so has the source of the technology that produced the form baffled them. It has been suggested that the whole corpus was produced around the thirteenth and four-teenth centuries A.D.

The bronzes consist of portrait heads of (probably) kings and queens, with half- and full-length figures of the king; all produced by the lost-wax method. The terra cottas, of which there are infinitely more than the bronzes, depict human heads, animal heads such as rams, sheep and elephants, full-length figures and seated figures on stone stools. There are carvings in quartz of stone stools, of which there are also representations in terra cotta and bronze. One of the latter is in the form of a figure coiled round a vessel placed on a stone stool. This is an indication that the production of art forms in bronze, terra cotta and stone were con-temporaneous. There are also granite stone carvings of figures and monoliths, the largest of which is the staff of Oranmiyan. Other staffs, such as those on Okemogun where the king of Ife celebrates the Olojo festival annually, still feature in ceremonials.

Representations of human figures in bronze and terra cotta indicate a lavish use of beaded decoration. It is therefore not surprising to find bead-making crucibles. The facial striations on some of the figures have also been found on representations of animal heads. Other forms of striation have been found on terra-cotta figures. They could have served decorative functions. Potsherd pavements can be found all over present Ife, including places not yet swallowed up in urban development but which in the past were presumably occupied by houses or were the sites of sacred groves and shrines.

One gets the impression that the art of Ife was produced for the king and his hierarchy of chiefs and priests. In this connection, it may be mentioned that there have been surface finds, and that there are plenty of potsherd pavements around the residence of Obalufe, the second in rank to the king of Ife. The art was probably an embellishment of secular and religious ceremonial, still a prominent feature of Ife today.

Benin Art

A persistent tradition, accepted by some scholars but disputed by others, tells us that bronze-casting (that is, by the lost-wax method) was introduced to Benin from Ife at the request of a Benin king. In any case, Benin developed a characteristic art of her own and a wider range of subject matter than Ife. Remains of potsherds pavements in Benin have been dated to the thirteenth and fourteenth centuries. There is evidence of the artistic use of copper by the thirteenth century, although this was smithing rather than casting. Now, if there was a distinctive culture by the fifteenth century and the peak of cultural excellence was in the sixteenth and seventeenth centuries, it has been suggested that there must have been some centuries of development before these three centuries.

Attempts have been made to divide the art of Benin into periods. The first, from about 1300, witnessed the supposed introduction of bronze casting from Ife to Benin. The second period is from 1485, and marked the coming of the Portuguese whose arrival was a catalyst to Benin art in that they provided a more plentiful supply of copper as well as additional subject matter for the artist. This period was the high water mark of Benin culture. The third period was marked by civil war and a consequent lull in artistic activities. The fourth and last period was marked by a revival in the eighteenth century, but following the decline of royal power, there was artistic decadence, and with the death of King Adolo in 1888 the last royal bronze heads were cast. Yet the production of Benin art has survived there until the present day. This survival, in contrast to the position of Ife art, is explicable by the fact that the city of Benin seems to have been occupied continuously from early times, whereas the site of Ife has been abandoned on more than one occasion on account of invasions.

Art objects from Benin include bronze heads, simple at first (if Fagg's periodization is accepted) but becoming more and more elaborate and heavy as (presumably) the supply of metal increased. Some of the heads with large holes on the top supported large, carved ivory tusks, and were placed on ancestral shrines with other objects. There were very many plaques (flat bronze reliefs), showing the king supported by attendants, warriors, hunters and the Portuguese. These plaques may have been nailed to wooden pillars in the king's palace. There were hip masks, bronze bells and stools, animal figures such as leopards and cocks, compositions with animals and human figures; ivory gongs, trumpets and bracelets. Benin mythology and folklore feature in the representations. Such representations include those of elephants whose trunks end in human hands.

Essentially an adjunct of the royal court, art in Benin was a prerogative of the king. Only the king could use bronze objects. This may be one of the reasons why bronze stools supported by snakes are associated with the king, and wooden stools showing the same iconographic motifs are associated with chiefs. The various craft guilds—weavers, wood and ivory carvers, smiths in various metals—supplied the king's needs by way of art objects which provided an impressive background to court ceremonial.

Igbo Ukwa Art

The objects which were excavated here consist mainly of bronzes and highly decorated pottery as well as objects used in personal decoration. Apart from earthenware pots, there is a representation in bronze of a roped (presumably earthenware) pot. Other objects in bronze include snake ornaments, ornamental bronze scabbards and hilts, bronze bowls shaped like calabashes and snail shells, and pendants in the form of animal and human heads. There are also beaded armlets, copper fan holders, anklets, and elephant tusks. Some of these objects may have been the regalia of an important chief, and others the grave property of a royal burial.

Cast by the lost-wax method, these bronze objects have been dated to between 700 and 1000 A.D. In looking for parallels between archaeological finds and surviving analogues in the area, it was found that some excavated objects have traits in common with what is known about the present-day peoples in the area, leading to the conclusion that the objects are probably connected with the institution of the Eze Nri, a priest king in Igboland.

Remarks on Bronze

At this point, it will be apposite to make a distinction between bronze and brass objects. Objects in the three case studies above have been referred to as bronze in conformity with previous practice. They are in fact not all bronzes. Igbo Ukwu objects are heavily leaded bronze with up to 12 percent tin and 16 per cent lead. Other objects are of pure copper.

Bronze is an alloy of 90 percent copper and 10 per cent tin, whilst brass is an alloy of 70 percent copper and 30 per cent tin. Copper in its pure state is easily worked, but bronze and brass are much harder; the former can be smithed, and the latter is used for casting in its molten state.

Benin objects are made of brass with a high percentage of zinc, and of the Ife objects analyzed so far, five are of almost pure copper, while twelve are of leaded brass. In passing, it may be mentioned that copper and its alloys were in use before the advent of Europeans but became plentiful only with European importation.

Nupe Bronzes

These are also known as the Tsoede bronzes, Tsoede being the legendary hero and founder of the Nupe kingdom. Here we have perhaps an articulate link between art objects and the nation's history. The bronzes are located in Tada and Jebba. They are described by tradition as part of the relics of Tsoede, who is reputed to have been born to an Attah of Igala in (or about) the fifteenth century when the Nupe people were subject to the Attah. After his death Tsoede is said to have been bequeathed the insignia of his rule to the Nupe people. Brass chains and bangles associated with him are still found today in most Nupe towns.

The bronzes consist of three figures in Jebbe, with strong iconographic and stylistic affinities to Benin works, and other figures in Tada, the latter including a seated male with striking stylistic resemblance to life work. All the bronzes are sacred objects which feature in ceremonies throughout the year. Because of their stylistic heterogeneity, it seems that these Nupe bronzes come from different sources.

Recent Art

Ekpu Figures

There are at least six hundred figures in the museum at Oron in Nigeria. Such figures are no longer carved, nor does anyone remember having seen them carved. Like other objects, they were not originally conceived as works of art for art's sake. Although they have great aesthetic merit, they now serve essentially as records of Oron's history, a storehouse of vanished customs and habits such as the wearing of long beards, the possession of ivory horns and other symbols of authority and wealth. Their purpose seems to have been to perpetuate the ancestors of lineage groups, since they are kept in special shrines where sacrifices were made to them, and in carving them the hardest wood was used to ensure durability.

Mbari Houses

Perhaps the best example of the association of art with social life is the houses of images (*mbari*), built by the Igbo of Nigeria in response to major crises such as famine, plague, warfare and other calamities which were regarded as signs of divine displeasure. Some of the deities depicted are Amadioha, god of thunder, who is now represented in European clothes to show the march of progress; and Otamiri and Ekwunoche, river goddess and providers of large families.

The erection of an *mbari* is a communal project in which each family in a town nominates men and women who will stay on the site until the project, which may take more than a year, is finished. In the past, an *mbari* was built with local material such as mats, but nowadays corrugated iron sheets are used for the roofing. It is larger than a normal dwelling house, and falls to pieces in as many years as it took to build it. During the construction, there are sacrifices, dancing, singing, and body painting—all forming an integral part of the building activities. Those working on the site are led by a professional artist, but the finished product is regarded as communal work.

Inside the *mbari* is represented every aspect of life from birth to death, and even beyond. The building may contain from thirty-five to over a hundred figures depicting things which are beautiful, good, terrifying, forbidden or humorous. There are representations of family wealth and productivity, traditional and modern diurnal activities as well as terrifying images from mythology and nature and the underworld of spirits. The central figure is that of the deity to whom the *mbari* is built; there may be other deities, representation of myths and typical scenes such as the ideal mother represented by a goddess, and with the advent of the white man there are representations of him too.

Images of both the Igbo and the white man change with time to incorporate the latest advances in housing, clothing and technology. Thus, *mbari* houses mirror changes in the social environment. In an *mbari* house dedicated to Ala in Owerri are representations of Amadioha; Ekwunoche with a large family; Mammy Water, a capricious creature which can bestow wealth or insanity; leopards and pythons, which in dreams and in reality are regarded as a threat to man. Forbidden things are also represented. These include masquerades which can be inspected by women and children at close quarters, a thing that can never happen in real life; also erotic and sexual imagery, whereas in ordinary daily life overt reference to sexual matters is forbidden.

Ikenga

Personal shrine (*ikenga*) sculptures among the Igbo vary from schematized (outlined, semi-abstract) to naturalistic human figures with a pair of horns on the head. Some are simply blocks of wood terminating with horns or schematized heads with a pair of horns. More elaborately carved *ikenga* are in the form of horned human figures holding a staff in one hand and a severed human head in the other. Sometimes the horns are carved to represent those of a ram. Whatever the type or degree of complexity, all *ikenga* have horns.

For the Igbo, if an individual derives his accompanying soul (*chi*) from God (*Chuku or Chineke*), it is the *ikenga* that serves as intermediary between him and his *chi*. Because the chi may either be good or bad, to *chi* is attributed good or bad luck. Success or failure is caused by chi which operates through *ikenga*, the symbol of an individual's progress and achievement.

It has been suggested that the word *ikenga* is a combination of three Igbo works, my power (*ike mu ga*), which has been shortened to two words, *ikem ga* and eventually one word *ikemga* and pronounced *ikenga*. It is therefore not surprising that it is the abstract concept of the power of the individual.

Every Igbo man looks forward to the day when he will have his own *ikenga*, simple at first, but becoming more elaborate as the owner's status improves. In annual *ikenga* feasts, the owner reviews his achievements during the previous year, and when he dies, the *ikenga* is brought out and the owner's achievement recounted. Sacrifices are offered to *ikenga* after every successful venture, the end of the yearly yam harvest, the attainment of high social status, escape from danger or illness.

As objects, *ikenga* are never carved unless commissioned. They are carved from trees which are believed to have special powers. Offerings are made before the carving begins, and when it is delivered, the owner also makes more offerings. The decorative and other features of *ikenga* are significant for the Igbo. The *ichi* scarifications on some *ikenga* are symbols of a titled man, while the horns refer to the role they play in the animal world. The raised matchet in the right hand is associated with success in farming, formerly the main occupation. But in a wider context, *ikenga* is associated with a man's right hand which controls the 'spirit force' of *ikenga*, and without which there can be no success in farming, fishing, hunting, war, trade, title taking—in short, in all aspects of a man's endeavor.

Lega Art

Art objects among the Lega, a Central African people, are found in the context of *bwami*, a closed body of people who share esoteric knowledge, seeking wisdom and moral excellence. There is a special relationship between the *bwami* association and sculpture. The association patronizes the arts, creating, using and explaining thousands of pieces of sculpture which consist of human and animal figures in wood, ivory, bone and clay. These and other paraphernalia, both natural and manmade, are tokens of membership and insignia of status. Senior members hold large ivory figures and masks which are regarded as the ultimate symbols of the unity, autonomy and solidarity of each community. Ivory and well-polished wood (equated with ivory), are associated with the highest grades of the *bwami*. These objects are valued as insignia of rank, and a person's status is enhanced by the possession of them in large quantities.

The objects are inherited patrilineally—that is, along the male line in a family. Individual carvers of objects are not remembered unless they happen to be high-ranking members of the *bwami*. Carvings are traced through lines of inheritance and succession to grades in the *bwami*, the line ending with the name of real or alleged first owner and not the maker. These objects serve as links between the living and the dead, even when the original objects have been replaced with new ones.

All arts taken together—plastic (sculpture), theatrical, choreographic, musical and oral (proverbs, aphorisms, paraphrases and other verbal utterances)—are essential to the understanding of *bwami*. Conversely, Lega art can only be understood within the context of *bwami*, which has exclusive ownership of art objects and dance paraphernalia. *Bwami* has charge of a body of specialized knowledge; this is condensed into proverbs and aphorisms which are interpreted by means of music, dance, dramatic performance and the display of the art objects.

Lega artifacts are made exclusively for the *bwami* whose members use and interpret them, and when not in use are, like ritual objects in other parts of Africa, secreted away. When the objects appear in rites verbal utterances help to identify and interpret them. The artist does not know the precise meaning of the work unless he is a high-ranking member of *bwami*. In any case, the meaning of Lega sculpture can only be understood when analyzed in the total context. Form alone does not convey meaning, but rather the activities that surround the form. The form and its details are the focal points of symbolism. The objects are iconic devices which play essential roles, singly or in groups, with other natural and manufactured objects.

Because *bwami* share common purposes which underlie the political, economic, religious, artistic and other aspects of the social life of the Lega people, the explanation of objects indicates what they are and their use, and relates them to the social system. The objects are storehouses of symbols which translate the essence of Lega thinking. Lega art objects in their social, ideological and ritual contexts stress relationship with oral literature, non-artistic objects and patterns of action.

Conclusion

From the case studies above, following Macquet, we have attempted to show that some of the objects labelled 'art' are not art by design but by metamorphosis. They were not originally made for disinterested aesthetic contemplation. Like medieval European sculptures and Egyptian mortuary art, African ritual objects have been metamorphosed into art by those who are historically and geographically distant from the users and makers. This transformation was meant originally for western eyes, but it carries the assumption that it is also art for the African. This assumption is based on the premises that art is a universal phenomenon and that the definition of art is so broad as to be able to accommodate African masks, carvings and similar objects.

In this way, artifacts are transformed into art objects. But the process can be arbitrary, depending upon the whims of the individual. As Schlesinger puts it, attempts to describe conditions necessary to raise an artifact to the level of a work of art have not always been successful. There is nothing common to all members of the concept labelled 'works of art'; nevertheless the items are held together by having some family resemblance or common denominator binding them together.

The problem here is perhaps that the aesthetic sense of the word 'art' is quite recent. The Greeks and Romans did not distinguish between art and craft, and what we now call art was regarded merely as a group of crafts. Viewed this way, perhaps we can label all the things we have described above as craft. But again, the question arises as to whether Africans regard them as crafts. For as Collingwood eloquently put it, if a people have no word for a certain kind of thing it may be that they are not aware of it as a distinct kind.

This is all the more reason why cultures have to be studied in their own terms and not as assimilated by Europeans. In this chapter, therefore, we have been concerned more with art as a social category, as part of social reality, than as a philosophical notion. Yet we find that in Africa art for art's sake does exist and much art exists for the sake of religion—that is, as accessories of religious cults.

Art has varying forms and functions in different parts and in different epochs of Africa. Apart from its antiquity, rock art has social dimensions in that through it, we have a glimpse of the everyday life of the rock shelter dwellers. Like rock art, Nok,

Ife, Benin and Igbo-Ukwu art serve as historical documents. They also have a social component in that there is evidence, slight in the case of the Nok, that the products were used in the embellishment of some aspect or other of social life. In the case of Ife, Benin and Igbo Ukwu, there is little doubt that these objects were connected with the king, chiefs and priests.

When the more recent objects were examined in their social ramifications, we found that the historical dimension was not lacking. Ekpu figures are records of lineage history, Afikpo maskers representing Aro slave traders serve as a reminder of the nineteenth-century internal slave trade, while the representation of equestrian motifs in north-east Yoruba art reminds us in wider context of the turbulent history of Yorubaland.

African art also reflects social change. Even *mbari* houses, with their painted ephemeral sculptures, mirror changes in the social environment. The creators are aware of social change which they incorporate into the *mbari*. The relation of art to the various aspects of culture is not fixed, therefore, and change in religious, economic, political and other aspects of social organization is reflected in the arts.

Note: Even though for descriptive purposes the word 'art' has been stretched to cover diverse forms of artifacts, it has been impossible to treat such objects as basketry in various media, beadwork such as the type used as ornaments in Kenya and as royal regalia by the Yoruba of Nigeria; calabash engraving; cloth weaving such as the Kente of Ghana, Akwete in Nigeria, and the wool blankets of the Peul in Mali.

Excerpt from: Richard Olaniyan, editor, *African History and Culture* (New York: Longman Group Ltd., 1982) pp. 206-212.

19. African Languages: Indigenous, Foreign and Creole

ADEBESI AFOLAYAN

In this brief excerpt, Adebesi Afolayan outlines the diverse languages currently used throughout the continent of Africa. The multilinguism in Africa, although it forms a rich mosaic representing the cultural diversity of the continent, nevertheless presents one of the difficulties in the achievement of political and economic unity.

There is a dichotomy among the languages of Africa. Generally, there are two kinds of languages in any given African country. Some are foreign to the community, whereas others are indigenous. Usually, those that are foreign are fewer in number than those that are indigenous.

This concept, however, is too simple, and for two main reasons. First, there are languages that are strictly neither foreign nor indigenous in the sense above, pidgins and creoles. Secondly, from the functional points of view, the distinction between the foreign and the indigenous is sometimes blurred.

Pidgin and Creole Languages

Pidgins are simple languages developed and used for limited communication between two sets of people with different languages. For example, pidgin English in West Africa is a simple language developed from English under the influence of local West African languages and Portuguese for the restricted purpose, initially for commercial transactions among English traders and coastal West African peoples and later for communication among the various peoples of the local multilingual West African communities. On the other hand, creoles are pidgins that have become so rooted that they become the mother tongues of some people just as indigenous languages are. Such are Krio of Sierra Leone in West Africa and Swahili in Tanzania, Kenya and Uganda in East Africa; but whereas the process of creolization is full and complete for Krio, it is not yet so with regard to the use of Swahili by every socio-cultural group everywhere in East Africa.

Foreign Languages

The languages that are foreign subdivide into two groups from the point of view of function and usage or social role. Some of them are used in conducting everyday life, whereas others are used only for restricted purposes.

Languages that are used for some aspects of everyday life but which are not primary languages of the people are technically referred to as second languages. In most African countries, these second languages were introduced into the countries by the former colonial masters. Thus they are generally modern European languages. Four of them are most commonly used: English, French, Spanish and Portuguese. Of these four, the two most dominant are English and French. Consequently, the Anglophone countries and the Francophone countries together include most of the black African countries.

Although the languages of Africa may number hundreds or perhaps thousands, from the typological point of view they belong to only a small number of language groups. As given by Greenberg, all the languages of Africa (and he lists as many as 730) can be assigned to only four large families; these are Congo-Kordofanian, Nilo-Saharan, Afro-Asiatic and Khoisan.

Excerpt from: Richard Olaniyan, *African History and Culture* (New York: Longman Group Ltd., 1982) pp. 176, 180.

20. Introduction to Music in Africa

AKIN EUBA

The following discussion focuses on traditional African music south of the Sahara Desert. In this succinct, yet, comprehensive survey Akin Euba describes the general characteristics, variety of instruments and the social context of traditional African music.

Introduction to Music in Africa

There are some people who believe that African music has always remained the same as we know it today. First, not all the music practiced in Africa today can be categorized as African music, for, in addition to the indigenous types of music, many new types have developed which are clearly foreign in origin. Secondly, even the indigenous types, which are usually described as traditional music and are often assumed to have been handed down intact through various generations of Africans, have been subject to change. One assumption that can be made with some certainty is that changes in the social structure of Africa, whether resulting from peaceful or violent causes, have usually been reflected in the music.

One element which almost inevitably produced changes in African music was the interaction between Africans and non-African peoples as well as that which occurred internally among the peoples of Africa. It would be a mistake to think that Africans did not make contact with one another before the advent of Europeans.

The two most important and best-documented sources of foreign influence in Africa are the Arabic and the European. Claims have also been made for a southeast Asian influence. Africans have been in contact with arabs for many centuries, and elements of Arabic music have become so well integrated into African traditional music that they no longer seem foreign. By contrast, the first contacts between Europe and Africa are comparatively recent, and consequently, European musical traits found in Africa stand out because they have not yet been integrated into the main musical culture.

One reason why African traditional music is assumed to have remained unaltered is that changes which occur in the music take place over long spans of time and are imperceptible except under the 'microscope' of the musical analyst. Another point that needs to be borne in mind is that different categories of music within the same African ethnic group are subject to different rates of change. For example, religious music is less likely to undergo change than secular music.

Traditional Music

Traditional music may be defined as the music which has been practiced in Africa from pre-colonial times. It is the oldest type of music in Africa, and, in spite of the new musical types which developed during the colonial period and in post-colonial times, traditional music remains by far the most widespread and the most popular of all the various types of music existing in Africa today.

Africa is a multilingual society, and, partly because of this, African traditional music may be said to exist in several idioms. The number of idioms may be roughly categorized in terms of the number of ethnic groups and the number of speech languages. (More will be said later with regard to the relationship between music and speech.) The statement about the multiplicity of ethnic idioms should not be interpreted to mean that there is no underlying unity in the music of black Africa. African traditional music represents a fine balance between unity and diversity, and there are enough unifying principles to enable us to speak of an African music in the same way in which we identify a European or Chinese music.

General Characteristics

As far as is known, black Africans have no indigenous musical notation. Music is an oral tradition and, in order to gain musical knowledge, it is necessary in traditional practice for the student to be in physical contact with the originators of the music. Moreover, although the musicians can and do describe the structure and practice of their art when questioned, there exists no indigenous theoretical literature on music, a point that needs little emphasis since written literature of any kind is a recent development in black Africa. In view of the absence of a notational system, traditional music is largely performed from memory.

One characteristic of the traditional music which has been noted even by casual observers is its sophisticated rhythmic organization. Yet while it is true that rhythm is a striking element, its importance is often exaggerated. The tonal structure of African music is equally important.

Drums are popularly regarded as being the most common musical instrument in Africa but, as Merriam has shown, the most common form of instrumental accompaniment is in reality hand clapping, followed by percussive instruments of the class known as idiophones, while drums occupy third place. It should be acknowledged, however, that the overall traditional instrumental music is essentially percussive.

One of the most important characteristics of traditional music is its integration with other arts (to a degree which often approaches the concept of total art) and the realization of the resultant multi-art complex within the framework of social events. In other words, music and other arts are often presented as an embellishment of events which are otherwise non-artistic. More will be said later about the social context of music and about the relationship between music and other arts.

Other characteristics of traditional African music that may be mentioned here are firstly the use of musical instruments to reproduce human speech and convey signals, and secondly a tendency to conceive of music as a combination of voices and instruments. This is not to imply that unaccompanied vocal music and purely instrumental music do not exist as separate entities, but that the majority of musical occasions are those in which voices and instruments are integrated.

Musical Instruments

Contrary to the belief that African musical instruments consist mostly of drums, there is a surprisingly large variety of instruments in Africa. First, all of the four categories which musicologists commonly use in the classification of the world's musical instruments are represented in Africa. Secondly, the instruments in each category are of many different types. The reason for such a profusion of instruments in Africa could be that while some instruments have a fairly wide distribution, there are others which are restricted to specific communities and sometimes even to specific social contexts within the same community.

Before discussing the instruments found in Africa, it would be well to define the four main categories commonly used in the classification of musical instruments from all over the world. These are idiophones, aerophones, chordophones and membranophones.

(1) Idiophones are instruments in which unstretchable materials are made to produce sound (e.g., rhythm sticks).

(2) Aerophones are instruments in which sound is produced through the excitation of a column of air (e.g., flutes).

(3) In chordophones, sound is produced through the excitation of stretched strings (e.g., violins).

(4) Membranophones are instruments in which sound is produced when stretched membranes are excited (e.g., membrane drums).

The following list gives examples of African instruments under the four categories:

Idiophones

Percussion Idiophones

(a) Percussion beam — for instance, a log of wood placed on the ground and beaten with sticks;

(b) Percussion trough — an example is a log of wood hollowed out on one side and beaten with sticks;

(c) Xylophones — with either fixed or loose keys;

(d) Percussion sticks (rhythm sticks) — for example, Yoruba apepe;

(e) Percussion gourd and rod — and example is the hemispherical gourd placed inverted on the ground and beaten with sticks among the Hausa of northern Nigeria. Also, found among the Tuaregs is a hemispherical gourd placed inverted inside an earthenware basin containing water and struck with sticks. The harder the striking, the greater the displacement of water and hence the higher the pitch.

(f) Percussion pots — these are sometimes filled with water for tuning. The *udu* of the Igbo of Nigeria is an example of the waterless percussion pot.

(g) Percussion reeds — examples of these are found among the Lango of Uganda. Lango boys who have no access to proper drums are able to practice drumming through the use of six reeds of different sizes (and pitches) which are stuck in the ground and struck with sticks.

(h) Slit drums — these are often erroneously referred to as slit gongs. Slit drums usually have one slit and two tones (as, for example, the *ikoro* of the Igbo of Nigeria), but are sometimes found with more than two slits, consequently producing more than two tones (as, for example, the five-tone slit drum of the Mande of Sierra Leone).

(i) Gourd on gourd — two halves of a gourd each sealed with membrane and containing two small pebbles. This instrument is used by Topoke girls of the Congo region.

(j) Stamping tubes — these are tubular objects struck on the ground to produce sound. The Badouma of Equatorial Africa use bamboo tubes of different sizes with their joint membranes removed (except at the ends which are struck on the ground) and having different tones according to their lengths and diameters. The tone of a tube is sometimes modulated by holding a hand over the opening at the top.

(k) Bells — these are often erroneously called gongs. There are three main varieties, namely (i) natural bells (such as seed shells of the borassus palm used by the Amba and the Karamoja of Uganda and tortoise shells with clappers made from twigs, found among the Gishu and Karamoja of Uganda); (ii) wooden bells (the Konjo of Uganda carve wooden bells with two clappers made of bone); and (iii) forged bells (made of iron and either having clappers inside them or beaten with sticks) — those beaten with sticks exist as single or double bells; sets of bells tuned to different tones are also found.

Rattles

(a) Gourd rattles with narrow necks and no openings, having seeds inside; (b) gourd rattles externally strung with seeds or beads; (c) rattling objects attached to the bodies of dancers; (d) concussion rattles — for instance, two oncoba fruit shells filled with dry seeds and joined together by a chain; this instrument is found in Uganda where it is restricted to girls.

Plucked Idiophones

These consist mainly of the *sanza* or *mbira* (which are popularly described as 'hand pianos' and whose Nigerian varieties include the Igbo *ubo*, the Yoruba *agidigbo* and the *ogumh* of the Igede of Benue State). *Sanzas* are found with gourd or wooden resonators and with keys made or iron or strips of bamboo. Large *sanzas* can have up to seventeen keys, and there are some instruments with two manuals . . . that is, having the keys arranged on two levels.

Friction Idiophones

Examples of these are found in Uganda, and include:
(a) a gourd rubbed against a board or stone;
(b) a stick rubbed against a board; and
(c) a stick rubbed against a box whose opening is placed in contact with the ground; pitch can be varied through changes in the pressure of rubbing.

Aerophones

(a) Flutes — these may be either end-blown or side-blown and with an open or closed end. They could either be straight or globular. In addition to single flutes, sets of flutes (pan-pipes) are also found.

(b) Trumpets — these may be defined as instruments having flared ends and in which sound is produced through lip vibration. By this definition, horns of animals are classified as trumpets. There are other trumpets which are made of metal. Like the flutes, trumpets are either end-blown or side-blown.

(c) Bull roarers — these consist of flat pieces of wood of varying lengths to which are attached strings by which they are whirled round and round in the air. Bull roarers are described as 'free aerophones' because the column of air involved in the production of sound is the open air.

(d) Reed aerophones — these are instruments whose sound resembles that of the European oboe. An example is the *algaita* of the Hausa of Nigeria.

Chordophones

(a) Musical bows — these are ordinary archer's bows which are made to produce sounds through the striking of their strings. They are found either with or without resonators. Typical resonators are the mouthes of gourds. In resonating by mouth the strings are held between but without touching the open lips of the player; such bows are sometimes called 'mouth bows'.

(b) Zithers — these have either single strings or multiple strings. Varieties of the African zither include:

(i) Raft zither — shaped like a raft (for example, the *molo* of the Hausa of Nigeria);

(ii) Board zither - having a rectangular board as its resonator:

(iii) Trough zither — with a trough-shaped resonator;

(iv) Flat bar zither — with the bar mounted on a gourd resonator;

(v) Tube zither — with a tubular object as its resonator (an example of the tube zither is the *valiha* of Malagasy).

(c) Harps.

(d) Lyres.

(e) Fiddles — the single-string fiddle, which probably came from Arabia is very common in Africa. It consists of a gourd resonator covered with skin (as, for example, the *goge* of the Hausa of Nigeria). Fiddles are either bowed or plucked.

Membranophones

Membrane drums are either single-headed (with one membrane) or double-headed (with two membranes). A single-headed drum is either open or closed at the other end. Some drums have tuning pegs while others are braced. There are drums which are stood on the ground when played and others which are held. Also, drums are either played with sticks, or with hands or with a combination of stick and hand. Varieties of drum sticks include straight sticks, curved sticks, spoon-shaped sticks, leather sticks and angular sticks.

Some drums have fixed tones while others have variable tones. The typical variable-tone drum is the tension drum whose tone can be altered through the application of pressure to strings which are connected to the drum heads. The tension drum has an hour-glass shape, and most examples of this drum have two heads. There are some, however, with single heads, such as the *koso* of the Yoruba and the *kotso* of the Hausa. In the case of the double-head *bata* of Nigeria, the two heads are of different sizes and consequently produce different tones.

Even when a drum has a single fixed tone, this basic tone can be altered through muting (that is, the application of pressure to the head with the hand or stick).

Membrane drums can be further categorized by virtue of the kinds of resonators which they have. Although most resonators are made of wood, others consist of earthenware pots or gourds.

There is a certain kind of drum, the friction drum, whose sound is produced in a way other than by the beating of its head. In the friction drum, a stick is affixed to the underside of the head, inside the resonator, and sound is produced when this stick is rubbed between the palms of the hands.

Stylistic Elements

In this section it is necessary first to make some observations concerning rhythmic and tonal organization in African traditional music.

Rhythm

Rhythm in traditional music may be broadly classified under two categories, namely (1) free rhythm, and (2) strict rhythm.

Free rhythm may be described as rhythm which has no regular metre and is 'non-danceable'. This kind of rhythm is usually found in chanting with no instrumental accompaniment. In strict rhythm there is a regular metre which enables one to move or dance easily to the rhythm.

African instrumental music is often described as having complex rhythms. Rhythmic complexity arises from the use of the principle of polyrhythms simultaneously.

Tonal Organization

With respect to tonal organization, many writers have attempted to define the scales used in African music. If the concept of the scale implies a predetermined order to precisely measured tones, then this concept is probably irrelevant in African music, except perhaps in regard to individual instruments (or instrumental ensembles) with multiple fixed pitches.

Whenever Africans sing in multiple parts, Europeans often assume that this is a result of the influence of their music. This is not necessarily true, since Africans have an indigenous vocal polyphony (part-singing) which is distinct from European polyphony. It is likely that, except for Islamized areas which are characterized by choral music in unison (as is typical of Arabic music), African choral music is essentially polyphonic. One of the most sophisticated styles of vocal polyphony is to be found in Central Africa.

Other notable elements of tonal organization existing in Africa are heterophony and the hocket technique. Heterophony may be described as partial polyphony. In heterophony, the musicians perform in unison most of the time and only occasionally diverge into multiple parts. The hocket technique involves two or more musicians playing the same tune by sharing the notes of the tune. Each of the musicians on his own is able to supply only a fraction of the total number of notes required to produce the tune.

Repetition and Variation

The basic style of African traditional music is characterized by a careful balance between repetition and variation. This principle is as applicable in vocal as in instrumental music and may be clearly observed in the so-called 'call-and-response' technique commonly used in vocal music all over Africa. This technique involves an alteration between a soloist and a chorus, in which the chorus part consists of a short phrase which is repeated over and over with little or no change, while the soloist's part changes. The following is the text of a Yoruba song which illustrates the call-and-response technique:

> Solo: *Omo ki o ye jowo o*
> Chorus: *Omo jowo*
> Solo: *Mo kunle mo be o o*
> Chorus: *Omo jowo*
> Solo: *Mo fekuru be o o*
> Chorus: *Omo jowo*
> Solo: *Mo fakara be o o*
> Chorus: *Omo jowo*
> Solo: *Ki o ye jowo o*
> Chorus: *Omo jowo*
> Solo: *Ki o ye jowo o*
> Chorus: *Omo jowo*

A similar system of organization is also found in ensemble instrumental music. Typically, it is the function of the leader of an orchestra to provide variation while each other member of the orchestra has a pattern which he repeats over and over again. Foreigners sometimes complain about the monotony of African traditional music and this is because, being unable to understand texts which the leading instrument plays, it is the repetitive structure of the secondary instruments that dominate their attention. For those who can understand the texts played by the leading instrument, the repetitive structure of the secondary instruments merely serves as a background against which the textual-musical variation of the leading instrument stands out clearly.

Speech Texts

The preceding statement leads naturally to a discussion of the importance of speech texts in traditional instrumental music. In most cultures of the world, the use of texts in vocal music only is assumed, but in Africa both vocal and instrumental music have a textual basis. This is what gave rise to the popular concept of the African talking drum, except that drums are not the only talking instruments. Any instrument that is able to produce multiple tones is potentially a talking instrument in Africa.

A musical instrument is able to talk by simulating the rhythm and intonation of ordinary speech. The element of intonation is so crucial that one is led to postulate that talking instruments are probably preponderant in African communities which use tone languages. Customarily, it is the leading instrument in an orchestra that does most of the talking. Since intonation has a semantic function in tone languages, it is important that a talking instrument is understood in the same way as ordinary speech. Consequently it is necessary for the talking instrument to observe the movement of speech tones, and, therefore, the musical patterns of the instrument arise from the natural contours of speech tones.

The speech tone principle is equally applicable in vocal music, and the structure of song melodies is usually conditioned by this principle. It should be noted, however, that whether in vocal or in instrumental music, the principle is never followed dogmatically, and now and then departures are made from it either for emphasis or for better musicality.

The Social Context of Music

Traditional music is usually realized within the context of social events. Although there are many occasions when music is performed purely for its own sake, the greater proportion of musical activity is that which takes place as part of social ceremonies.

From this point of view, the form which a given musical performance takes is determined by the structure of the social ceremony. As Nketia has observed in his discussion of vocal music in Ghana, form is derived partly from the context of a song and partly from verbal texts. Room is always left for improvisation and for the re-arrangement of the order of verses, and therefore, the actual shape of a song depends on the particular situation in which it is sung. In view of this, a distinction should be made between the basic form, basic pattern and basic length of a song on the one hand and its resultant form, resultant pattern and the duration of a particular performance at a particular time, on the other hand.

The various social events with which music is most usually associated include religious worship, war, therapy, magic, work, children's games, sports, installation of chiefs and kings, festivals and ceremonies pertaining to the life cycle (such as birth rites, infant rites, puberty rites, marriage and funeral rites).

Apart from embellishing social events, music has other important social functions. In a society which, as far as we know, had no written literature until recently, music has served as one of the most important means of documenting history. Moreover, day-to-day new and other items of information are often transmitted through music. Indeed, music is indispensable in traditional society in the acquisition of general education pertaining to customs, life style, philosophy and other aspects of culture.

Music also plays a major role in politics. Kings and important chiefs usually have personal musicians whose duties include image-making for their employers. Musicians are particularly gifted in the subtle use of praise texts designed to enhance the prestige of their clients while castigating the clients' opponents.

One of the most important aspects of the social context of music is that the community at large has ample opportunity to participate in music-making. While certain areas of music are extremely difficult and can only be executed by specially trained artists, there are others which are simple enough for the average member of the community to join in. One obvious example of collaboration between specialists and non-specialists is in the call-and-response type of song in which the solo part is performed by trained musicians while the choral part may be sung by any onlookers who care to join in.

Certain musical instruments are identified with specific social contexts or personalities, and since such instruments are in some cases never used outside these contexts, this partly accounts for the large number of musical instruments in Africa. For example, percussion sticks are used in circumcision rites in Uganda and in initiation rites among the Bantu. According to Merriam, drums are reserved for royalty among the Tutsi and, apart from the king, only the Queen Mother is allowed to keep a drum set. Bull roarers are commonly reserved for initiation ceremonies or activities of cult groups. In general, trumpets are regarded as symbols of royalty while bells are sometimes played to indicate the presence of divinities. Finally, among the Yoruba of Nigeria, *igbin* drums are identified with Obatala, the god of creation; *agere* drums with Ogun, the god of warfare and or iron implements; and *ipese* drums with Orunmila, the god of the Ife divination.

Excerpt from: Richard Olaniyan, editor, *Introduction to Music in Africa* (New York: Longman Group Ltd., 1982) pp. 224-233.

21. Lament of the Drums

CHRISTOPHER OKIGBO

The drum is the best known African musical instrument. In traditional African society it was the principal means of long-distance communication between villages and communities. The following poem "Lament of the Drums" by Christopher Okigbo uses metaphors and allusions to tell of the disruption of the traditional way of life, and bewails that change.

Lament of the Drums

I

LION-HEARTED cedar forest, gonads for our thunder,
Even if you are very far away, we invoke you:

Give us our hollow heads of long-drums ...

Antelopes for the cedar forest, swifter messengers
Than flash-of-beacon-flame, we invoke you:

Hide us; deliver us from our nakedness ...
Many-fingered canebrake, exile for our laughter,
Even if you are very far away, we invoke you:

Come; limber our raw hides of antelopes ...

Thunder of tanks of giant iron steps of detonators,
Fail safe from the clearing, we implore you:

We are tuned for a feast-of-seven-souls ...

II

AND THE DRUMS once more
From our soot chamber,
From the cinerary tower
To the crowded clearing;

Long-drums, we awake
Like a shriek of incense,
The unheard sullen shriek
Of the funerary ram:

Liquid messengers of blood,
Like urgent telegrams,
We have never been deployed
For feast of antelopes ...

And to the Distant - but how shall we go?
The robbers will strip us of our tendons!

For we sense
With dog-nose a Babylonian capture,
The martyrdom
Blended into that chaliced vintage;

And savour
The incense and in high buskin,
Like a web
Of voices all rent by javelins.

But distant seven winds invite us and our cannons
To limber our membranes for a dance of elephants ...

III

THEY ARE FISHING today in the dark waters
Where the mariner is finishing his rest ...

Palinurus, alone in a hot prison, you will keep
The dead sea awake with nightsong ...

Silver of rivulets this side of the bridge,
Cascades of lily-livered laughter,
Fold-on-fold of raped, naked blue -
What memory has the sea of her lover?

Palinurus, unloved in your empty catacomb,
You will wear away through age alone ...

Nothing remains, only smoke after storm -
Some strange Celaeno and her harpy crew,
Laden with night and their belly's excrement,
Profane all things with hooked feet and foul teeth -

Masks and beggar-masks without age or shadow:
Broken tin-gods whose vision is dissolved ...

It is over, Palinurus, at least for you,
In your tarmac of night and fever-dew:

Tears of grace, not of sorrow, broken
In two, protest your inviolable image;

And the sultry waters, touched by the sun,
Inherit your paleness who reign, resigned

Like palm oil fostered in an ancient clay bowl;
A half-forgotten name; like a stifled sneeze ...

Fishermen out there in the dark - O you
Who rake the waves or chase their wake -

Weave for him a shadow out of your laughter
For a dumb child to hide his nakedness ...

IV

AND THE DRUMS
Once more and like masked dancers,
On the orange -
Yellow myth of the sands of exile -

Long-drums dis-
Jointed, and with bleeding tendons,
Like tarantulas
Emptied of their bitterest poisons,

And to the Distant - but how shall we go?
The robbers will strip us of our thunder ...

- So, like a dead letter unanswered,
 Our rococo
 Choir of insects is null
 Cacophony
 And void as a debt summons served
 On a bankrupt;

- But the antiphony, still clamorous,
 In tremolo,
 Like an afternoon, for shadows;
 And the winds
 The distant seven cannons invite us
 To a sonorous

Ishthar's lament for Tammuz:

V

FOR THE FAR *removed there is wailing:*

For the far removed;
For the Distant ...

The wailing is for the fields of crop:

The drums' lament is:
They grow not ...

The wailing is for the fields of men:

For the barren wedded ones;
For perishing children ...

The wailing is for the Great River:

Her pot-bellied watchers
Despoil her ...

Excerpt from: Christopher Okigbo, *Labyrinths* (New York: Holmes and Meier
    Publishers, Inc., 1971) pp. 45-50.

22. "Congo"
LEOPOLD SENGHOR

This poem by Leopold Senghor, the Senegalese philosopher, poet and politician, celebrates the African Motherland. Sexual symbols are employed by Senghor to emphasize the importance of life associated with the productivity of the land and the fertility of the people.

Congo
Lament for three koras and a balafong

OHO! Congo oho! I move the voices of the koras of Koyate to make
your great name their rhythm
Over the water and rivers, over all I remember (the ink of the scribe remembers nothing).

OHO! Congo, asleep in your bed of forest, queen over Africa made
subject
Phalli of mountains, hold high your pavilion
By my head by my tongue you are woman, you are woman by my belly
Mother of all things in whose nostrils is breath, mother of crocodiles and hippopotami
Manatees and iguanas, fishes and birds, mother of floods that suckle the harvests.
Great woman! Water wide open to the oar and the canoe's stem

My Sao my lover with maddened thighs, with long calm
     waterlily arms

Precious woman of ouzougou, body of imputrescible oil, skin
     of diamantine night.

Calm Goddess with your smile that rides the dizzy surges of
     your blood
Malarious by your descent, deliver me from the surrection of
     my blood.
Drum drum you drum, from the panther's spring, the ant's
     strategy
From the viscous hates risen on the third day from the mud of
     the
marshes
Ah! above all, from the spongy soil and the soapy songs of the
     Whiteman.
But deliver me from the night without joy and keep watch
     over the
silence of the forests.
So I may become the splendid haft and the twenty-six cubit
     leap
In the wind, be the flight of the canoe on the supple surge of
     your belly.
Clearings in your bosom islands of love, hills of amber and
     gongo
Seaflats of childhood of Joal, of Dyilor in September
Nights of Ermenonville in Autumn—the weather so fine and
     gentle.
Serene flowers of your hair, white petals of your mouth
And above all, gentle talk at the newmoon feast, drawn out till
     the mid-night of the blood.
Deliver me from the night of my blood, for watch is kept by
     the silence of the forests.

My lover at my side, whose oil makes docile my hands my
     heart
My strength is set up in abandon, my honour in submission

And my wisdom in the instinct of your rhythm. The leader of
the dance makes fast his vigour
To the prow of his sex, like the proud hunter of manatees.
Ring out bells, sing out tongues, beat out oars the dance of
the Master of oars.
And his canoe is worthy of the triumphant choirs of Fadyoutt
And I call for twice two hands at the drums, for forty virgins to
sing his deeds.
Beat the rhythm of the arrow glowing red, the Sun's claw at
noon
Sound, cowrie-rattles, the rhythm of the rumble of Mighty
Waters
Of death on the crest of exultation, the irrecusable call of the
deep.

But the canoe is to be born again among the lilies of foam
To float above the sweetness of bamboos in the transparent
morning of the world.

Excerpt from: Leopold Sedar Senghor, "Congo: Lament for Three Koras and
a Balafong," in *Selected Poems* (New York: Holmes and Meier Publishers,
Inc., 1964) pp. 65-66.

STUDY QUESTIONS

1. What is the role and importance of the traditional African family? How is unity strengthened and maintained?

2. What is the religious and social meaning of the practice of circumcision among the Gikuyu of Kenya?

3. What is the "ontological transformation" which occurs when Ndembu girls and boys go through their rites of passage to become women and men?

4. Identify the four fundamental spiritual forces in Zulu religion. What are the eight major religious roles of appointed persons in relation to these forces and functions?

5. Differentiate between African Rock, Nok, Ife, Benin Igbo and Lega art in Africa.

6. Indicate the differences between African indigeneous and creole languages? What is the importance of foreign languages in Africa today?

7. What are the unique features of African music?

8. Identify the most important African musical instruments and how they are used.

9. How would you describe the special stylistic features of African music?

10. What is meant by the "social context" of African music?

11. Christopher Okigbo employs several literary devices to express sadness over the disruption of the African traditional way of life in his poem, "Lament of the Drums". Identify some of the images, metaphors and allusions which he uses.

12. By what literary means does Leopold Senghor express concepts for the productivity of the land in Africa and the fertility of the people in his poem "Congo"?

Part III

The European Presence in Africa

The seventeenth century marked a turning point in Africa's history. By 1600 major African empires gave way to smaller kingdoms that found themselves constantly struggling to retain a traditional way of life while fighting off, first Arabic and later European, invaders. Since the seventh century, Africans, especially in the north, increasingly came under the influence of Arabic culture. This Arabic penetration of Africa only subsided with the European penetration, exploitation and ultimate colonization of the continent.

The trans-Atlantic slave trade from 1451 to 1870 and the colonization of Africa by Belgian, British, French, German, Italian, Portuguese and Spanish settlers between 1880 and 1960, without regard to African peoples, institutions, land or culture, characterize the essence of the European presence on the continent. Thus Part III—the European Presence in Africa—contains six readings that examine how these two forces altered traditional African societies.

The first two sections discuss the origins of the African slave trade to the "New World," i.e. the western hemisphere, as a means of meeting the demand for a labor force and detail the operations of the Portuguese slave trade. Two eyewitness accounts of the slave trade are provided by Alexander

Falconbridge, a slave ship physician, and Venture Smith, an enslaved African. These two first hand accounts offer interesting insights into this "peculiar institution" of human bondage.

At the 1885 Berlin Conference, convened by Kaiser Otto von Bismarck, fourteen European countries completed their scramble for Africa by declaring that no African territory could be claimed unless it was effectively occupied. This section concludes with two brief excerpts concerning the European settlement, political domination and economic exploitation of Africa that finally compelled Africans to reclaim control of the continent and their destiny by overturning European colonialism in Africa.

23. The Beginning of the Trans-Atlantic Slave Trade

ROBERT I. ROTBERG

In this brief excerpt historian Robert I. Rotberg sets the stage for the European contest for Africa and the New World. The demand for sugar and other "new world" commodities on the one hand, and a ready supply of labor on the other precipitated a world drama that is yet unfolding.

Two Distinct Africas

Between the 17th and the 19th centuries, there were two Africas. The first consisted of the bulk of the interior of the continent. This Africa was only indirectly influenced by the economic, social, and political trends of Europe. The second was coastal Africa, where Africans first interacted with both Europeans and arabs and where the impact of new ideas, new theologies, and new organizational methods was initially felt. It was coastal Africa also where Africans initially and for many years to come confronted the realities of exploitation. The second Africa ultimately encompassed the first, and western and middle eastern ideas were introduced to the interior of the continent.

From Sugar to Slaves

The first Africa merged into the second Africa in and because of the clash of armies. From the 17th century onward, coastal Africa was thoroughly involved with the wider world, especially with the arabs in the east and Europe in the south after the settlement of the Dutch at the Cape of Good Hope in mid-century. Its predominant involvement was the enslavement and sale of men and women. The combat of armies supplied captives; and, as the needs of the Americas increased, the frontier of European and arab influence expanded. If we seek an underlying villain for this process, it was sugar. Only in the 17th century did sugar begin to be cultivated successfully and extensively in the West Indies. Sugar demands backbreaking labor, especially during the cane-cutting season. Without ready supplies of African labor, it would have proved costly—perhaps impossible—to grow cane successfully in the West Indies and Brazil.

Fueled by this foreign demand, the slave trade enveloped Africa throughout the 17th and 18th centuries and for a large part of the 19th century. . . . The apparatus necessary for obtaining slaves; walking them to the marshalling yards of the coast; fattening and feeding them there; and selling them, individual by individual, to ship captains for transport overseas, demanded entrepreneurial initiative and managerial competence of a high and complex order. It presumably also required a strong stomach and a hard heart on the part of Europeans and Africans alike. Certainly the treatment of slaves in the African ports was degrading. Even more inhumane were the shackling and cramming of cramped ships with anxious, potentially rebellious slaves, and their transport across often stormy seas to an auction yard in the Americas. If enslavement were an abomination— even by the standards of the day—the sea voyage, the so-called Middle Passage of six to ten weeks, was totally destructive.

Excerpt from: Robert I. Rotberg, *The Africans: A Reader* (Westport, CT: Greenwood Publishing Group, Inc., 1986) pp. 108, 109, 112.

24. The Portuguese Slave Trade

KATIA M. MATTOSO

Katia Mattoso provides abundant and detailed factual infor-
mation about the slave trade practiced by the Portuguese in this selec-
tion. She explains the operations of the slave trade from capture to
incarceration on the coast to extremely dangerous and life-threatening
ocean passage and finally to auction block and lifelong bondage tied to
hard labor. This was the fate of millions of Africans taken and enslaved
against their will.

Commercial Operations

By the time the African slave trade had been organized on
a fairly extensive scale, the practice of hunting and capturing men
for sale as slaves had almost disappeared. Europeans purchased
slaves from African kings and merchants. Accordingly, from the
early part of the sixteenth century, when the traffic in blacks began
to increase, European slave traders concentrated mainly on the
Gold Coast, where it was easiest to find Africans accustomed to
European merchandise; fabrics, hardware of various kinds, alco-
holic beverages, and above all firearms were highly prized and
much in demand, indeed necessities. Guinean merchants, accustomed to trading gold for European knickknacks, naturally turned
to supply slaves when the demand increased.

At first the trade was rather disorganized, but by 1650 it
had become a major enterprise involving the new kingdoms

around the Gulf of Guinea; these kingdoms, which ranged over the interior, slowly moved their centers away from the coasts. New slave markets were established farther to the south, in the Congo, Angola, Benguela, even as far away as the East African coast. The Europeans limited themselves to establishing depots, warehouses, and fortresses along the coasts of territories that were left to the control of local African states, such as the Yoruba empire of Oyo, the empire of the Ashanti, and the kingdom of Dahomey. These kingdoms quite predictably became increasingly warlike; their power was based on military might, and they needed weapons. The centers of power moved inland in order to secure a monopoly on the profitable trade in slaves. As we saw earlier, the Portuguese managed to convert the king and leading families of the Congo to Catholicism. But by 1575, owing to the increased demand for slaves for Brazil, the Portuguese changed their policy and lost interest in fostering a Christian state in Africa. It was as a conquistador that Paulo Dias de Novais was sent to the Congo, and missionaries gave way to soldiers sent to conquer Angola, which in the seventeenth and eighteenth centuries became the center of the Brazilian slave trade. The slave trade in Guinea did not lead to devastation or catastrophic depopulation; indeed, it increased the wealth of the more advanced Guinean communities at the expense of weaker ones. By contrast, in Angola, as well as in East Africa later on, the slave trade quickly brought disaster in its wake, turning the country into a veritable desert: major population shifts deprived the region of manpower while enriching the black and white merchants who sold laborers to rapidly growing Brazil. The depletion of manpower in those areas of Africa affected by the Portuguese trade—Angola, the Congo, lower Zambesi, Monomotapa—was not compensated by the trade's one positive contribution, the introduction (by the Portuguese in the sixteen century) of new crops, such as maize and manioc, which provided coastal dwellers with a better-balanced diet, thus stabilizing the population. But this single contribution could hardly make up for the sterilizing effects of the slave trade, which halted the social, economic, and cultural development of black Africa. There can be no doubt that the chiefs of the coastal tribes bear a heavy responsibility in this pillage. European traffickers were clever enough to take advantage of the situation and to assist in the development of a well-oiled machine that was to transform the African captive into the Brazilian slave, with handsome profits for everyone involved in the process.

Slaves were "recruited" for the trade in a variety of ways. It was customary to dispose of village hotheads, men who had broken the laws of the community by stealing or committing adultery, by selling them into slavery; children, regarded in hard times as idle mouths to feed; the debtors; and the losers in fratricidal wars waged between half brothers vying for their late father's crown. Thus slaves stemmed from all social categories— an important point to bear in mind. In addition, during periods of famine, common enough in the Sahel and the Gold Coast which often suffered from prolonged periods of drought or heavy rains, entire families sometimes sold themselves into slavery so as not to die of hunger. But in the seventeenth and eighteenth centuries, wars—military campaigns undertaken to conquer not land but men—remained the major source of new slaves. Such wars also proved to be an excellent way for the chiefs of coastal tribes to get rid of the energetic and hence dangerous young men of hostile inland tribes.

Captives destined for eventual sale were brought to the coast. Traditional African chieftains sometimes used these prisoners as money to pay the taxes or tribute they owed to Portuguese colonizers. But usually it was without obligation, and solely in pursuit of profit, that the African chieftain personally led his slaves to the European port to be sold to the slave dealers. Sometimes he dealt through intermediaries, usually halfbreeds but commonly enough blacks, who took it upon themselves to lead the captives from the interior to the port cities. The agents were known as *tangomau* in Guinea and as *pombeiro* or *lancado* in Angola. Unlike the *pombeiro*, the *lancado* resided in the court of a native king or chieftain. He was generally white or mulatto, and his job was to sell the king's (or local chieftain's) slaves. Sometimes the *lancado* resold his slaves to the *pombeiro* instead of selling them directly to Europeans in the ports. Thus the organization of the trade was very flexible yet

efficient and highly structured, with official intermediaries sup-
plying the traffickers; the system was well adapted to the
requirements of European merchants.

There were three ways of organizing slave commerce in
the Portuguese empire: slave trading as private enterprise on a
large of small scale, slave trading in conjunction with other commercial activities carried on by large trading companies, and
slave trading under the terms of a form of commercial contract
that Iberians called the *assiento*. Remember that from 1580 to
1640 the Portuguese and Spanish crowns were combined. The
combined kingdom granted the *assiento* first to the Portuguese,
then to the Dutch, then to the French, and finally to the English.
The *assiento* was a farm on licenses to export slaves from African
ports, fees for which were paid to a *contratador*, who could be a
person or corporation. The *contratador* who received the *assiento* obtained a virtually monopoly on the slave trade in a particular area: Guinea, Angola, Cape Verde, or all three combined. In
return, he agreed to provide to the colonies a specified number
of slaves on terms set forth in his contract. The *contratador* was
not required to do the work himself, however. He issued licenses (*avencas*) to individuals who then outfitted ships for use as
slavers. The *assiento* was used mainly in Spanish colonies. Until
1640, metropolitan Portugal does not seem to have been undu-
ly concerned about the supply of slaves to its Brazilian colony,
and none of the *assientos* signed before that date was valid for
the Portuguese possessions. The first written contract of which
we have knowledge dates from 1587; it granted the *contratadores*
Pedro de Sevilla and Antonio Mendes de Lamego a monopoly
on barter for slaves (*resgate*) in Angola and its dependencies in
the Congo and Benguela. But the Portuguese who had settled
in Brazil took it upon themselves as early as 1559 to furnish their
Brazilian estates with a supply of black manpower. Bahia, with
its port Salvador, and Pernambuco, with its port Recife, became,
thanks to their merchants, major centers for the importation of
slaves, indispensable for the economic development of the
sugar-producing hinterland. This take-over of the slave trade by
private enterprise was the first break in the monopoly, and the
history of the slave traffic in Brazil would thereafter be one of

constant struggle between private initiative and the Portuguese trading companies that were established, with a fair amount of success, from the second half of the seventeenth century on. Significantly, it was dynamic and adaptable private entrepreneurs who helped to establish direct commercial ties between Brazil and Africa, thus eliminating the European leg in the classic triangular trade. This was a crucial development, and it explains why state trading companies and private traders fought bitterly throughout the seventeenth and eighteenth centuries. In theory, in order to trade directly with Africa one required a special license generally issued by the Portuguese monarch, who was thus forced to arbitrate between competitors both holding privileges he himself had granted. This competition for licenses and royal grants of privilege ultimately led, in the eighteenth century, to institutionalization of the private slave trade and to authorization of trading companies with headquarters in Brazil.

The slave trade was essentially based on barter. The *vats, cowries,* and *zimbos* that natives used among themselves as money and that Europeans used in the early days of the trade played a dwindling role and eventually fell into disuse. The unit of barter was quite varied: "packs," "packets," "bars," and other units generally contained powder, weapons, fabrics, hardware, and trinkets if the ship came from Europe. If it came from a Brazilian port, it usually carried, in varying proportions, tobacco, sugar, manioc flour, and spirits. As mentioned earlier, tobacco became a prized item among both Europeans and blacks. In any case, no ship ever carried just slaves. Vessels had to carry basic food supplies for the crew for both the voyage out and often the return voyage as well, since many needed supplies could not be obtained along the African coast. The ships engaged in the slave trade were equipped with immense cauldrons for cooking the captives' food. Barrels of water also occupied a great deal of space. The equipment of a slaver included irons for securing slaves and stockades for keeping them confined. We know very little about the voyages between Lisbon and Africa in the sixteenth and seventeenth centuries. But we are well informed about those that departed from Nantes in the eighteenth century. The passage from Nantes to Angola normally took around two months, though six-month voyages were not unusual. Proceeding from port to port, via Madeira or Tenerife in the Canary Islands or Gorree, ships reached the coast of Africa. Ships sailing from Brazil could make ports in the Congo, Angola, Benguela, and Mozambique without any stops.

Portuguese navigators found varied opportunities along the four to five thousand miles of African coastline. On the coast to Guinea, that is, between the mouth of the Senegal and Orange rivers, the Portuguese had to compete with other Europeans. What is more, all the installations necessary for the slave trade had to be authorized by local kings and chieftains, who generally offered wholesalers long-term leases on port and market facilities. Foreigners paid landing fees and other duties and also made personal gifts to kings, dignitaries, and chieftains, gifts that quickly became compulsory. Together, these dues, gifts, and so on were referred to as "customs." Add to this the fees that might have to be paid to brokers. In the eighteenth century these intermediaries played an important, indeed an indispensable, role. Called *tangomaus* by the Portuguese, they conducted the inland *resgate* and led their charges to the coast. Colorful, courageous characters, true adventurers little inclined to associate with their tamer compatriots, these agents were widely accused of blasphemy and dissolute ways.

Despite the existence of these brokers and of rudimentary treaties fixing the "customs," relations between Europeans and natives were not always peaceful. Native clients could turn into enemies and attack European buildings, forcing the personnel to take to the bush, where they were sometimes massacred or abandoned. Or apparently peaceful Portuguese merchants could turn into aggressors and fill out an incomplete cargo by "impressment," that is, by forcing free blacks seized close to the coast to embark for America. Still, there were numerous brokers available to meet the merchants' demands. Some lived in the ports, such as Annamambou or Ouidah. These were generally Europeans, who also served the traders as interpreters and procurers. Others were blacks chosen by their masters to act as official intermediaries. All these brokers were entrepreneurs in the end, dealers in men, and ships' captains often entrusted them with trade goods even before they delivered their captives.

The situation was a little simpler in territories belonging to Portugal. In the sixteenth and seventeenth centuries slaves were "discovered" by *pombeiros*. These were blacks or mulattoes, themselves slaves of white planters, who assigned them to go inland to buy slaves. The word *pombeiro* derives from the word for "carrier pigeon": like the bird, they carried messages and then returned faithfully to the nest from which they had been released. In native languages the *pombeiros* were referred to as "hawkers." The two interpretations of their role are both apt. These slave procurers seem to have vanished in the seventeenth century. Care must be taken to distinguish them from the *lancados*, whites or mulattoes who lived in the courts of native rulers, or *sovas*. There they lived in huts just like the villagers, but without any protection, entirely dependent on the good will of the *sovas*. They took it upon themselves to sell the *sovas'* slaves and were thus stationed at the very source of the slave trade.

As one moves forward into the eighteenth and nineteenth centuries, the number of ports of embarkation with permanent, fixed, and well-organized slave depots increases. The various fees and customs paid to native rulers along the Guinean coast are now replaced by exit duties paid to the government of Portugal. We shall see, in fact, how native populations were totally denied any share in the profits of slavery. When brokers brought in only two or three slaves at a time, slavers were obliged to collect their cargo at various ports along the coast, a process that could take months. This was an old system, but not very practical, since captives had to be maintained for long periods while awaiting the ocean crossing. Some slavers fitted out their steerage for this purpose, but this raised many problems of space, because merchandise had to be unloaded as new slaves were taken on board. More commonly slaves were held on shore, in a corral surrounded by pickets to prevent escape and ward off attacks. This system, too, had its disadvantages, because ships often moved long distances, more than two hundred leagues, which meant that the center of operations also had to be shifted constantly, with additional fees and customs paid at each new anchorage, thus reducing the profits of the voyage. Thus all slavers tried to avoid the collection process. The Portuguese, who had anchorages of their own in the Congo, Angola, Benguela, and Mozambique, were more successful at this than other Europeans, particularly after the end of the sixteenth century.

Thus the "fixed depot" system was in widest use: under this system, employees were permanently stationed at depots at certain points along the coast. They had plenty of time to gather up large numbers of captives to be delivered in groups to the slavers. This profitable method of operation became possible in Ouidah, for example, when Bahians set up depots there and a fort was built in the 1720s. Captives were assembled near the point of embarkation in wooden or stone barracks, many of which can still be visited today. Many came from far away, some from very long distances indeed. They often served as porters, carrying merchandise and supplies along the inland trails. In the depots the captives were specially cared for prior to embarkation. They were well fed and given palm oil to grease their skin. The sick were treated and isolated from the rest. If embarkation was delayed, captives worked the land to grow food needed for their upkeep. In a variant of this system, captives were held not on land but on a large ship permanently anchored in the port. The Portuguese used this method, which made the slave depot less vulnerable to attack, in Angola.

Regardless of the system used, it was always difficult to predict how long it would take for a slaver to complete its cargo, and the mortality rate was high among both captives and crew. Sailors were well aware of the dangers that awaited them along the African coast. It has been calculated that the death rate was higher among the crew of English slavers than among the captives, who after all constituted a precious cargo that had to be delivered in the best possible condition to the American market. Profits from slave trafficking varied widely, and merchants sought to multiply the number of voyages as much as possible.

The Perils and Risks of the Slave Trade

Coastal searches, fixed depots, apparently friendly relations with local natives, the presence of large numbers of dependable procurers and intermediaries, and all the well-oiled machinery for procuring and shipping slaves often concealed the many serious difficulties that made the slave trade a highly risky business, particularly in areas where Europeans lacked a firm foothold.

Sometimes native rulers were enticed into marauding, as in 1580 in Angola, when the local king managed to massacre thirty Portuguese and all their Christian slaves and then attacked the ten or twelve ships moored in the harbor in order to lay hands on the cargo he craved, some twenty thousand *crusados* worth of merchandise. Or a chieftain might wish to replenish his own stock of captives at little cost to himself, or to resell his prisoners to other slavers. This situation was quite common in areas where the slave trade was unregulated. Or again, a chief dissatisfied with the merchandise received in exchange for his captives might wish to take his vengeance. Merchants were also affected by wars in Europe; each country tried to use local rivalries and pent-up jealousies to its own advantage against the enemy of the moment. These ever-present dangers were aggravated by the fear of rebellion among the captives, much more common and terrifying on shore than on board ship, since the captives knew perfectly well that they did not know how to sail the vessels that were taking them to Brazil. Imagine the threat posed by the confinement in a small space of large numbers of strong men whose only thought was to regain their liberty, to flee. This situation explains why slavers took such care in guarding their prisoners: captives were segregated by sex and hotheads were kept in irons. Precautions were redoubled as the date of departure approached, since preparations could hardly be kept secret from the captives. The longer they were held in port, the greater the risk. As was mentioned earlier, the wait was inevitably fairly lengthy. It depended on how far a ship had to sail to meet its quota and above all on internal African struggles: political struggles, social struggles, struggles for survival during famine in drought-ridden areas. In any case, it does not seem possible to assert that the chronological development of the slave trade followed a geographic progression, that is, that the coast was the first area whose slave supply was depleted, followed by areas farther inland. Combinations of circumstance led to the capture of prisoners, so that at different times the markets were supplied with blacks from the interior and blacks from the coast. Only Angola, which was depopulated early and with great rapidity, may have been an exception to this rule. One factor never influenced the time it took to embark slaves, however: demand from the other side of the Atlantic, which increased steadily throughout the slave-trading period.

To be sure, European wars frequently disrupted the trade, but as the business became more and more highly structured, capture and storage of slaves came to be less and less governed by local circumstances, and the length of wait in the ports tended to increase, especially where Europeans had permanent installations. There was of course season variation: the number of captives was higher during the southern summer, when trading activities were most intense, and lower during the winter. Such epidemics as smallpox, which frequently cut down large numbers of captives, also depleted the slave reserves. Traders generally preferred to embark captives who had been held for a long period, who were thus "prepared," and who also posed the greatest threat of revolt. But if demand has high, slavers did not hesitate to take on newly arrived captives, who were less fit for the hardships of a long and difficult voyage. Wrenched out of their families, communities, clans, and tribes, wrested from their familiar spiritual, cultural, and physical surroundings, captive blacks were treated by their European captors as a human herd in transit; their legal status was ambiguous, because they would not really become slaves until they had been sold once more.

But were the captives really unorganized? To be sure, their first reactions were stupor and fear, prostration, dread, and horror before the unknown, in the face of harsh discipline and much that was strange. But gradually, painfully, they learned of the existence of a different and peculiar world. Used to living in an organized social framework that had become incorporated into the structure of their personalities, captives found themselves almost anonymous, lost in a mass in which one was distinguished from another only by sex, age, physical appearance, and behavior in the face of the unknown. The new masters were studied and their gestures examined. There was both active and passive resistance. Captives quickly learned that survival was the most important thing, and the desire to commit suicide or rebel was gradually overcome, in appearance at any rate, by European-imposed discipline.

Religion and surveillance were the best ways of taming the captive. Camps were always provided with an effective police force, assisted by informers. Above all, traders agreed on the value of Christianity, with its promise of a better world on the other side of the Atlantic. Indeed the Portuguese prohibited the embarkation of unbaptized slaves. Group baptisms were held, in which the entire ceremony involved having a priest give each captive a Christian name while placing a bit of salt on his tongue. Upon arrival at a Brazilian port of plantation, these baptismal rites were often repeated, for it was well known that harried captains frequently took on unbaptized blacks. A resolution of 1620 even ordered that chaplains be taken on board to catechize the blacks during the crossing. It hardly needs saying that these orders remained futile and that blacks who left Africa as "pagans" arrived as pagans in Brazil, even in the nineteenth century. In any case, when baptisms were held, the priest's interpreter spoke words similar to these, which date from the seventeenth century: "Know that you are now children of God. You are leaving for the lands of the Portuguese, where you will learn the substance of the holy faith. Think no more of your native lands, and eat no dogs, rats, or horses. Be happy."

Content or not, believing or not, the day of departure always came too quickly for the African facing the unknown prepared for him by his Portuguese masters. Sold once and destined to be sold again, he was compelled to embark upon a lengthy voyage.

From Captivity to Slavery: A One-Way Journey

The imminence of departure was heralded by the preparation of the transport ship. In the seventeenth century it was quite difficult to maintain vessels that rarely returned to Lisbon. In 1622, for example, the governor of Sao Thome explained to the king that of four ships dispatched in *resgate*, two were lost and two others delayed because of poor mending and caulking. Sao Thome had no real caulker or carpenter but "only a few negroes who take the place of one." By contrast, Brazilian slave ports were well equipped. But the merchants of Bahia and Pernambuco, intent on quick profits, often turned their ships around without adequate inspection. This situation continued into the eighteenth and nineteenth centuries, because reconditioning a ship required not just necessary repairs but cleaning the hull and checking the condition of the holds, irons, rails and stanchions, and rigging. Occasionally a worn anchor or mast had to be replaced.

When the supplies were brought on board: the indispensable fresh water was carried in "pipes"—one pipe contained five to six hundred liters, and at least twenty-five were required for every hundred captives. But many captains, eager to save space, sought to cut down on the amount of water loaded. The ship's carpenter-cooper was responsible for checking the condition of the barrels: a shortage of water was worse than a shortage of food. Besides the pipes of water, the ship took on wood for heating the stew of rice, dried vegetables, and manioc that was fed to the captives. A Portuguese law of 1684 required that captives be given three meals a day together with a *canada* (2.662 liters) of water. The law also required loading of medications needed for care of the sick and stipulated that a chaplain be taken along to say the mass. Violations of this law were to be punished, in theory, by a fine of two thousand *crusados* plus twice the value of the captives transported, together with ten years' exile. Food for the crew consisted mainly of flour, biscuits, fowl, and fruits, mainly bananas and lemons, which were necessary to counter the danger of scurvy.

The ship's surgeon then checked the health of all captives, who were marked with an iron on the shoulder, thigh, or chest, a scene which though often described by authors intent on showing how the slave was robbed of his human dignity, was but one stage in the lengthy process of enslavement. Once on board, captives were placed in irons until the coast of Africa was out of sight. The promiscuity and horror of this imprisonment have also been described in terms to wrench the heart of any sensitive reader, and it is indeed true that the conditions in which captives were confined were frightful. But one should be careful not to generalize, for the treatment of prisoners varied from ship to ship, as did the degree of discomfort, hunger, thirst, and filth. The number of captives carried by a ship of course depended on the capacity of the vessel. For the sixteenth and seventeenth century we have little information about the types of ships used in the slave trade, their tonnage, transport capacity, frequency of voyages, and age and sex of slaves transported, nor do we know anything about the economic organization of this traffic. In this period Dutch slavers ran from 450 to 1,000 tons, but Portuguese ships were apparently smaller, better organized, and cleaner (which is not to say that they were clean). The Portuguese carried 500 captives on one caravel, whereas the Dutch put only 300 on a large vessel. A small Portuguese brigantine could carry up to 200 slaves, a large vessel up to 700.

It took thirty-five days to sail from Angola to Pernambuco, forty to Bahia, fifty to Rio de Janeiro. But if the winds died and the ship in full canvas was caught in the silence of the equatorial calms, who knows how many anxious days the sailors, themselves prisoners and sharing their captives' hunger, spent scanning the heavens and the endless ocean? We hear of crossings that lasted three, four, or even five months, by which time food had run short and tempers were stretched to the breaking point. Even if the crossing was smooth and quick, without major problems, it was horribly painful for the captives. Brother Carli describes one ship loaded with 670 captives in the following terms. "Men were piled in the bottom of the hold, chained for fear that they would rise up and kill all the whites aboard. Women were held in the second steerage compartment, and those who were pregnant were grouped in the rear cabin. Children were crowded into the first steerage like herring in a barrel. If they tried to sleep, they fell on top of one another. There were bilges for natural needs, but since many were afraid of losing their place they relieved themselves wherever they happened to be, especially the men who were cruelly cramped. The heat and stench became unbearable."

This concise, dry, eyewitness account is more eloquent than any bombastic commentary. Equally eloquent are the vain attempts of the Portuguese Crown to regulate the trade: the law of 1684, for example, required that the number of negroes embarked not exceed five to seven "head" for every two tons of ship's weight, and that ships must be equipped with portholes so that the captives could breathe. The regulation added that the upper portions of the vessel could carry an additional five "little heads" (that is, children) per ton. The regulations were easily evaded: slave traders listed as children young blacks who had reached adult height.

Who died during the long forced voyage? In these conditions the mortality rate was high. Life was hard for the ship's crew as well as the slaves. It has been suggested that the latter suffered an average mortality of 15 to 20 percent. In fact, there are virtually no quantitative studies, and we have little accurate information to go on. From isolated cases we can, however, establish orders of magnitude for the sixteenth and seventeenth centuries; for the eighteenth and nineteenth centuries there are some excellent studies, but they are limited to a few years' duration. In 1569 Frei Tome de Macedo mentioned one ship that carried 500 captives. In one night it lost 120 of them, or 20.4 percent of the cargo. In 1625, the governor of Angola, Joao Correa de Souza sent five slavers to Brazil, for which we have the following figures:

Number of Captives	Number who died	Percentage who died
195	85	44.4
220	126	57.2
357	157	43.9
142	51	35.2
297	163	54.8

Thus, in a total cargo of 1,211 captives, only 628 survived the crossing (49.2) percent. And 68 more died immediately after the landing. Of the 195 "pieces" on the first vessel, we are told that 110 survived, 25 of them elderly, sick black men, 55 elderly black women, and 30 youths and children. Were such high mortality rates common? Was this disastrous voyage typical? It is hard to say, for we know nothing about the tonnage of the five vessels, the composition of the cargo by age and sex, the duration of the voyage, the health conditions on board, or the state of health of the captives when they boarded. The oldest and youngest passengers in any case seem to have weathered the crossing best, which suggests that death struck mainly young adults! Great caution is therefore advisable in dealing with these reports. Other reports of other crossings give very different indications. Most historians who have attempted to separate true from false in these accounts today agree that the average mortality rate was 15 to 20 percent. We hear of one ship in which only two captives died in the crossing. In any case, a mortality rate in excess of 20 percent would have made it very difficult for most ships to have turned a profit.

We are much better informed for the eighteenth and nineteenth centuries, thanks to recent work by Pierre Verger and Herbert Klein. Their answers to questions about the organization, pace, direction, and volume of the slave trade have shed new light on certain fundamental aspects of the subject. But their research is limited in space and time: it covers no more than a twenty-year period and is limited to Angola, Benin, and Mozambique. Still, this work is invaluable and useful.

Angola, as we have seen, continued to be the principal supplier of slaves to Brazil in the eighteenth century. Between 1723 and 1771, 51 percent of imports from Angola went mainly to Rio de Janeiro, compared to 27.3 percent to Bahia, 18.2 percent to Pernambuco, and a modest .2 percent to Santos. During the period when the slave trade was supposed to be controlled by the Maranhao e Para Company, these would-be monopolies accounted for just 2.2. percent of the traffic! Once the privileges and monopolies were abolished, Pernambuco, Maranhao, and Para saw their share in the trade increase: in the years 1812, 1815, 1817, and 1822-1826 they received 37 percent of the blacks imported. In this same period, the figure for Rio increased to 54 percent, while that for Bahia declined to 6 percent. The reason for this was that Bahia drew its supplies mainly from the Mina Coast, and for it Angola was only a secondary source at this time.

The eighteenth century was the age of heavy galleys and maneuverable corvettes. Eighteen different kinds of vessels have been counted that plied the Atlantic in the slave trade. Fifty-five percent of these were galleys and corvettes, though at the end of the century there was a sharp increase in the number of brigantines sailing from the port of Rio. The bulk of the traffic moved between July and November, and as in the previous century voyages to Rio took 35-40 days from Angola and 50-70 days from Mozambique, assuming that no major difficulty cropped up during the crossing. But the number of voyages made by each vessel varied: it appears that ships belonging to the monopoly companies made fewer crossings than those belonging to free merchants. Herbert Klein gives the following figures:

> between 1790 and 1811, 43 vessels belonging to independent merchants made 1975 voyages in 32 years, or 4 voyages per ship;
>
> 25 other vessels made 125 voyages in 27 years, or five per ship;
>
> For the company of Grao Para e Maranhao, the average was two voyages per ship, and for the company of Pernambuco and Paraiba it was 3 voyages;
>
> after the abolition of the companies' privilege, in the period 1723-1728, the free merchants with 61 vessels made 118 voyages, or 1.9 voyages per ship, and from 1762-1767 with 63 vessels they made 140 voyages, or 2.2 voyages per ship.

It is relatively easy to explain these differences. The monopolistic companies were obliged to import a fixed number of captives, set by the terms of their contract. The free merchants were motivated by nothing other than profit. Furthermore, the capacity of vessels varied. Free traders could carry an average of 420 captives per vessel (their vessels ranged from 120 to 168 tons), whereas the company of Pernambuco and Paraiba carried an average of 397 captives per ship and that of Grao Para e Maranhao, 160, owing to regulations imposed by the law of 1684, which, as was mentioned earlier, limited the number of "head" on board to 2.5-3.5 per ton, depending on the fitting of the ship.

Slavers always carried more men than women: the ratio was generally about two men for each woman. We know almost nothing about the age of the captives. No tax was paid on nurslings, and small children went for half the normal tax. Thus it was tempting for slave traders to say that older children and even adolescents were younger than they actually were, or even to leave them out of the passenger list altogether. In letters of manumission and wills left by Africans in Brazil, most former slaves maintain that they came to Brazil when still very young. Thus the number of children listed as passengers on slave ships was probably much smaller than the number actually carried. In any case the number must not have been very large: between 1734 and 1769, children officially accounted for 6 percent of the 156,638 captives exported from the port of Luanda. They counted for 3.1 percent of the captives exported through the port of Benguela between 1758 and 1784, compared with 8-13 percent of Dutch cargoes during the eighteenth century. At the destination, Rio de Janeiro on the other side of the Atlantic, the number of captive children officially disembarked fell to .5 percent of the total imported between 1795 and 1811! Was this due to extremely high mortality during the crossing? Apparently not, for during the same period we know from reliable data that the mortality rate was 6.2 percent for children and 9.5 percent for adults. It seems that children were quite simply not counted as part of the ship's cargo because they could not be sold or were difficult to sell. The question of why seems difficult to answer. Let me suggest, at any rate, that the child was not immediately productive; indeed, on the contrary, he or she was a burden. What is more, the child mortality rate was high in Brazil, so that there was great risk of seeing one's investment disappear.

By contrast, the adult mortality rate of 9.5 percent during the crossing, calculated by Klein, agrees quite well with the figure of 10 percent calculated by Goulart. The most lethal voyages were thus undertaken during autumn and winter. Since the total mortality rate, from the time of capture until the day of sale in Brazil, was around 15-20 percent, more than half the losses in human lives occurred during the crossing itself, which seems fairly plausible. The figure represents, in any case, an improvement of 10 percent over the previous two centuries. The improvement was only by comparison with earlier years, since the mortality rate was still quite high, especially when compared with mortality rates in European countries during the same period: for England and Wales between 1780 and 1810, the mortality rate range from 2.3 to 2.8 percent. For France from 1770 to 1790 it varied from 2.7 percent to 4.4 percent. But figures for stable populations, during a period in which the great killer epidemics had disappeared, cannot really be compared with figures for the herd of uprooted captives who were packed on board the slave ships. During the seventeenth century, France, too, experienced mortality rates as high as 25.3 percent during periods of crisis, compared with a normal mortality rate for the same period that fluctuated around 3.4 percent.

During the nineteenth century the mortality rate during passage improved somewhat. It declined from the previous 9.5 percent to about 7.1 percent during the period 1825-1830, even though these were difficult years for the slave trade, which since 1815 had become illegal north of the equator.

All these averages, whatever they may have been, must not be allowed to obscure the realities, the extreme, indeed exceptional, cases. Mortality rates of more than 20 percent were not rare (they occurred on 5.6 percent of the ships leaving Angola and Mozambique for Rio de Janeiro). During the eighteenth and nineteenth centuries it was mainly galleys, corvettes, and brigantines that confronted the dangers of the Brazilian trade, and they were usually overloaded. The average number of captives carried per voyage from the ports of Congo (Malembo, Cabinda, the Zaire River) to Rio was 359.1. For Angola (Ambriz, Loanda, Benguela) the figure was 407.9. Even more crowded were slavers sailing from far-off Lourenco Marques Inhanbanes, Quelimane, and Mozambique, which carried an average of 558.9 captives per vessel; the reason for this overcrowding was that these longer voyages were expensive. By carrying more captives, ship owners could keep profit margins as high as those obtained by ships sailing from East African ports. Higher-than-average mortality rates can be explained by any number of causes, which in extreme cases combined to produce the catastrophic voyages of which slave traders have left accounts. These may of course be exaggerated, for in magnifying their losses traders may have been trying to avoid various taxes or duties. Among the leading cause of mortality, the length of the voyage and the port of origin of the captives seem to have been the most important factors. If the voyage was prolonged beyond a certain length, mortality increased. The threshold was fifty days for West African sailings, seventy days for East African. Beyond that time, lack of food and above all lack of water made survival difficult above decks as well as below. The supplies taken on board, in amounts based on the length of an "ideal" voyage, represented a heavy investment by ships' captains, who tried to take as little as possible with them. When rations had to be reduced, obviously those of the captives were reduced more than those of the crew. Exceptionally bad weather or pursuit by pirates could force a ship off its normal course and thus dangerously prolong the length of the crossing. In the nineteenth century, when most European nations declared all traffic in slaves to be illegal, slave traders attempted to use smaller, faster, more maneuverable vessels, but this forced them to crowd a part of their human cargo onto the open decks, which considerably complicated the manipulation of the sails. We learn as much from the account of a man named Hill, who served as chaplain on board the slave ship Progresso. He reports that the ship lost fifty of its captives in one day. They had been carried on the deck, but a storm arose that forced the captain to order the sails attached. The captives crowded on the deck made this impossible, and they had to be sent below, into a hold too small to hold such a crowd.

On board the slaver, the captive was a man exposed to every kind of risk and defenseless against death. His diet changed suddenly. He lacked physical exercise, even when he was forced to walk or dance on deck during the crossing. The promiscuity of the holds was unbearable. Fear and despair rent his heart. Shipboard hygiene was generally poor. To be sure, the captive washed daily and was supposed to clean his "quarters." But he passed his nights in horribly crowded steerage, where the air was barely breathable. During the day he was somewhat freer to move about, but his movements were closely watched and depended on the weather, the size of the cargo, and above all on the crew's assessment of the captives' mood, for rebellion and mutiny were a constant worry. In fact, we know of no case of slave mutiny on board a Brazilian slaver; if any attempt were made, they were apparently quickly and easily put down. The one exception to this statement dates from 1823. It involves the fantastic story of a slave ship carrying black Macuas to the port of Bahia. Rebellion is said to have broken out on the high seas, instigated by a black *ladino* (one who already spoke Portuguese) by the name of Jose Toto of Jose Pato. Jose had told the blacks that they would be eaten by the whites once they reached land. The blacks rose, we are told, killed the whites, and managed to reach Bahia, a feat made possible by the presence on board of several slave sailors who knew a little bit about navigation. In any case, the atmosphere on board a slaver was one of suspicion and hostility. It was a hermetic universe divided into two parts, and tension was constant. For the crew the voyage was long. How much longer was it for the captive, clamped in irons and knowing that he was on a one-way journey, where each passing hour took him farther and farther from his native country until he was delivered, bound hand and foot, to a strange and brutal oppressor?

Debarkation and Fattening for Market

Whether he arrived from some remote port after a month or two or even longer at sea or was shifted about in a dangerous and sometimes clandestine coastal trade, the captive generally left the ship in an easily imaginable state of physical and moral exhaustion. If he came from across the ocean he had suffered the psychic trauma of capture and the long marches required in some cases to reach the slave ports. He had been placed in irons and often been forced to wait long periods for the arrival of the *tumbeiros*. Imprisoned on board ship, he had experienced the ups and downs of a hard passage only to be disembarked, more dead than alive, in strange and hostile territory. The slave who came from less far away did not necessarily suffer less, for he may have been forced to leave friends and relatives behind and to abandon a way of life to which he had become more or less accustomed, only to be chained up and dragged off once again to face an unknown future, in a state of anguish equaled only by the physical exhaustion that surely followed his forced voyage, within accompanying promiscuity, hunger, and brutality. But for his new master—a temporary master to be sure, and in fact more owner than master—he represented a major investment of capital on which it was natural to seek the greatest possible return. Slaves therefore had to be shown to prospective buyers in the best possible physical and even moral condition, because buyer and seller would inevitably bargain, and bargain hard, over the price, which could hinge on the health of the merchandise. Thus prior to sale the captive was always well cared for and fed. He was rubbed down with palm oil to hide any wounds he might have, conceal skin diseases, and above all to give his black body that luster which was always taken as a sign of vigor. Teeth and gums were often rubbed with astringent roots, which gave the mouth a healthy appearance. Exercises helped to overcome the stiff joints and muscular atrophy brought on by long voyages in uncomfortable positions, and in quarters so cramped that the captive often had to sleep on his side.

In the early days of the trade, in the sixteenth and seventeenth centuries, when the Brazilian ports of entry were still modest villages with plenty of open space on their outskirts, newly arrived captives were held in open barracks whose roofs afforded the only protection against the winds and rains so common in the tropics. But as the trade developed in the second half of the seventeenth century, and as the outskirts of the cities became more and more urbanized, it became necessary to establish permanent slave depots, sometimes even whole districts, whose purpose was to house new arrivals: a good example is the commercial parish of Pila in Salvador (Bahia) in the eighteenth and nineteenth centuries.

We do not know the precise capacity of these depots. Let me suggest, as a hypothesis, that they could hold 400-500 slaves, a number equivalent to the average cargo of a slave ship. Actually, to be unloaded into a depot or warehouse was a privilege reserved for captives arriving in well-established ports. In other ports of entry there were no permanent shelters, and the slave market was an open-air affair, exposed to the elements. Sometimes slaves were sold in the streets and squares; local merchants displayed their human wares at the doors of their shops and sold them at auction to the highest bidder. A German traveler by the name of Freyreiss, who visited Bahia in the middle of the nineteenth century, has left this description of a slave market and depot: "The slaves, packed by the hundreds into a sort of hut, are scantily clad, wearing a bit of cloth or wool around the stomach. As a matter of hygiene their heads have been shaved. Thus, naked and shorn, seated on the ground, looking curiously at passersby, they are not much different in appearance from macaque monkeys. . . . Some arrive from Africa branded with hot irons like animals."

Little remains today of these slave market depots. Urbanization, abetted by guilty consciences, has destroyed these vestiges of the past. In Olinda, Recife's sister city in the state of Pernambuco, however, an old slave market still stands with its original structure almost intact. It is a large rectangle enclosing a square. On two sides slave depots form the walls of the enormous stone building. The facades are protected by a beautiful arcaded gallery. The depots had only one gate, which served as both door and window and which was the main source of ventilation; at night it was securely locked for obvious security reasons. Small openings in the tops of the walls allowed just enough air to enter for the captives to breathe at night. The central square was naturally the marketplace where auctions were held, but in its center was a pillory, still standing today, which could be used to tie and whip slaves from the city sent for punishment, thereby inspiring fear and terror in the minds of the new arrivals. Thus the market, for all its harmonious proportions, was a place to sell and discipline slaves; for the new arrival it was a horrible ghetto, a sordid place in which he was isolated, put on display, palpated, and sold.

It is clear that permanent depots were established in the major ports of entry. With the development of an internal slave traffic, traders began to build lodgings on the major roads which could be used as way stations and rest stops for slaves to be sold in nearby cities: some were final stopping places, physical conditioning stations, around which developed small villages that eventually grew into fairly large towns. Later, when the now illegal slave trade became too difficult and too dangerous to practice on land, the slave ship itself was used as warehouse and marketplace. Buyers—in these circumstances almost always intermediaries—came on board to make their transactions, and "the merchandise" was unloaded furtively at night, at some secure site safe from prying eyes. In all these market depots, whatever their nature or location, Africans were cared for, groomed, and well fed, by force it necessary. Dried meat and fish, manioc flour, and bananas and oranges were supposed to restore their health and appearance. The important thing was to avoid death and disease and obtain the best possible price.

How Slaves Were Sold

Public auction and private sale were the two systems of selling slaves used throughout Brazil's three-hundred-year history of slave labor.

Auctions were used chiefly with captives newly arrived in Brazil. They were generally held in the ports of entry, starting ten to fifteen days after the unloading of cargo and lasting until all the Africans on board had been sold, which could take quite some time. When the demand for labor was high, sellers took advantage of the situation by putting hard-to-sell captives on the block first. The best of the lot were saved until last. Three examples, selected from the few pieces of relatively detailed information we have, will illustrate this technique, which was well established and advantageous to shrewd dealers and sharp buyers.

There is a surviving *certidao*, or record, of an auction sale held in 1612, involving seven of a lot of ten captives brought in from Angola. The three others died during the crossing. The seven survivors sold for 28,000 reis a piece, or 196,000 reis for the lot. The shipper, who was selling the slaves on behalf of a third party, received from the ship owner as reimbursement for the transport of the three deceased captives 7,200 reis, to be paid in Angola in fabric (48 panos at 200 reis each, or 9,600 reis in all, less a discount of 2,400 reis). Thus the seller received a total of 196,000 from the auction plus 7,200 reis, or 203,200 reis in all. What were his outlays? To begin with, a duty of 40,000 reis, or 4,000 per head, dead or alive), plus 1,000 reis in costs for the five days prior to the sale, plus the cost of transport of 9,600 reis per living slave. The seller's profits thus came to 95,000 reis, or 13,571 reis per slave. This was the gross profit, from which deduction must also be made for the cost of purchasing the slaves in Angola. This cost was generally expressed in terms of goods bartered, and we do not know what it was in this case. It has been asserted that the Portuguese bought their captives at very low prices.

Our second example comes from the second half of the eighteenth century. It involves seven captives sent to Rio de Janeiro in 1762 by Captain Joao Proenca e Sylva. Here is the tally for the sale:

Receipts (in reis)

2 young females, dead at sea	—
1 adult negro sold to Ignacio Martins on 30 May	90,000
1 molecao (young man) sold to Manoel Francisco dos Santos on 4 June	64,000
1 molecao sold to Francisco Lobo on 14 June	70,000
1 moleque (child) died after debarkation on 14 June	—
1 moleque sold to Manoel Machado Borges on 30 June	51,600
Total Receipts	275,600

Expenditures (in reis)

Sea transport and costs paid to captain	100,295
Services of a priest who baptized five captives	7,500
Medicine and fees for the treatment of a sick captive after debarkation	2,120
Food for slaves for 76 days at 60 reis per day	4,560
Commission for sale at 6 percent	16,536
Total Expenditures	131,011
Gross profit	144,589

What is striking in this account is first of all the high mortality rate in this lot: three out of seven died before any profit could be made. It is also surprising that it took a month to sell these four slaves, who went separately to different buyers. The cost of baptizing five captives is exorbitant, whereas the cost of food and the medical fees seem reasonable.

Let us compare the 1762 example with the 1612 example. The account for 1762 makes no mention of import duties. Were these included under the head of "sea transport and costs paid to captain"? In that case, the transport costs from Angola to Brazil—14,326 per captive in 1762 compared with 9,600 in 1612—would be a composite of import duties and costs of the voyage.

The time elapsed between arrival and sale increased considerably. It took five days to sell the seven slaves in the 1612 lot. For the captives of 1762 it took at least one month (30 May to 30 June), and perhaps as much as 76 days, since there is a reference to 76 days of food after debarkation. Admittedly, 1762 was a year in which the demand for slaves was relatively low. It was a bad moment: mining was in decline and there was a crisis in the sugar market. Furthermore, the document does not state whether the slaves were sold at auction or privately.

The 1762 sale, moreover, was made by an agent who received a commission of 6 percent of the total receipts. In the 1612 sale no agent seems to have been involved.

Finally, we have no idea in either case how much was paid for the captives in Angola.

Our third case dates from the eighteenth century. We know about it from a tally sheet presented by Manoel Ferreira concerning fourteen captives sent to Bahia by Captain Manoel Jose da Rocha, a resident of Angola. These fourteen captives were brought to Salvador in 1795 by the galley Sao Marcos, commanded by Captain Jose de Matos da Costa and fitted out by Felis Francisco Ferreira:

Expenditures (in reis)

Duties on aforementioned 14 slaves at 8,700		121,800
Freightage for same		87,010
Paid in medical expenses at sea		7,000
Expenses connected with the death of 1 slave		800
Food for all until 12 August		12,680
Expenses (text is illegible)		58,500
	Total	287,790
For monies belonging to above-named party		640,000
For monies to be given to		
Captain Manoel Roiz Barreto		48,000
	Total Expenditures	976,000

Receipts

1 negro molecao (young man) sold		110,000
1 negro molecao sold		90,000
1 negro molecao sold		93,000
1 negress molecona (young woman) sold		70,000
1 negress molecona sold		70,000
1 negro molecao sold		90,000
1 negress molecona sold		80,000
1 negro conferado sold		70,000
1 negress sold		64,000
1 negress sold		69,000
1 negress sold		56,000
1 negress sold		70,000
1 negro with two fistulae on the face and a wound on the leg		40,000
1 negro who died on 12 July		—
	Total Receipts	976,000

This account is quite different in form from the other two. It tells us about the duties paid on captives imported into Brazil, duties that more than doubled during two centuries (from 4,000 reis in 1612 to 8,700 reis in 1795). The freightage of 6,215 reis per head reflects a sharp drop in the cost of transportation compared with the 9,600 reis per head of 1612, especially considering the depreciation in the value of the real, which contained 0.007 grams of 22-carat gold in 1612 but only 0.002 grams at the beginning of the nineteenth century. What was the reason for this drop? Was the trade better organized? Was there increased competition among a larger number of ships? On the other hand, the selling price of a slave in 1795 was roughly equal to the 1762 price, with the slight rise, from 68,900 to 75,076 on the average, no doubt due to increased demand for labor: this was a period of prosperity for the sugar *engenhos*. Compared with 1612, the average price per slave had almost tripled.

The 1795 document makes no mention of a commission or agent, unless the sixty item under expenses, which is illegible, is in fact the total commission on the sale, which would come to 4,875 reis per captive or 5.79 of the total sale, a figure close to the 6 percent paid in 1762. On the other hand, we do not know the significance of the 48,000 reis paid to Captain Manoel Roiz Barreto. As for the 640,000 real figure, this was probably the gross profit earned by Manoe Jose da Rocha, the Angolan merchant who consigned to the vessel his cargo of fourteen captives, who no doubt traveled in the company of a good many other anonymous and precious "negroes" and "negresses."

Here are three examples, then: unfortunately, we have absolutely no idea whether or not they were representative nor can we say with confidence that between 1612 and 1795 the price of imported slaves tripled and import duties more than doubled while the cost of transport declined.

Auction sales were not limited to Africans newly arrived in the ports of entry. Slaves were sold at auction after default on a mortgage, something that happened fairly often to sugar planters who were frequently forced to borrow from important merchants. These merchants, residents of the port cities engaged in the import-export business, made shrewd loans to *senhores de engenho*, offering advances against future harvests evaluated at well below the market price. These "advances" were generally in the form of commodities indispensable to the running of the plantation: tools, consumption items, and even slaves. If the sugar planter later found himself unable to pay back the loan, his slaves would be seized immediately and sold at public auction. This explains why the Portuguese government, convinced by the just arguments of the sugar growers, introduced as early as the second half of the seventeenth century a number of measures intended to prevent the ruin of growers stripped of needed manpower. The whole situation was a vicious circle that seems to have been hard to break, as the repetition of similar measures throughout the colonial period shows. Regulations alone could not do the job. The practice of seizing the slaves of debtors and selling them at auction continued in the nineteenth century, as we see from the following notice published in the Jornal da Bahia in 1854:

Notice—Dr. Jose Joaquim Simoes, municipal judge of the third civil chamber of this city of Bahia and its territory . . .

Know that on 14 March inst., after session of this tribunal in its chambers on Direita do Palacio Street at ten o'clock in the morning, there will be sale by public auction of this tribunal, to whoever offers the most and makes the highest bid, of the following property:

Francisco, Nago, palanquin bearer and field hand, in good health, evaluated at 600,000 reis.

David, Nago, same description, in good health, evaluated at 600,000 reis.

Bruno, Nago, same description, evaluated at 600,000 reis.

Julio, Ussa (Hausa), field hand, with hernia, evaluated at 400,000 reis.

An ass with a serious flaw in its left hoof and undernourished, estimated at 200,000 reis.

As in all auctions, the price of the slave was set by the highest bidder. But we do not know whether imported slaves were always sold to the highest bidder: a public sale is not necessarily a sale to the highest bidder. But all signs suggest that whenever a seller had a particularly robust or skilled lot of slaves on his hands, or whenever demand exceeded supply, slave sales were true auctions.

Private sales were based on a prior understanding between buyer and seller, and the selling price was set in advance. We do not know when such a system was first established. Obviously it allowed for a certain flexibility in transactions. Private sales do not seem to have been practiced in Brazil until the slave trade was fairly well organized and the country enjoyed a relatively plentiful supply of labor. In my view the recourse to private sale was probably linked to urban development, which began in the late seventeenth century, for initially we find it being practiced almost exclusively in the cities, where large numbers of buyers required only a few slaves, either for domestic work or for jobs in construction and transportation. If a buyer acquired a skilled slave—a mason, carpenter, painter, cooper, carter, or fruit and vegetable seller—he might hire out that slave's services. The master would then live off the slave's earnings. This practice was widespread in large cities and in developed secondary and tertiary sectors of the economy. It gave urban life in Brazil a particular cast. In the nineteenth century, especially after slave trading became illegal, private sales tended to replace public sales. The massive transfer of slave labor out of the northern and northeastern sections of the country after 1850 seems to have been accomplished through private sales. This does not rule out the possibility that there were also auction sales in periods of high demand. That auctions did not disappear completely after 1850 is shown by newspaper advertisements such as the following: "B. Ariani will hold an auction on the 11th inst. at noon in Nova do Comercio Street to sell several slaves, several horses, and an ass" (Jornal da Bahia, 9 May 1855).

Ten years later, the newspaper Diario da Bahia published the following advertisement: "Sale at auction of furniture, slaves, fabrics. At the Estella house, largo da Alfandega. Saturday 14 October [1865] at 11 o'clock, Joao Vigilio, tourinho, will sell at auction in his warehouse various items of furniture, china, glasses, fabrics, dry goods, watches, and a good slave, a light-skinned mulatto, age 21, excellent appearance, for valet or coachman."

Why were private sales held? A slave owner who found himself in financial difficulties might be obliged to sell off his capital in order to pay his debts or to obtain cash to meet his everyday needs. Others might wish to sell aging and relatively unproductive slaves, or else they might yield to a particularly attractive offer for a talented slave. After the middle of the nineteenth century, moreover, there was another reason for the increase in the number of private sales: the growth of banking institutions had made available new opportunities to those with capital to invest. This was especially true in Bahia, where a slump in the sugar-cane industry was compounded by the growth of a large body of free laborers, whose ranks were swelled by increasing numbers of freed slaves. Many of the traditional markets for slave labor therefore disappeared, both in the cities and in the surrounding countryside. The growth of banking made available other outlets for capital that would once have been used to buy slaves to hire out as laborers. The banks tempted Bahians with the prospect of less risky investments. By 1870 this led to a sharp decrease in the number of slaves owned by residents of the city and to a rise in the amount of capital invested in urban real estate, bank stocks, and government bonds.

Excerpt from: Katia M. Mattoso, *To Be a Slave in Brazil* (New Brunswick, NJ: Rutgers University Press, 1986) pp. 18-21, 27-32, 33-40, 52-54, 55-61.

25. An Eyewitness Account

ALEXANDER FALCONBRIDGE

The following selection is a firsthand description of the slave trade on the coast of Africa by Alexander Falconbridge. Falconbridge was a physician, serving in the late 18th century on British slave ships plying the West African Coast and taking their captives to the West Indies. He later became an opponent of the slave trade, and wrote an account of its horrors.

Account of the Slave Trade on the Coast of Africa

After permission has been obtained for breaking trade, as it is termed, the captains go ashore, from time to time, to examine the negroes that are exposed to sale and to make their purchases. The slaves are bought by the black traders at fairs, which are held for that purpose, at the distance of upwards of two hundred miles from the sea coast; and these fairs are said to be supplied from an interior part of the country. Many negroes, upon being questioned relative to the places of their nativity, have asserted that they have travelled during the revolution of several moons (their usual method of calculating time) before they have reached the places where they were purchased by the black traders. At these fairs, which are held at uncertain periods, but generally every six weeks, several thousands are frequently exposed to sale who had been collected from all parts of the country for a very considerable distance round. During one of my voyages, the black traders brought down, in different canoes, from twelve to fifteen hundred negroes which had been purchased at one fair. They consisted chiefly of men and boys, the women seldom exceeding a third of the whole number. From forty to two hundred negroes are generally purchased at a time by the black traders, according to the opulence of the buyer, and consist of all ages, from a month to sixty years and upwards. Scarcely any age or situation is deemed an exception, the price being proportionable. Women sometimes form a part of them, who happen to be so far advanced in their pregnancy as to be delivered during their journey from the fairs to the coast; and I have frequently seen instances of deliveries on board ship. . . .

As soon as the wretched negroes fall into the hands of the black traders, they experience an earnest of the sufferings which they are doomed in the future to undergo. And there is not the least doubt that even before they can reach the fairs, great numbers perish from cruel usage. They are brought from the places where they are purchased, to Bonny, &c., in canoes, at the bottom of which they lie, having their hands tied with a kind of willow twigs and a strict watch is kept over them. Their usage in other respects during the time of passage, which generally lasts several days, is equally cruel. Their allowance of food is so scanty that it is barely sufficient to support nature and they are also much exposed to the violent rains which frequently fall, being covered only with mats that afford but a slight defense; and as there is usually water in the bottom of the canoes they are scarcely every dry. . . .

And after they become the property of Europeans their treatment is no less severe. The men, on being brought aboard ship, are immediately fastened together, two and two, by handcuffs on their wrists and by irons riveted on their legs. They are then sent down between the decks and placed in a space partitioned off for that purpose. The women also are placed in a separate space between decks, but without being ironed. An adjoining room, on the same deck, is set apart for the boys.

At the same time, however, they are frequently stowed so close as to admit of no other position than lying on their sides. Nor will the height between decks, unless directly under the grating, allow them to stand; especially where there are platforms on either side, which is generally the case.

The diet of the negroes while on board, consists chiefly of horse-beans boiled to the consistence of a pulp; of boiled yams and rice and sometimes of a small quantity of beef or pork. The latter are frequently taken from the provisions laid in for the sailors. They sometimes make use of a sauce composed of palm-oil mixed with flour, water and pepper, which the sailors call slabber-sauce. Yams are the favorite food of the Eboe or Bight negroes, and rice or corn of those from Gold and Windward Coasts; each preferring the produce of their native soil.

In their own country the negroes in general live on animal food and fish, with roots, yams and Indian corn. The horse-beans and rice, with which they are fed aboard ship, are chiefly brought from Europe.

Upon the negroes refusing to take food, I have seen coals of fire, glowing hot, put on a shovel and placed so near their lips as to scorch and burn them. And this has been accompanied with threats of forcing them to swallow the coals if they persisted in refusing to eat. This generally had the desired effect. I have also been credibly informed that a certain captain in the slave-trade poured melted lead on such of his negroes as obstinately refused their food.

Exercise being considered necessary for the preservation of their health they are sometimes obliged to dance when the weather will permit their coming on deck. If they go about it reluctantly or do not move with agility, they are flogged; a person standing by them all the time with a cat-o'-nine-tails in his hand for that purpose. Their music, upon these occasions, consists of a drum, sometimes with only one head; and when that is worn out they make use of the bottom of one of the tubs before described. The poor wretches are frequently compelled to sing also; but when they do so, their songs are generally, as may naturally be expected, melancholy lamentations of their exile from their native country.

A certain Liverpool ship once took on board at Bonny, at least seven hundred negroes. By shipping so large a number, the slaves were so crowded that they were obliged to lie on upon another. This occasioned such a mortality among them that without meeting the unusual bad weather or having a longer voyage than common, nearly one half of them died before the ship arrived in the West Indies.

That it may be possible to form some idea of the almost incredible small space into which so large a number of negroes were crammed, the following particulars of this ship are given. According to Liverpool custom she measured 235 tons. Her width across the beam was 25 feet. Length between the decks, 92 feet, which was divided into four rooms, thus:

Store room in which no negroes were placed	15 feet
negroe's rooms—men's rooms-about	45 feet
women's ditto—about	10 feet
boy's ditto—about	22 feet
Total room for negroes	77 feet

Excerpt from: Ali A. Mazrui and Toby K. Levine, editors, *The Africans: A Reader* (New York: Praeger, 1986) pp. 120-123.

26. Taken from the Guinea Coast as a Child

VENTURE SMITH

When this narrative was composed, Venture Smith was an old man, living in East Haddam, Connecticut. He had taken his surname from Colonel Oliver Smith, his last owner, who had permitted him to work evenings in order to buy his freedom. After freeing himself, he had bought his wife and children from their master and settled in Connecticut.

The events Smith describes here took place in Africa, the home that he left at the age of six. Though he surely did not have total recall of his life in Africa, his general description is probably quite accurate. Perhaps the most important aspect of this narrative is its depiction of the warfare between the states of the coast and those of the interior, where Smith was born. This commercial warfare, waged for the slave trade, brought about great changes in the political life of Africa.

A Narrative of the Life and Adventures of Venture

I was born at Dukandarra, in Guinea, about the year 1729. My father's name was Saungm Furro, Prince of the tribe of Dukandarra. My father had three wives. Polygamy was not uncommon in that country, especially among the rich, as every man was allowed to keep as many wives as he could maintain. By his first wife he had three children. The eldest of them was myself, named by my father, Broteer. The other two were named Cundazo and Soozaduka. My father had two children by his second wife, and one by his third. I descended from a very large, tall and stout race of beings, much larger than the generality of people in other parts of the globe, being commonly considerable above six feet in height, and every way well proportioned.

The first thing worthy of notice which I remember was, a contention between my father and mother, on account of my father marrying his third wife without the consent of his first and eldest, which was contrary to the custom generally observed among my countrymen. In consequence of this rupture, my mother left her husband and country, and travelled away with her three children to the eastward. I was then five years old. She took not the lest sustenance along with her, to support either herself or children. I was able to travel along by her side; the other two of her offspring she carried one on her back, and the other being a sucking child, in her arms. When we became hungry, our mother used to set us down on the ground, and gather some of the fruits which grew spontaneously in that climate. These served us for food on the way. At night we all lay down together in the most secure place we could find, and reposed ourselves until morning. Though there were many noxious animals there; yet so kind was our Almighty protector, that none of them were ever permitted to hurt or molest us. Thus we went on our journey until the second day after our departure from Dukandarra, when we came to the entrance of a great desert. During our travel in that we were often affrighted with the doleful howlings and yellings of wolves, lions, and other animals. After five days travel we came to the end of this desert, and immediately entered into a beautiful and extensive interval country. Here my mother was pleased to stop and seek a refuge for me. She left me at the house of a very rich farmer. I was then, as I should judge, not less than one hundred and forty miles from my native place, separated from all my relations and acquaintance. At this place my mother took her farewell of me, and returned to my own country. My new guardian, as I shall call the man with whom I was left, put me into the business of tending sheep, immediately after I was left with him. The flock which I kept with the assistance of a boy, consisted of about forty. We drove them every morning between two and three miles to pasture, into the wide and delightful plains. When night drew on, we drove them home and secured them in the cote. In this round I continued during my stay here. One incident which befell me when I was driving my flock from pasture, was so dreadful to me in that age, and is to this time so fresh in my memory, that I cannot help noticing it in this place. Two large dogs sallied out of a certain house and set upon me. One of them took me by the arm, and the other by the thigh, and before their master could come and relieve me, they lacerated my flesh to such a degree, that the scars are very visible to the present day. My master was immediately sent for. He came and carried me home, as I was unable to go myself on account of my wounds. Nothing remarkable happened afterwards until my father sent for me to return home.

Before I dismiss this country, I must just inform my reader what I remember concerning this place. A large river runs through this country in a westerly course. The land for a great way on each side is flat and level, hedged in by a considerable rise in the country at a great distance from it. It scarce even rains there, yet the land is fertile; great dews fall in the night which refresh the soil. About the latter end of June or first of July, the river begins to rise, and gradually increases until it has inundated the country for a great distance, to the height of seven or eight feet. This brings on a slime which enriches the land surprisingly. When the river has subsided, the natives begin to sow and plant, and the vegetation is exceeding rapid. Near this rich river my guardian's land lay. He possessed, I cannot exactly tell how much, yet this I am certain of respecting it, that he owned an immense tract. He possessed likewise a great many cattle and goats. During my stay with him I was kindly used, and with as much tenderness, for what I saw, as his only son, although I was an entire stranger to him, remote from friends and relations. The principal occupations of the inhabitants there, were the cultivation of the soil and the care of their flocks. They were a people pretty similar in every respect to that of mine, except in their persons, which were not so tall and stout. They appeared to be very kind and friendly. I will now return to my departure from that place.

My father sent a man and horse after me. After settling with my guardian for keeping me, he took me away and went for home. It was then about one year since my mother brought me here. Nothing remarkable occurred to us on our journey until we arrived safe home.

I found then that the difference between my parents had been made up previous to their sending for me. On my return, I was received both by my father and mother with great joy and affection, and was once more restored to my paternal dwelling in peace and happiness. I was then about six years old.

Not more than six weeks had passed after my return, before a message was brought by an inhabitant of the place where I lived the preceding year to my father, that the place had been invaded by a numerous army, from a nation not far distant, furnished with musical instruments, and all kinds of arms then in use; that they were instigated by some white nation who equipped and sent them to subdue and possess the country; that his nation had made no preparation for war, having been for a long time in profound peace; that they could not defend themselves against such a formidable train of invaders, and must therefore necessarily evacuate their lands to the fierce enemy, and fly to the protection of some chief; and that if he would permit them they would come under his rule and protection when they had to retreat from their own possessions. He was a kind and merciful prince, and therefore consented to these proposals.

He had scarcely returned to his nation with the message, before the whole of his people were obliged to retreat from their country, and come to my father's dominions.

He gave them every privilege and all the protection his government could afford. But they had not been there longer than four days before news came to them that the invaders had laid waste their country, and were coming speedily to destroy them in my father's territories. This affrighted them, and therefore they immediately pushed off to the southward, into the unknown countries there, and were never more heard of.

Two days after their retreat, the report turned out to be but too true. A detachment from the enemy came to my father and informed him, that the whole army was encamped not far out of his dominions, and would invade the territory and deprive his people of their liberties and rights, if he did not comply with the following terms. These were to pay them a large sum of money, three hundred fat cattle, and a great number of goats, sheep, asses, &c.

My father told the messenger he would comply rather than that his subjects should be deprived of their rights and privileges, which he was not then in circumstances to defend from so sudden an invasion. Upon turning out those articles, the enemy pledged their faith and honor that they would not attack him. On these he relied an therefore thought it unnecessary to be on his guard against the enemy. But their pledges of faith and honor proved no better than those of other unprincipled hostile nations; for a few days after a certain relation of the king came and informed him, that the enemy who sent terms of accommodation to him and received tribute to their satisfaction, yet meditated an attack upon his subjects by surprise, and that probably they would commence their attack in less than one day, and concluded with advising him, as he was not prepared for war, to order a speedy retreat of his family and subjects. He complied with this advice.

The same night which was fixed upon to retreat, my father and his family set off about the break of day. The king and his two younger wives went in one company, and my mother and her children in another. We left our dwellings in succession, and my father's company went on first. We directed our course for a large shrub plain, some distance off, where we intended to conceal ourselves from the approaching enemy, until we could refresh ourselves a little. But we presently found that our retreat was not secure. For having struck up a little fire for the purpose of cooking victuals, the enemy who happened to be encamped a little distance off, had sent out a scouting party who discovered us by the smoke of the fire, just as we were extinguishing it, and about to eat. As soon as we had finished eating, my father discovered the party, and immediately began to discharge arrows at them. This was what I first saw, and it alarmed both me and the women, who being unable to make any resistance, immediately betook ourselves to the tall thick reeds not far off, and left the old king to fight alone. For some time I beheld him from the reeds defending himself with great courage and firmness, till at last he was obliged to surrender himself into their hands.

They then came to us in the reeds, and the very first salute I had from them was a violent blow on the back part of the head with the fore part of a gun, and at the same time a grasp round the neck. I then had a rope put about my neck, as had all the women in the thicket with me, and was immediately led to my father, who was likewise pinioned and haltered for leading. In this condition we were all led to the camp. The women and myself being pretty submissive, had tolerable treatment from the enemy, while my father was closely interrogated respecting his money which they knew he must have. But as he gave them no account of it, he was instantly cut and pounded on his body with great inhumanity, that he might be induced by the torture he suffered to make the discovery. All this availed not the least to make him give up his money, but he despised all the tortures which they inflicted, until the continued exercise and increase of torment, obliged him to sink and expire. He thus died without informing his enemies where his money lay. I saw him while he was thus tortured to death. The shocking scene is to this day fresh in my mind, and I have often been overcome while thinking on it. He was a man of remarkable stature. I should judge as much as six feet and six or seven inches high, two feet across his shoulders, and every way well proportioned. He was a man of remarkable strength and resolution, affable, kind and gentle, ruling with equity and moderation.

The army of the enemy was large, I should suppose consisting of about six thousand men. Their leader was called Baukurre. After destroying the old prince, they decamped and immediately marched towards the sea, lying to the west, taking with them myself and the women prisoners. In the march a scouting party was detached from the main army. To the leader of this party I was made waiter, having to carry his gun, &c. As we were a-scouting we came cross a herd of fat cattle, consisting of about thirty in number. These we set upon, and immediately wrested from their keepers, and afterwards converted them into food for the army. The enemy had remarkable success in destroying the country wherever they went. For as far as they had penetrated, they laid the habitations waste and captured the people. The distance they had now brought me was about four hundred miles. All the march I had very hard tasks imposed on me, which I must perform on pain of punishment. I was obliged to carry on my head a large flat stone used for grinding our corn, weighing as I should suppose, as much as twenty-five pounds; besides victuals, mat and cooking utensils. Though I was pretty large and stout for my age, yet these burdens were very grievous to me, being only six years and a half old.

We were then come to a place called Malagasco. When we entered the place we could not see the least appearance of either houses or inhabitants, but upon stricter search found, that instead of houses above ground they had dens in the sides of hillocks, contiguous to ponds and streams of water. In these we perceived they had all hid themselves, as I suppose they usually did on such occasions. In order to compel them to surrender, the enemy contrived to smoke them out with faggots. These they put to the entrance of the caves and set them on fire. While they were engaged in this business, to their great surprise some of them were desperately wounded with arrows which fell from above on them. This mystery they soon found out. They perceived that the enemy discharged these arrows through holes on the top of the dens directly into the air. Their weight brought them back, point downwards on their enemies heads, whilst they were smoking the inhabitants out. The points of their arrows were poisoned, but their enemy had an antidote for it, which they instantly applied to the wounded part. The smoke at last obliged the people to give themselves up. They came out of their caves, first spatting the palms of their hands together, and immediately after extended their arms, crossed at their wrists, ready to be bound and pinioned. I should judge that the dens above mentioned were extended about eight feet horizontally into the earth, six feet in height and as many wide. They were arched over head and lined with earth, which was of the clay kind, and made the surface of their walls firm and smooth.

The invaders then pinioned the prisoners of all ages and sexes indiscriminately, took their flocks and all their effects, and moved on their way towards the sea. On the march the prisoners were treated with clemency, on account of their being submissive and humble. Having come to the next tribe, the enemy laid siege and immediately took men, women, children, flocks, and all their valuable effects. They then went on to the next district which was contiguous to the sea, called in Africa, Anamaboo. The enemies' provisions were then almost spent, as well as their strength. The inhabitants knowing what conduct they had pursued, and what were their present intentions, improved the favorable opportunity, attacked them, and took enemy, prisoners, flocks and all their effects. I was then taken a second time. All of us were then put into the castle, and kept for market. On a certain time I and other prisoners were put on board a canoe, under our master, and rowed away to a vessel belonging to Rhode Island, commanded by Captain Collingwood, and the mate Thomas Mumford. While we were going to the vessel, our master told us all to appear to the best possible advantage for sale. I was bought on board by one Robertson Mumford, steward of said vessel, for four gallons of rum, and a piece of calico, and called VENTURE, on account of his having purchased me with his own private venture. Thus I came by my name. All the slaves that were bought for that vessel's cargo, were two hundred and sixty.

Excerpt from: Thomas R. Frazier, editor, *Afro-American History -Primary Source* (Belmont, CA: The Dorsey Press, 1988) pp. 5-10.

27. Colonial Policies

OLUWOLE OMANI

Despite the differences in the policies pursued by the European colonial governments in Africa, their basic goal appeared to be essentially the same: the political domination and economic exploitation of the Africans. This implies that the colonial system in Africa was one of dependence of the exploited African majority on the dominant but few European imperialists, who treated the colonial peoples as social inferiors incapable of governing themselves. However, it was only after the drawing of political boundaries in Africa in the 1880s that colonial policies started to take shape.

British Policy

In many of her African colonial territories Britain (at different periods) adopted a system of indirect rule. In their efforts to maintain law and order for effective free trade, the British depended on the traditional institutions, especially the traditional government of the colonized peoples. The officials believed that African traditional systems of government were the most suitable for the Africans, provided that these were rid of features which did not conform with the British sense of justice. This belief formed the core of the respect which the British officers accorded the African chiefs, who were treated as separate yet equal colleagues. It must be noted, however, that this British dependence on traditional political institutions arose less from a theory of the government of dependent territories and people than as a pragmatic and economical solution to the financial, personnel, defense and communication problems which confronted them. Bearing this in mind, the British may, to a small extent only, be regarded as more 'liberal' than the French or any other colonial power in the style of their colonial policy.

It would appear also that the British had the intention of preparing their colonies, especially the large ones (Nigeria and the Gold Coast, for example), for independence at a future date, though this future remained remote. They hoped to do this by imposing their particular brand of parliamentary government on the African peoples. This is why the colonies inherited Houses of Assemblies and Chiefs along the patterns of their British overlords. Although the British may have accepted the self-imposed burden of bearing responsibility for the advancement of their colonies in Africa, they did not assume that Africa would one day become an extension of Britain, or that Africans would one day become 'Britons'.

The relationship between the British officers and the African elite forms another basic feature of British colonial policy. The British officer usually felt uneasy before the educated African, and sometimes expressed contempt for the few educated elements in the colonies. The irony of this situation was that it was Britons who trained these Africans, mostly in their mission schools, and Britons who now disowned them, regarding the supporters of the 'radical' nationalists especially as mere 'verandah boys'.

French Policy

The administration of French African colonies was highly centralized. France treated her colonies as a political and economic unit, and simply regarded them as 'Overseas France.' This meant that the territories under the French empire were legally part of France proper even though they were culturally different, and physically separated by water and distance. The French officially had the basic aim of assimilating the inhabitants of their colonies into French culture and civilization—a civilization which they assumed to be the best in the world. This policy, in which, however, they in large measure failed, was informed by egalitarian ideas which had been gaining ground

ever since the French Revolution. As a result, the French started out with the intention of creating a system that would transform Africans into French citizens in order to enjoy the same
rights and privileges as those actually born in France proper.

The French assimilation policy never took account of the
diversities of the African peoples. This is not surprising because
the colonial administration was intended to make French citizens of Africans. Compared, therefore, with the British policy,
it is clear that France had no aim of granting independence to
her colonies. She believed in retaining the colonies as an annex
to the homeland or metropolis, allowing them to send their political representatives to the French National Assembly in Paris.

To pursue the policy of assimilation, educational opportunities in the colonies were designed for advancement within the
French system. These opportunities, however, remained limited. This implies that the French failed to provide adequately
for the means through which the African was supposed to be
assimilated into French society and culture. Only those colonial
subjects who fulfilled all the requirements stipulated by the
French authorities would be accepted as French citizens. Such
requirements included: the passing of a test in the French language; becoming a Christian; and assimilating French customs
and traditions. This dual policy divided the colonial peoples into
two categories: the assimilated French citizens who enjoyed all
the rights and privileges of French citizenship, and the colonial
subjects to whom the 'Indigenat' applied. The 'Indigenat' was
a system introduced in the 1880s, whereby any commandant in
the colonies could summarily punish the Africans for certain specific offenses without trial. No appeal was allowed under this
system.

Excerpt from: Richard Olaniyan, editor, *African History and Culture* (Essex,
England: Longman Group, 1982) pp. 81-83.

28. The Changed Situation in the Nineteenth Century

J. D. OMER-COOPER

Slavery was officially abolished in Europe and the New World during the course of the nineteenth century. The political reasons for this are due, as J. D. Omer-Cooper recounts, largely because of major shifts in the economic base of society. Modern technology became readily available to replace the hand labor of the slaves who in turn again became expendable. Also, by this time, the moral outrage against the brutality of slavery was becoming more strident and more articulate.

The Changed Situation in the Nineteenth Century

During the nineteenth century . . . Africa underwent a dramatic period of revolutionary change which is still continuing. Part of this process was due to external factors. The Industrial Revolution was already under way in Britain, and Europe would soon be looking to Africa as a source of raw materials and as a market for the goods produced by the new factories. Europe was also acquiring technical means which would make it relatively easy to break down the physical barriers to penetration into Africa and an overwhelming military power sufficient to annihilate resistance. At the same time the social changes brought about by the Industrial Revolution aroused stirrings of conscience. A more vital attitude to religion sprang up, a hostility to the slave trade, and a desire to convert the heathen which went well with a situation in which it seemed more profitable to trade with Africans in Africa than to export them elsewhere, and in which Christian conversion seemed necessarily to imply the adoption of European tastes and a demand for European goods. Thus through traders and dedicated missionaries Europe began to exert an influence by actually changing African societies in the light of Christian ideas. This inevitably brought with it political consequences. European political authority gradually extended itself until under the influence of almost hysterical competition between the European powers it culminated in the Scramble for Africa which brought the vast preponderance of the continent under the control of European states.

It must not be thought, however, that the revolutionary changes in African history were all the result of external influence. By the beginning of the nineteenth century internal stresses within the continent were preparing the way for two massive movements. In West Africa the inevitable tensions occurred between Muslims and rulers who practiced traditional religions. These resulted from the situation caused by the fall of Songhai and were coming to a head, preparing the way for a whole series of religious movements known as the West African jihads. In modern South Africa population pressure in Zululand had already set in motion a process which was to culminate in the dramatic rise of the Zulu as a military power and a vast series of wars and migrations which vitally affected the whole history of Southern and Central Africa.

Excerpt from: A. E. Afigbo, E. A. Ayandelo, J. D. Omer-Cooper, R. Palmer, editors, *The Making of Modern Africa*, Vol. I (New York: Longman Group Ltd., 1986) pp. 30-31.

STUDY QUESTIONS

1. Why does Robert Rotberg describe the continent of Africa in terms of "two distinct Africas" from the seventeenth to the nineteenth? How did this distinction break down?

2. Identify the origin, organization and the operations of the trans-Atlantic slave trade?

3. What specific aspects of the British slave trade with the West Indies appear in Alexander Falconbridge's firsthand account?

4. What, according to Venture Smith, were the events that led to his being captured and sold into slavery in America in the early eighteenth century?

5. Indicate the new economic conditions which emerged in the nineteenth century that paved the way for the abolishment of slavery.

6. What were the new events that occurred both inside and outside of Africa which paved the way for colonialism?

7. What were the similarities and differences between the colonial policies of the British and the French in Africa?

Part IV

Nationalism, Independence and Nation-Building

The people of Africa today are in the process of reclaiming their land, and reasserting their heritage, culture, and destiny. The fighting of World War II and aftermath prompted a resurgence in African nationalism and a renewed opportunity for resistance and independence that had been subdued just prior to the outbreak of World War I. This section begins with a discussion of the impact of World War II on colonial Africa and a description of factors influencing the rise of nationalist movements in Africa. The section also contains selected writings and thoughts of historical and contemporary African nationalist leaders who inspired and led, and who are continuing to lead and inspire, the African masses in the overturning of the European oppressors and brought/are bringing their peoples and nations to independence.

These nationalist leaders also developed ideas or philosophies that served as models and set the tone for nation-building in a modern, secular world. Marcus Garvey expressed the importance of Africans taking the initiative in the struggle for freedom and liberty, while Kwame Nkrumah insisted that a realistic approach to rebuilding Africa involves the recognition of the Islamic Euro-Christian and indigenous African experience as the current reality on the continent.

Since Africa will not be completely liberated until black majority rule comes to South Africa, this section contains the writings of Steve Biko, Bishop Desmond Tutu and Nelson Mandela, and their vision of a fully-liberated, empowered black South Africa. The section concludes with Julius Nyerere's (former President of Tanzania) assertion that the future of Africa is contingent upon Africa belonging to all Africans with rights, freedom, and justice being extended to all Africans as well. In sum, these selections reflect the frustrations, struggle and hope of African peoples and nations as they confront and attempt to address effectively the internal and external demands of modern nation-building.

29. Ending the Colonial Era

Norman R. Bennett

The end of WWII in 1945 set the stage for the close of European colonialism in Africa. As Norman R. Bennett clearly points out, the European colonial powers were no longer major world powers; they had to turn to rebuilding at home. And, in the meantime, the African colonies had become a seedbed for nationalist and independence movements.

Ending the Colonial Era

The shattering global conflict of World War II had a much greater impact on colonial Africa than did the 1914-1918 war. In the Far East the Japanese quickly conquered the European possessions, vividly illustrating the fragile nature of European rule. The graceless collapse of the Third Republic led to the conflicting governments of Philippe Petain and Charles de Gaulle, thus forcing the colonial administrators of France's African empire to choose one or the other as the legitimate government of France. Most of the colonial governors opted for Petain's Vichy state, but in French Equatorial Africa the governor of the colony of Chad, Felix Eboue, a black from France's South American territory of Guyane, threw his support to de Gaulle's Free French government-in-exile. Eboue's decision provided de Gaulle with a first significant power base in French territory in his difficult campaign to be recognized as a legitimate leader of the French nation. And from the equatorial region a Free

French military expedition led by Jacques Leclerc gave de Gaulle one of his first victories through a successful attack on the Italians in Libya. Following the Allied landings in North Africa in 1943, French West Africa also declared for de Gaulle. Consequently, de Gaulle and other Frenchmen were fully aware that changes in the African policy of France, reflecting African support for the Free French war effort, had to follow the conflict's termination. Britain's colonial governments were not required to undergo a similar dramatic course. Nevertheless, the colonies supplied important manpower, both black and white, and materials for campaigns ranging from Italy to Burma, as well as for liberation of Ethiopia and the conquest of Somaliland from the Italians in speedy operations during 1941.

The propaganda machine organized for World War II by the Allied Powers was as significant in its colonial influences as the similar effort of World War I. The third clause of the Atlantic Charter, the result of a 1941 meeting between Winston S. Churchill and Franklin Delano Roosevelt, recalled Wilson's Fourteen Points and his campaign to make the world safe for democracy. The Charter of the United Nations, adopted by the Allies in 1945, further enshrined such principles as a people's right to the free determination of its own government. Equally important to some Africans was the presence of Allied troops in Africa. The American invaders of North Africa, with their tradition of hostility to other nations ruling subject peoples, led North African nationalists to hope for postwar changes in the colonial structures of Morocco, Algeria, Tunisia, and Libya. The Allied conquest of Vichy Madagascar in 1942 was also an unsettling factor in the French island colony.

Nevertheless, no startling changes for most of Africa's peoples followed the peace settlements with Germany, Japan, and their allies. Only the former Italian colonies were affected directly. Ethiopia had been restored, after some British hesitation, to Haile Selassie's government in 1941. Great Power rivalry prevented Libya, Eritrea, and Somaliland from falling to any new colonial rulers. By its peace treaty in 1947, Italy renounced all rights to its former colonies. Since the major powers were unable to agree on their future, the issue was decided in the United

Nations. Libya gained independence in 1951, while Eritrea was federated to Ethiopia in 1952, and Somaliland was placed under Italy as a United Nations trust territory in 1950. The Somali Republic, a union of British and Italian Somaliland, gained independence in 1960.

In other African dependencies the former mandated colonies of the defunct League of Nations became trust territories of the United Nations. The Union of South Africa, however, refused to acknowledge the authority of the United Nations in South West Africa, a move which the United Nations, despite a ruling in its favor by the World Court, has proved powerless to reverse. In the other trust territories, however, the new international organization was so constituted as to treat its dependencies in a manner far different from the League of Nations. Both of the major Great Powers of the postwar period, the United States and the Soviet Union, had, for their own different reasons, a hostility to the continuance of colonial rule in an Africa where neither had colonies. And the membership of the United Nations, with its representation of Asian, Latin American, and African nations, contained many lesser powers even more dedicated to the ending of European colonial empires. The new climate of opinion was represented particularly among the members of the organization directly concerned with the former mandates, the Trusteeship Council. The period of limited and comfortable debate over colonial territories between the holders of the mandates—the system of the League of Nations—was now replaced by an increasingly active intervention by the Trusteeship Council to ensure that the occupying powers were doing all that was possible to prepare their charges for independence.

Even more significant for Africa was the change in the world climate of opinion concerning the future of the overseas colonial empires. The European nations possessing subordinate territories were no longer important major powers. Colonial questions were of far less importance to them than internal struggles to rebuild war-shattered economic and social fabrics. Above all, there was the example of the crumbling European domination of Asia. India was given independence as the two nations of India and Pakistan by the British Labor government in 1947. British rule ended also in Ceylon and Burma, while many of the remaining Asian territories of other European nations similarly underwent dramatic changes in status. The United States participated in the process by its long-delayed granting of independence to the Philippines in 1946. The British decisions were especially significant for Africa. Once these initial steps were taken in Asia, it is clearly only a matter of time before all of Britain's dependencies were treated similarly. An indication of the new British attitude was the Development and Welfare Act of 1945, a measure based on a similar act of 1940, inspired by conditions in the West Indian colonies. It was designed to supply financial resources for social and economic development from the budget of the metropolitan power. The act, for example, favored the organization of African trade unions, an important step in the rise of effective nationalism. A successful general strike of 1945 in Nigeria demonstrated the consequent new strength of such organizations. The British may have considered that what they regarded as their backward African colonies would achieve independence only in the most distant future, but events were not to follow this comfortable pattern.

Excerpt from: Norman R. Bennett, *Africa and Europe* (New York: Africana Publishing Company, 1984) pp. 154-157.

30. Redeeming the African Motherland

MARCUS GARVEY

The speech shows Marcus Garvey at his most eloquent. The second Universal Negro Improvement Association (UNIA) convention, at which the speech was given, was to some extent overshadowed by the mounting scandal over Garvey's shipping line, the Black Star Line. The shipping line's managers were accused of misappropriating the company's funds and of failing to live up to the great promises Garvey had made about the line's future. Within several months of the UNIA convention, the Black Star Line went bankrupt and Garvey was arrested for mail fraud. Although Garvey left troubles and shattered dreams behind him, the impact of his ideas and words outlived and outshone the man himself. The following speech was delivered in Liberty Hall in Harlem during the second international UNIA convention in August of 1921. It is representative of Garvey's lifelong belief in the importance of Africa for black men and women everywhere.

Redeeming the African Motherland

Four years ago, realizing the oppression and the hardships from which we suffered, we organized ourselves into an organization for the purpose of bettering our condition, and founding a government of our own. The four years of organization have brought good results, in that from an obscure, despised race we have grown into a mighty power, a mighty force whose influence is being felt throughout the length and breadth of the world. The Universal Negro Improvement Association existed but in name four years ago, today it is known as the greatest moving force among negroes. We have accomplished this through unity of effort and unity of purpose, it is a fair demonstration of what we will be able to accomplish in the very near future, when the millions who are outside the pale of the Universal Negro Improvement Association will have linked themselves up with us.

By our success of the last four years we will be able to estimate the grander success of a free and redeemed Africa. In climbing the heights to where we are today, we have had to surmount difficulties, we have had to climb over obstacles, but the obstacles were stepping stones to the future greatness of this cause we represent. Day by day we are writing a new history, recording new deeds of valor performed by this race of ours. It is true that the world has not yet valued us at our true worth but we are climbing up so fast and with such force that every day the world is changing its attitude towards us. Wheresoever you turn your eyes today you will find the moving influence of the Universal Negro Improvement Association among negroes from all corners of the globe. We hear among negroes the cry of "Africa for the Africans." This cry has become a positive, determined one. It is a cry that is raised simultaneously the world over because of the universal oppression that affects the negro. You who are congregated here tonight as delegates representing the hundreds of branches of the Universal Negro Improvement Association in different parts of the world will realize that we in New York are positive in this great desire of a free and redeemed Africa. We have established this Liberty Hall as the centre from which we send out the sparks of liberty to the four corners of the globe, and if you have caught the spark in your section, we want you to keep it a-burning for the great cause we represent.

There was a mad rush among nations everywhere towards national independence. Everywhere we hear the cry of liberty, of freedom, and a demand for democracy. In our corner of the world we are raising the cry for liberty, freedom and democracy. Men who have raised the cry for freedom and liberty in ages past have always made up their minds to die for the realization of the dream. We who are assembled in this convention as delegates representing the negroes of the world give out the same spirit that the fathers of liberty in this country gave out over one hundred years ago. We give out a spirit that knows no compromise, a spirit that refuses to turn back, a spirit that says "Liberty or Death," and in prosecution of this great ideal—the ideal of a free and redeemed Africa—men may scorn, men may spurn us, and may say that we are on the wrong side of life, but let me tell you that way in which you are travelling is just the way all peoples who are free have travelled in the past. If you want liberty you yourselves must strike the blow. If you must be free you must become so through your own effort, through your own initiative. Those who have discouraged you in the past are those who have enslaved you for centuries and it is not expected that they will admit that you have a right to strike out at this late hour for freedom, liberty and democracy.

At no time in this history of the world, for the last five hundred years, was there ever a serious attempt made to free negroes. We have been camouflaged into believing that we were made free by Abraham Lincoln. That we were made free by Victoria of England, but up to now we are still slaves, we are industrial slaves, we are social slaves, we are political slaves, and the new negro desires a freedom that has no boundary, no limit. We desire a freedom that will lift us to the common standard of all men whether they be white men of Europe or yellow men of Asia, therefore, in our desire to lift ourselves to that standard we shall stop at nothing until there is a free and redeemed Africa.

I understand that just at this time while we are endeavoring to create public opinion and public sentiment in favor of a free Africa, that others of our race are being subsidized to turn the attention of the world toward a different desire on the part of negroes, but let me tell you that we who make up this organization know no turning back, we have pledged ourselves even unto the last drop of our sacred blood that Africa must be free. The enemy may argue with you to show you the impossibility of a free and redeemed Africa, but I want you to take as your argument the thirteen colonies of America, that once owed their sovereignty to Great Britain, that sovereignty has been destroyed to make a United States of America. George Washington was not God Almighty. He was a man like any negro in this building, and if he and his associates were able to make a free America, we too can make a free Africa. Hampden, Gladstone, Pitt and Disraeli were not the representatives of God in the person of Jesus Christ. They were but men, but in their time they worked for the expansion of the British Empire, and today they boast of a British Empire upon which "the sun never sets." As Pitt and Gladstone were able to work for the expansion of the British Empire, so you and I can work for the expansion of a great African Empire. Voltaire and Mirabeau were not Jesus Christs, they were but men like ourselves. They worked and overturned the French Monarchy. They worked for the democracy which France now enjoys, and if they were able to do that, we are able to work for a democracy in Africa. Lenin and Trotsky were not Jesus Christs, but they were able to overthrow the despotism of Russia, and today they have given to the world a social republic, the first of its kind. If Lenin and Trotsky were able to do that for Russia, you and I can do that for Africa. Therefore, let no man, let no power on earth, turn you from this sacred cause of liberty. I prefer to die at this moment rather than not to work for the freedom of Africa. If liberty is good for certain sets of humanity it is good for all. Black men, colored men, negroes have as much right to be free as any other race that God Almighty ever created, and we desire freedom that is unfettered, freedom that is unlimited, freedom that will give us a chance and opportunity to rise to the fullest of our ambition and that we cannot get in countries where other men rule and dominate.

We have reached the time when every minute, every second must count for something done, something achieved in the cause of Africa. We need the freedom of Africa now, therefore, we desire the kind of leadership that will give it to us as quickly as possible. You will realize that not only individuals, but governments are using their influence against us. But what do we care about the unrighteous influence of any government? Our cause is based upon righteousness. And anything that is not righteous we have no respect for, because God Almighty is our leader and Jesus Christ our standard bearer. We rely on them for that kind of leadership that will make us free, for it is the same God who inspired the Psalmist to write "Princes shall come out of Egypt and Ethiopia shall stretch out her hands unto God." At this moment me thinks I see Ethiopia stretching forth her hands unto God and me thinks I see the angel of God taking up the standard of the red, the black and the green, and saying "Men of the negro race, men of Ethiopia, follow me." Tonight we are following. We are following 400,000,000 strong. We are following with a determination that we must be free before the wreck of matter, before the crash of worlds.

It falls to our lot to tear off the shackles that bind Mother Africa. Can you do it? You did it in the Revolutionary War. You did it in the Civil War; You did it at the Battles of the Marne and Verdun; You did it in Mesopotamia. You can do it marching up the battle heights of Africa. Let the world know that 400,000,000 negroes are prepared to die or live as free men. Despise us as much as you care. Ignore us as much as you care. We are coming 400,000,000 strong. We are coming with our woes behind us, with the memory of suffering behind us—woes and suffering of three hundred years—they shall be our inspiration. My bulwark of strength in the conflict of freedom in Africa, will be the three hundred years of persecution and hardship left behind in this western hemisphere. The more I remember the suffering of my fore-fathers, the more I remember the lynchings and burnings in the southern states of America, the more I will fight on even though the battle seems doubtful. Tell me that I must turn back, and I laugh you to scorn. Go on! Go on! Climb ye the heights of liberty and cease not in well doing until you have planted the banner of the red, the black and the green on the hilltops of Africa.

Excerpt from: Amy Jacques-Garvey, editor, *Philosophy and Opinions of Marcus Garvey* (New York: Macmillan, 1925) pp.70-74.

31. Factors Contributing to the Rise of Nationalist Movements in Africa

OLUWOLE OMANI

Independence movements flourished all over the continent of Africa after WWII, sometimes violently, and sometimes nonviolently until they reached their peak in the 1960s. Within a few years thereafter almost every former European colony of Africa had established its sovereign independence. Oluwole Omani in this excerpt lists six important reasons why the people of Africa became so insistent on establishing their independence.

(1) Widespread discontent among the people

In spite of the economic benefits which some Africans might have derived from colonial rule, ultimately these failed to satisfy the needs and aspirations of the majority. Even where Africans were allowed to keep their land and improve their standard of living by providing raw materials for European consumption, they were angered by the low prices paid them by the foreign firms. In other places, their lands were confiscated by their European masters, and many Africans were driven into the small, infertile and sometimes unhealthy reserves, as in Kenya and most other territories in East Africa. The Africans watched helplessly the exploitation of their natural resources by the alien imperialists; they felt the weight of unemployment, slave labor and heavy taxation—all of which featured prominently in South Africa. As a result of their experience under colonial rule, Africans came to believe that the early white missionaries in their midst taught them only how to say the 'Lord's Prayer' with the Bible firmly held to their chests, while their other white brothers robbed them of their wealth.

All the above factors combined with others to make the Africans dissatisfied. This widespread discontent was demonstrated in various ways. Africans began to realize the strength that they could draw from their ancestral history, and wanted to build a new and free future on the foundation of their pre-colonial past. Their desire was to remove the myth of white superiority and assert the natural equality of mankind, especially in respect of relations between the white and black races. This desire was expressed in the scholarly activities and achievements of men like E. W. Blyden, a West Indian of African descent who argued against the European belief that Africans had achieved nothing in the past until the arrival of the Europeans. A spectacular demonstration of discontent by the rural population was the organized Cocoa Hold-up of 1937, mainly in the Gold Coast (Ghana), during which the cocoa farmers refused to sell their cocoa to the Europeans until the prices were increased.

The tendency to resist was shown not only in the economic but also in religious arenas. Many churches broke away from the missionary organizations. Although some still adhered to the orthodox doctrines of Christianity, they accepted only Africans as their leaders. The independent African church movements could not reconcile the Christian doctrine of brotherhood and equality with the discriminatory attitudes of the Europeans, many of whom were clergymen. The prophetic movements, which also emerged as resistance groups, paid less respect to orthodoxy in their doctrines. They looked upon only African prophets as their leaders, and on African ideals as their yardstick.

(2) The Second World War and its effects

The Second World War and its aftermath contributed greatly to the emergent nationalist upsurge in Africa. The war acted as a catalyst, producing two processes: the emergence of a new radical leadership, and the creation of a large group of supporters for the new African leadership.

The Allied defeats in the early stages of the war at the hands of Germany and Japan and the German occupation of France indicated clearly that the colonial powers were not as formidable as was previously believed in Africa. The Africans appreciated now, more than ever, how much the Europeans depended on African troops and material aid. For instance, Nigeria contributed immensely to the ultimate victory of Britain and the Allied Forces during the Second World War (as they had done too in the First). Nigerians served in the armed forces, others toiled in the construction of airfields and roads for wartime communications and the production of vital raw materials. Although a relatively poor people, they also contributed money towards the war effort.

Furthermore, Africans, during the war, learned new technical skills, gained a wider perspective of world affairs, and met and exchanged ideas with Asians then engaged in the struggle to remove the European yoke. With this experience, the basis of European justification for continued domination of Africa was further undermined.

Allied propaganda during the war centred on the claim that they were fighting for freedom and the right of mankind to have a government of their choice. This was contained in the Atlantic Charter of 1944. After the war, the Africans became aware that the principle of self-determination as contained in the Charter was not meant to apply to Africa. Their political consciousness and nationalist sentiment were thus aroused and they started to think how best they could gain their freedom. The United Nations Organization with its anti-colonialist, anti-imperialist and anti-racist policies also helped to keep the desire for self-government constantly in the minds of the Africans.

(3) The rise of nationalist associations

Before the Second World War, a number of significant organizations, which can be described as precursors of the nationalist movements, sprang up, especially in West Africa. Here we will examine those that emerged in British West African territories, where their activities were probably best organized.

(a) The Aborigines' Rights Protection Society (ARPS)

The ARPS was formed in 1897 at Cape Coast to protest against the Land Bill of that same year. In 1898, it sent a delegation of three prosperous merchants to London to protest against the bill on behalf of the natural rulers. The delegation met the British Prime Minister, Chamberlain, who finally decided to withdraw the bill. A jubilant ARPS therefore decided to form itself into a permanent organization to protect the rights of the rulers and peoples of the Gold Coast.

(b) The West African Students Union (WASU)

It may be said that modern militant nationalism in West Africa was initiated by student organizations. One such organization was the WASU, formed in Britain by a Nigerian, Ladipo Solanke, in the 1920s. The Union was endowed with a hostel in 1928 by Marcus Garvey, and it published a journal. This journal afforded great opportunities to nationalist writers. The WASU served until the 1940s as an important pressure group in the agitation against colonial rule, and as the training ground in militant nationalist politics for African youths studying in Britain. Its members became the more militant as a result of their experience and contacts overseas.

(c) The National Congress of British West Africa (NCBWA)

The NCBWA was formed in 1919 as a result of a meeting called in Accra by J. E. Casely-Hayford (a Gold Coast lawyer) in co-operation with Nana Ofori Atta and R. A. Savage. The first Congress, held in 1920, attracted delegates from many parts of West Africa. The Congress envisaged a large and united nationalist forum for all the British West African territories. It demanded the introduction of universal adult suffrage; equal employment and promotion opportunities for both Europeans and Africans in the civil service; higher educational opportunities, especially the establishment of a west African university and a compulsory free education system; and finally, a clearer separation of the judiciary from the colonial administration.

(d) The youth organizations

The emergence of youth organizations was a reaction to the conservatism of the older associations and politicians. The youth organizations wanted to involve many more people in their activities than had the older associations.

The Union of Young Nigerians was inaugurated under the leadership of Dr. J. C. Vaughan, Ayo Williams and Ernest Ikoli for the purpose of informing the youth about conditions in their country. In 1932, Eyo Ita organized the Nigerian Youth League at Calabar. Its main objective was to forward educational reforms. Consequently, the West African People's Institute was established to prepare young men for self-supporting employment instead of dependence on foreign establishments for employment. In 1935, the Lagos Youth Movement was formed by Ernest Ikoli, Dr. J. C. Vaughan, Samuel Akinsanya (now the Odemo of Ishara) and Chief H. O. Davies. This organization agitated for higher education generally and protested against the alleged inferior status of the Yaba Higher College which it wanted to see raised to the status of a university. The name of the movement was changed in 1936 to the Nigerian Youth Movement. Throughout the inter-war period, the NYM tried to unite Nigerians, through ethnic co-operation, to educate the public in political consciousness, and to achieve complete autonomy for Nigeria. It called upon the colonial government to revise the Nigerian constitution and also agitated for social and economic reforms. The introduction of tribalism into Nigerian politics, however, brought about the collapse of this movement.

(4) The rise of political parties

Ultimately between the world wars, a large number of political parties emerged in Africa. They included the Nigerian National Democratic Party (NNDP) founded by Herbert Macaulay in 1923, the Moroccan League (1926), the New Destour Party in Tunisia reorganized by Bourguiba in 1934, the Algerian Popular Party founded in 1937 by Messali after breaking away from the French Communist Party, and the National Council of Nigeria and the Cameroons, later called the National Council for Nigerian Citizens (NCNC) founded in 1944. Other important ones were the Action Group (AG) 1951, led by Chief Obafemi Awolowo, the Northern People's Congress (NPC) 1949, both in Nigeria, the United Gold Coast Convention (UGCC) 1947, led by Dr. Danquah, and the Convention People's Party (CPP) in the Gold Coast organized in 1949 by the late Dr. Kwame Nkrumah. In Sierra Leone, there was the Sierra Leone People's Party (SLPP) 1951; and in the Gambia the Progressive People's Party (PPP) founded in 1962. The Rassemblement Democratique Africain (RDA), formed in 1946 primarily on the initiative of Felix Houphouet-Boigny of the Ivory Coast, eventually became the dominant political party of French West Africa. In East Africa, Jomo Kenyatta founded the Kenya African National Union; in Uganda there were the Uganda Nationalist Congress (1952) and Milton Obote's Uganda People's Congress; the Tanganyika African National Union was formed in 1954 under the leadership of Julius Nyerere. All these political parties developed as a result of the nationalist feelings and agitation which were widespread at the time. The willingness of the British and French colonial powers to concede some measure of self-government was also a contributory factor in the development of parties. The failure of such parties to emerge in the Portuguese territories at that time might lend some weight to the point made above.

(5) The roles of the African elite

The traditional elite of Africa were the rulers and the chiefs. Their attitude to European domination depended on the political situation in the different areas. There were great rivalries among the rulers, and these, rather than patriotism, dictated their attitude to European presence. By and large, many of the traditional rulers found themselves leading the resistance against the early European penetration and rule. Because many of them were stripped of most, or at times all, of their political powers and land, these allied with a new elite that was then emerging. This was the nationalist or educated elite. For instance, in West

Africa, the Aborigines' Rights Protection Society, which protested against the Land Bill of 1897, was supported by chiefs and religious leaders; the National Congress of British West Africa was formed in 1919 in consultation with a traditional ruler of the Gold Coast (Ghana), Nana Ofori Atta; while in 1915 when Lord Lugard asked the Eleko of Lagos to persuade his people to pay the unpopular water rate, the Eleko refused after being advised by the new elite. Herbert Macaulay, a member of the new nationalist elite group, championed the cause of the chiefs and people of Lagos against the Lagos High court ruling that the 1861 cession of Lagos to the British implied that all lands which were by then not privately owned should be Crown Land. A test case was brought by Chief Oluwa, the Eleko, under the guidance of Herbert Macaulay. The Privy Council in London which heard this case ruled in favor of Chief Oluwa.

(6) The role of the press

The writings of educated men of African descent contributed greatly to the independence movements as their inspiration. Many of these writers began to deepen their knowledge of the traditions of their people in an effort to discover their cultural heritage. In 1903, Casely-Hayford published his *Gold Coast Native Institutions* and in 1911, *Ethiopia Unbound;* while John Payne Jackson, a Liberian settled in Lagos, edited the Lagos Weekly Record from 1891 to 1918. Also in Nigeria the following news papers were started: Nigerian Pioneer, 1914; Lagos Standard, 1903; Nigerian Chronicle, 1908; and Nigerian Times, 1914.

The press helped to keep the elite in Africa in contact and united, though it was never profitable economically. The newspapers and journals especially were intended to educate the African masses and to influence public opinion, but only a few could read them. More seriously, only a few could afford even to buy them. Thus the practice of passing the same copy of a newspaper from hand to hand grew up, and few copies were actually sold.

Excerpt from: Richard Olaniyan, editor, *African History and Culture* (New York: Longman Publishing Group Ltd., 1982) pp. 85-94.

32. African Nationalism and Nationhood

John N. Paden

In this selection John N. Paden develops useful definitions of terms associated with the concepts of nationalism, nation, and nation-state which are relevant to the movement toward independence in Africa in the mid-twentieth century. Paden also makes a useful distinction between the stages of proto-nationalism, independence movements and nationalism/supranationalism.

African Nationalism and Nationhood

In the European context, the term nationalism usually refers to those movements, feelings, and ideologies which demand that the basic political boundaries and identities of a people be contained within the framework of a sovereign state. Sovereignty, as the concept emerged in the nineteenth and twentieth centuries, reflects an international system wherein states are accorded complete autonomy on internal matters, legal equality and inviolability within the external (or international) context, and some precise delimitation of territoriality.

If a sovereign state is based on a single national identity we refer to it as a nation-state. A sovereign state which comprises several national identities may be called a multinational state. The idea of nation refers to a people, or volk, who regard themselves as sharing common values and goals, as sharing a common history and a common future, and as being somehow distinguishable in various ways from other peoples. Within the European context, the characteristics which have been used most frequently to distinguish different peoples have included the following: language, culture, proximity (or territorial identification), religion, political system, and economic interdependence. While none of these characteristics is necessarily essential to the consolidation of a nation-state, some combination of them is usually present.

The concept of a people sharing common values and a common identity clearly relates the issue of nationality (and nationalism) to the issue of ethnicity. Ethnicity may be regarded as communal (as opposed to associational) loyalty or identity and is usually accompanied by the claim of kinship or common origin (real or assumed). The notion of ethnicity does not necessarily require political independence, sovereignty, or territoriality. Ethnic groups, such as the Bakongo (Congo-Kinshasa) or the Tswana (Botswana), which have petitioned for separate political status are expressing what may be called ethnic nationalism. The terms ethnic group and nationality group ... often have overlapping meanings. In general usage, however, an ethnic group is a smaller scale unit than a nationality group. Also, ethnic groups emphasize kinship, a notion which may be transmuted in various ways in the concept of nationality.

Nationalism need not preclude certain types of subnational loyalties, either in the nation-state context or in those cases of the multinational state where a sufficient commonality of interest reinforces the legitimacy of the national state (rather than the component nationalities) as the seat of sovereignty. Peoples usually have multiple identities or loyalties, each relative to different needs or situations. Thus, for example, within Germany the Bavarians and the Prussians (peoples associated with specific geographical regions, religions, and cultures) are significant subnational identity groups, but only if these peoples demanded secession from the nation-state of Germany would we regard this as nationalism in the fullest sense.

A conceptual category which relates the notion of nationality to that of sovereignty is irredentism. This would occur if an international (or sovereign-state) boundary divided a people or nation and the members of this nation were dissatisfied or frustrated enough to actively demand reunion. An irredentist movement usually originates with a minority group resident in a state neighboring their homeland state. Examples would include the Turks in Cyprus, the Ewe in Ghana, or the French in Alsace-Lorraine between 1870 and 1914.

In trying to explain how national identity emerges, a major branch of theory concentrates on definition by reference to the external context; a "we" group for instance, is distinguished from a "they" group which is usually in relative proximity. Thus, to a certain extent, Polish nationalism emerged as a response to the Russians along Poland's eastern border. Since nationality is ultimately a matter of social definition rather than of objective definition, the self-ascriptive identity process and the external-ascriptive process are always interrelated. The question of what constitutes a "German," "Pole," "Russian" will vary with the time context, the spatial context, and a variety of subject perceptions. This process was clearly demonstrated when members of these European groups migrated to America where new (usually more general) categories of national identities were ascribed to them.

Another major process in the emergence of national identity is the extension of loyalties from smaller to larger scale units. Thus, the city-states of the Italian peninsula began to coalesce in the late nineteenth century into what finally emerged as the nation-state Italy. In cases where multinational empires have broken up, as with the Hapsburg Empire and the Turkish Ottoman Empire after World War I, and with the various colonial empires after World War II, the resultant components may regroup themselves into units smaller than the original empire but larger than the individual components. Thus Yugoslavia was formed after World War I from several peoples, such as the Croats, Serbs, Macedonians, Slovenes, and Montenegrins.

The Scope of African Nationalism

Three stages of nationalism accompanied the emergence of African states from colonial rule. These included the early proto-nationalistic phenomena, the drive to independence, and the post-independence period of nationalism and supranationalism.

Proto-nationalism

The idea of African proto-nationalism has been developed in recent years as a category for discussing phenomena related to demands for political autonomy (as opposed to sovereignty) in the period prior to the organization of African nationalist movements. In most African states this generally occurred in the time period from 1900 to 1935. The distinguishing feature of these phenomena was active rejection of the establishment and legitimacy of alien rule. Major manifestations of proto-nationalism have been resistance movements, rebellions, and individual protests.

Resistance movements usually occurred at the time of colonial conquest. Thus, the Fulani battle at Burmi (Northern Nigeria) in 1903 was a clear effort to resist alien (British) rule. The Ashanti wars of 1899 and the Islamic wars of Samory Toure were in a similar category.

Rebellions, or revolts, usually occurred shortly after the occupation of an area. They constituted early attempts to throw off alien rule once such rule had been established. Examples would include the Maji Maji rebellion (Tanganyika) against the rule of the Germans and the Zulu rebellion (South Africa) against the British in 1906.

Individual protest movements have taken a variety of forms. Frequently they involved leaders from the African Christian churches (such as John Chilembwe of Malawi, who, in Nat Turner style, was willing to "strike a blow and die"). Other protestors were leaders of nascent labor unions (as in the Copperbelt) or of ethnic voluntary associations (such as Harry Thuku of Kenya) who were willing to go to jail for petitioning against heavy taxation, poor work conditions, and land alienation. Nationalist literature of a later period has accorded these men both a real and a symbolic role in the independence movements.

The Independence Movements

African nationalism can be clearly identified in the period 1945 to 1960. In the late 1930s urban organizations began to emerge, often drawing on the new, western-educated, professional and skilled classes. These organizations raised the issue of increasing African participation in the civil service, administration, government, and in the modern economic sector. An example of such an organization would be the Lagos Youth Movement (Nigeria), founded in 1934, which later became the springboard for nationalist leaders such as Nnamdi Azikiwe.

During World War II the African colonies provided manpower and staging bases for the Allies, especially in the North African campaigns against Italy and Germany. In return for this assistance, Britain and France promised major reforms in the colonial system. But as a result of the war, the myth of European infallibility was broken, and the universalistic concepts of freedom, democracy, and justice, which had been part of the rhetoric of the Allied confrontation with fascism, were interpreted by the educated class of Africans as applicable within the African context.

With regard to this question of principles and values, Thomas Hodgkin comments on the political vocabulary of early African nationalists:

> The theoretical weapons with which African nationalists make their revolutions have been largely borrowed from the armouries of the metropolitan countries. Much of the political thinking of contemporary African leaders is bound to be derivative. They are themselves the products of European schools and universities. They are asserting claims of a kind that have already been asserted by Europeans, around which a European sacred literature has been built up. And they have to state their case in a language that will be intelligible to their European rulers. . . . [Three strains of western thought stand out: 1] the Christian idea of human brotherhood and the specifically Protestant conception of an "elect"; [2] the traditional democratic belief in "the right to choose our own governors . . ."; and [3] the socialist (not necessarily Marxian) conception of a society in which "economic exploitation," poverty and unemployment are abolished, and rewards are related to work.

Within a brief period of approximately fifteen years following World War II, African political parties were formed, self-government was demanded, and independence was won in most African states. The speed of change does not mean that the task was easy. In almost every case, the colonial power offered major resistance of some sort. It is a tribute to the organizational skill, and often charismatic inspiration, of the pre-independence African nationalists that they were able to mobilize enough support to enforce their demands and to do so, in nearly all cases, without resort to violence.

Nationalism and Supranationalism

The territorial units within which the nationalist movements developed were, for the most part, the colonial units. During the pre-independence nationalist period, however, a matter of considerable debate among nationalist leaders was the question of the most appropriate boundaries for future nation-states in Africa. In a few cases, it was suggested that units smaller than the existing colonial units, consisting primarily of ethnic nationalities, be the basis of nationhood in Africa. In most cases, however, the idea of using ethnic nationalities as a basis for future nationhood was rejected by the elites in favor of political groupings which were larger than the existing colonial units. The arbitrary nature of the inherited colonial boundaries militated against their acceptability to nationalist leaders who were intent on promoting a new order of things. But the acquired identities of the peoples constituting the former colonies, as well as objective factors such as the intracolonial structure of communications systems, tend to reinforce the originally arbitrary boundaries, and the viability of the former colonial boundaries has been stronger than had been anticipated. . . . In the immediate post-colonial nation-building period the major source of national unity in almost every case turned out to be the legacy of the nationalist party of the independence movement.

Yet certain pre-independence concepts of nationalism extended beyond the imposed framework of colonial boundaries associated with the inherited national state systems. It may be that when the birth pains of the new African states have lessened, the reservoir of ideas generated in the pre-independence period will regain importance in African nationalism.

Excerpt from: John N. Paden and Edward W. Soja, editors, *The African Experience*, Vol. I (Chicago: Northwestern University Press, 1970) pp. 403-407.

33. Consciencism

KWAME NKRUMAH

The first president of the independent nation of Ghana in West Africa in 1954, Kwame Nkrumah, was also a political philosopher and writer. In this excerpt from his book Consciencism, *Nkrumah defines the threefold concept of culture in Africa which is emerging based on African Traditional Society, Christianity and Islam.*

With true independence regained, however, a new harmony needs to be forged, a harmony that will allow the combined presence of traditional Africa, Islamic Africa and Euro-Christian Africa, so that this presence is in tune with the original humanist principles underlying African society. Our society is not the old society, but a new society enlarged by Islamic and Euro-Christian influences. A new emergent ideology is therefore required, an ideology which can solidify in a philosophical statement, but at the same time an ideology which will not abandon the original humanist principles of Africa.

Such a philosophical statement will be born out of the crisis of the African conscience confronted with the three strands of present African society. Such a philosophical statement I propose to name Philosophical Consciencism, for it will give the theoretical basis for an ideology whose aim shall be to contain the African experience of Islamic and Euro-Christian presence as well as the experience of the traditional African society, and, by gestation, employ them for the harmonious growth and development of that society.

Every society is placed in nature. And it seeks to influence nature, to impose such transformations upon nature, as will develop the environment of the society for its better fulfillment. The changed environment, in bringing about a better fulfillment of the society, thereby alters the society. Society placed in nature is therefore caught in the correlation of transformation with development. This correlation represents the toil of man both as a social being and as an individual. This kind of correlation has achieved expression in various social-political theories. For a social-political theory has a section which determines the way in which social forces are to be deployed in order to increase the transformation of society.

Slavery and feudalism represent social-political theories in which the deployment of forces is not a problematic question. In both slavery and feudalism, workers, the people whose toil transforms nature for the development of society, are dissociated from any say in rule. By a vicious division of labor, one class of citizen toils and another reaps where it has not sown. In the slave society, as in the feudal society, that part of society whose labors transform nature is not the same as the part which is better fulfilled as a result of this transformation. If by their fruits we shall know them, they must first grow the fruits. In slave and feudal society, the fruit-eaters are not the fruit-growers. This is the cardinal factor in exploitation, that the section of a society whose labors transform nature is not the same as the section which is better fulfilled as a result of this transformation.

In every non-socialist society, there can be found two strata which correspond to that of the oppressor and the oppressed, the exploiter and the exploited. In all such societies, the essential relation between the two strata is the same as that between masters and slaves, lords and serfs. In capitalism, which is only a social-political theory in which the important aspects of slavery and feudalism are refined, a stratified society is required for its proper functioning, a society is required in which the working class is oppressed by the ruling class; for, under capitalism, that portion of society whose labors transform nature and produce goods is not the portion of society which enjoys the fruits of this transformation and productivity.

Excerpt from: Kwame Nkrumah, *Consciencism* (New York: Monthly Review Foundation, 1970) p. 70.

34. The Definition of Black Consciousness

STEVE BIKO

During the 1970s in South Africa, Steve Biko emerged as an eloquent opponent of apartheid by building his own constructive and forceful, yet basically nonviolent, philosophy of Black Consciousness. He succeeded in winning over the support of numerous leading white South African citizens, including newspaper editor Donald Woods. Eventually Biko became a victim of apartheid as many opponents before him and others since. The story of Biko's life is told, in part, in Donald Wood's book Biko *and in a movie entitled "Cry Freedom."*

We have in our policy manifesto defined blacks as those who are by law or tradition politically, economically and socially discriminated against as a group in the South African society and identifying themselves as a unit in the struggle towards the realization of their aspirations. This definition illustrates to us a number of things:

1. Being black is not a matter of pigmentation - being black is a reflection of a mental attitude.

2. Merely by describing yourself as black you have started on a road towards emancipation, you have committed yourself to fight against all forces that seek to use your blackness as a stamp that marks you out as a subservient being.

From the above observations therefore, we can see that the term black is not necessarily all-inclusive; i.e. the fact we are all not white does not necessarily mean that we are all black. Non-whites do exist and will continue to exist and will continue to exist for quite a long time. If one's aspiration is whiteness but his pigmentation makes attainment of this impossible, then that person is a non-white. Any man who calls a white man "Baas", any man who serves in the police force or Security Branch is ipso facto a non-white. Black people—real black people—are those who can manage to hold their heads high in defiance rather than willingly surrender their souls to the white man.

Briefly defined therefore, Black Consciousness is in essence the realization by the black man of the need to rally together with his brothers around the cause of their operation—the blackness of their skin—and to operate as a group in order to rid themselves of the shackles that bind them to perpetual servitude. It seeks to demonstrate the lie that black is an aberration from the "normal" which is white. It is a manifestation of a new realization that by seeking to run away from themselves and to emulate the white man, blacks are insulting the intelligence of whoever created them black. Black Consciousness therefore, takes cognizance of the deliberateness of God's plan in creating black people black. It seeks to infuse the black community with a new-found pride in themselves, their efforts, their value systems, their culture, their religion and their outlook to life.

The interrelationship between the consciousness of self and the emancipatory programme is of paramount importance. Blacks no longer seek to reform the system because so doing implies acceptance of the major points around which the system revolves.

Blacks are out to completely transform the system and to make of it what they wish. Such a major undertaking can only be realized in an atmosphere where people are convinced of the truth inherent in their stand. Liberation therefore, is of paramount importance in the concept of Black Consciousness, for we cannot be conscious of ourselves and yet remain in bondage. We want to attain the envisioned self which is a free self.

The surge towards Black Consciousness is a phenomenon that has manifested itself throughout the so-called Third World. There is no doubt that discrimination against the black man the world over fetches its origin from the exploitative attitude of the white man. Colonization of white countries by whites has throughout history resulted in nothing more sinister than mere cultural or geographical fusion at worst, or language bastardization at best. It is true that the history of weaker nations is shaped by bigger nations, but nowhere in the world today do we see whites exploiting whites on a scale even remotely similar to what is happening in South Africa. Hence, one is forced to conclude that it is not coincidence that black people are exploited. It was a deliberate plan which has culminated in even so called black independent countries not attaining any real independence.

With this background in mind we are forced, therefore, to believe that it is a case of haves against have-nots where whites have been deliberately made haves and blacks have-nots. There is for instance no worker in the classical sense among whites in South Africa, for even the most down-trodden white worker still has a lot to lose if the system is changed. He is protected by several laws against competition at work from the majority. He has a vote and he uses it to return the Nationalist Government to power because he sees them as the only people who, through job reservation laws, are bent on looking after his interests against competition with the "Natives".

It should therefore be accepted that an analysis of our situation in terms of one's color at once takes care of the greatest single determinant for political action—i.e. color—while also validly describing the blacks as the only real workers in South Africa. It immediately kills all suggestions that there could ever be effective rapport between the real workers, i.e. blacks, and the privileged white workers since we have shown that the latter are the greatest supporters of the system. True enough, the system has allowed so dangerous an anti-black attitude to build up amongst whites that it is taken as almost a sin to be black and hence the poor whites, who are economically nearest to the blacks, demonstrate the distance between themselves and the blacks by an exaggerated reactionary attitude towards blacks. Hence the greatest anti-black feeling is to be found amongst the very poor whites whom the class theory calls upon to be with black workers in the struggle for emancipation. This is the kind of twisted logic that the Black Consciousness approach seeks to eradicate.

In terms of the Black Consciousness approach we recognize the existence of one major force in South Africa. This is white racism. It is the one force against which all of us are pitted. It works with unnerving totality, featuring both on the offensive and in our defense. Its greatest ally to date has been the refusal by us to club together as blacks because we are told to do so would be racialist. So, while we progressively lose ourselves in a world of colorlessness and amorphous common humanity, whites are deriving pleasure and security in entrenching white racism and further exploiting the minds and bodies of the unsuspecting black masses. Their agents are even present amongst us, telling us that it is immoral to withdraw into a cocoon, that dialogue is the answer to our problem and that it is unfortunate that there is white racism in some quarters but you must understand that things are changing. These in fact are the greatest racists for they refuse to credit us with any intelligence to know what we want. Their intentions are obvious; they want to be barometers by which the rest of the white society can measure feelings in the black world. This then is WHAT MAKES US believe that white power presents its self as a totality not only provoking us but also controlling our response to the provocation. This is an important point to note because it is often missed by those who believe that there are a few good whites. Sure there are a few good whites just as much as there are a few bad blacks.

shapeless, no definite form

However what we are concerned here with is group attitudes and group politics. The exception does not make a lie of the rule—it merely substantiates it.

The overall analysis therefore, based on the Hegelian theory of dialectic materialism, is as follows. That since the thesis is a white racism there can only be one valid antithesis i.e. a solid black unity to counterbalance the scale. If South Africa is to be a land where black and white live together in harmony without fear of group exploitation, it is only when these two opposites have interplayed and produced a viable synthesis of ideas and a modus vivendi. We can never wage any struggle without offer-

practical compromise, bypasses difficulties

ing a strong counterpoint to the white races that permeate our society so effectively.

One must immediately dispel the thought that Black Consciousness is merely a methodology or means toward an end. What Black Consciousness seeks to do is to produce at the output end of the process real black people who do not regard themselves as appendages to white society. This truth cannot be reversed. We do not need to apologize for this because it is true that the white systems have produced through the world a number of people who are not aware that they too are people. Our adherence to values that we set for ourselves can also not be reversed because it will always be a lie to accept white values as necessarily the best. The fact that a synthesis may be attained only relates to adherence to power politics. Someone somewhere along the line will be forced to accept the truth and here we believe that ours is the truth.

The future of South Africa in the case where blacks adopt Black Consciousness is the subject for concern especially among initiates. What do we do when we have attained our consciousness? Do we propose to kick whites out? I believe personally that the answers to these questions ought to be found in the SASO Policy Manifesto and in our analysis of the situation in South Africa. We have defined what we mean by true integration and the very fact that such a definition exists does illustrate what our standpoint is. In any case we are much more concerned about what is happening now, than what will happen in the future. The future will always be shaped by the sequence of present-day events.

The importance of black solidarity to the various segments of the black community must not be understated. There have been in the past a lot of suggestions that there can be no viable unity amongst blacks because they hold each other in contempt. Coloreds despise Africans because they, (the former) by their proximity to the Africans, may lose the chances of assimilation into the white world. Africans despise the coloreds and Indians for a variety of reasons. Indians not only despise Africans but in many instances also exploit the Africans in job and shop situations. All these stereotype attitudes have led to mountainous inter-group suspicions amongst the blacks.

What we should at all times look at is the fact that:

1. We are all oppressed by the same system.

2. That we are oppressed to varying degrees is a deliberate design to stratify us not only socially but also in terms of aspirations.

3. Therefore it is to be expected that in terms of the enemy's plan there must be this suspicion and that if we are committed to the problem of emancipation to the same degree it is part of our duty to bring to the attention of the black people the deliberateness of the enemy's subjugation scheme.

4. That we should go on with our programme, attracting to it only committed people and not just those eager to see an equitable distribution of groups amongst our ranks. This is a game common amongst liberals. The one criterion that must govern all our action is commitment.

Further implications of Black Consciousness are to do with correcting false images of ourselves in terms of culture, education, religion, economics. The importance of this also must not be understated. There is always an interplay between the history of a people i.e. the past, and their faith in themselves and hopes for their future. We are aware of the terrible role played by our education and religion in creating amongst us a false understanding of ourselves. We must therefore work out schemes not only to correct this, but further to be our own authorities rather than wait to be interpreted by others. Whites can only see us from the outside and as such can never extract and analyze the ethos in the black community. In summary therefore one need only refer this house to the SASO Policy Manifesto which carries most of the salient points in the definition of Black Consciousness. I wish to stress again the need for us to know very clearly what we mean by certain terms and what our understanding is when we talk of Black Consciousness.

Excerpt from: Steven Biko, *I Write What I Like* (New York: Harper and Row, 1978) pp. 48-53.

distinguishing character
sentiment moral nature
guiding beliefs

35. The Question of South Africa

DESMOND TUTU

In 1985 the Nobel Prize Committee awarded Bishop Desmond Tutu the Nobel Peace Prize for his role in the struggle to end apartheid in South Africa. The text of his acceptance speech is presented below in its entirety.

I speak out of a full heart, for I am about to speak about a land that I love deeply and passionately; a beautiful land of rolling hills and gurgling steams, of clear starlit skies, of singing birds, and gamboling lambs; a land God has richly endowed with the good things of the earth, a land rich in mineral deposits of nearly every kind; a land of vast open spaces, enough to accommodate all its inhabitants comfortably; a land capable of feeding itself and other lands on the beleaguered continent of Africa, a veritable breadbasket; a land that could contribute wonderfully to the material and spiritual development and prosperity of all Africa and indeed of the whole world. It is endowed with enough to satisfy the material and spiritual needs of all its peoples.

And so we would expect that such a land, veritably flowing with milk and honey, should be a land where peace and harmony and contentment reigned supreme. Alas, the opposite is the case. For my beloved country is wracked by division, by alienation, by animosity, by separation, by injustice, by avoid-

prevalent in a particular field (handwritten note)

able pain and suffering. It is a deeply fragmented society, ridden by fear and anxiety, covered by a pall of despondency and a sense of desperation, split up into hostile, warring factions.

It is a highly volatile land, and its inhabitants sit on a powder-keg with a very short fuse indeed, ready to blow us all up into kingdom-come. There is endemic unrest, like a festering sore that will not heal until not just the symptoms are treated but the root causes are removed.

South African society is deeply polarized. Nothing illustrates this more sharply than the events of the past week. While the black community was in seventh heaven of delight because of the decision of that committee in Oslo, and while the world was congratulating the recipient of the Nobel Peace Prize, the white government and most white South Africans, very sadly, were seeking to devalue that prize. An event that should have been the occasion of uninhibited joy and thanksgiving revealed a sadly divided society.

Before I came to this country in early September to go on sabbatical, I visited one of the trouble-spots near Johannesburg. I went with members of the Executive Committee of the South African Council of Churches, which had met in emergency session after I had urged Mr. P. W. Botha to meet with church leaders to deal with a rapidly deteriorating situation. As a result of our peace initiative, we did get to meet with two cabinet ministers, demonstrating thereby our concern to carry out our call to be ministers of reconciliation and ambassadors of Christ.

In this black township, we met an old lady who told us that she was looking after her grandchildren and the child of neighbors while they were at work. On the day about which she was speaking, the police had been chasing black schoolchildren in that street, but the children had eluded the police, who then drove down the street past the old lady's house. Her wards were playing in front of the house, in the yard. She was sitting in the kitchen at the back, when her daughter burst in, calling agitatedly for her. She rushed out into the living room. A grandson had fallen just inside the door, dead. The police had shot him in the back. He was six years old. Recently a baby, a few weeks old, became the first white casualty of the current uprisings.

Every death is one too many. Those whom the black community has identified as collaborators with a system that oppresses them and denies them the most elementary human rights have met cruel death, which we deplore as much as any others. They have rejected these people operating within the system, whom they have seen as lackies and stooges, despite their titles of town councilors, and so on, under an apparently new dispensation extending the right of local government to the blacks.

Over 100,000 black students are out of school, boycotting—as they did in 1976—what they and the black community perceive as an inferior education designed deliberately for inferiority. An already highly volatile situation has been ignited several times and, as a result, over 80 persons have died. There has been industrial unrest, with the first official strike by black miners taking place, not without its toll of fatalities among the blacks.

Some may be inclined to ask: But why should all this unrest be taking place just when the South African government appears to have embarked on the road of reform, exemplified externally by the signing of the Nkomati accord and internally by the implementation of a new constitution which appears to depart radically from the one it replaces, for it makes room for three chambers: one for whites, one for coloreds, and one for Indians; a constitution described by many as a significant step forward?

I wish to state here, as I have stated on other occasions, that Mr. P. W. Botha must be commended for his courage in declaring that the future of South Africa could no longer be determined by whites only. That was a very brave thing to do. The tragedy of South Africa is that something with such a considerable potential for resolving the burgeoning crisis of our land should have been vitiated by the exclusion of 73 percent of the population, the overwhelming majority in the land.

By no stretch of the imagination could that kind of constitution be considered to be democratic. The composition of the committees, in the ratio of four whites to two coloreds to one Indian, demonstrates eloquently what most people had suspected all along—that it was intended to perpetuate the rule of a minority. The fact that the first qualification for membership in the chambers is racial says that this constitution was designed to entrench racism and ethnicity. The most obnoxious features of apartheid would remain untouched and unchanged. The Group Areas Act, the Population Registration Act, separate educational systems for the different race groups; all this and more would remain quite unchanged.

This constitution was seen by the mainline English-speaking churches and the official white opposition as disastrously inadequate, and they called for its rejection in the whites-only referendum last November. The call was not heeded. The blacks overwhelmingly rejected what they regarded as a sham, an instrument in the politics of exclusion. Various groups campaigned for a boycott of the colored and Indian elections—campaigned, I might add, against very great odds, by and large peacefully. As we know, the authorities responded with their usual iron-fist tactics, detaining most of the leaders of the United Democratic Front (UDF) and other organizations that had organized the boycott—and we have some of them now holed up in the British Consulate in Durban, causing a diplomatic contretemps.

The current unrest was in very large measure triggered off by the reaction of the authorities to anti-election demonstrations in August. The farcical overall turnout of only about 20 percent says more eloquently than anything else that the Indians and coloreds have refused to be co-opted as the junior partners of apartheid—the phrase used by Allan Boesak, the founding father of the UDF and president of the World Alliance of Reformed Churches.

But there is little freedom in this land of plenty. There is little freedom to disagree with the determinations of the authorities. There is large-scale unemployment because of the drought and the recession that has hit most of the world's economy. And it is at such a time that the authorities have increased the prices of various foodstuffs and also of rents in black townships—measures designed to hit hardest those least able to afford the additional costs. It is not surprising that all this has exacerbated an already tense and volatile situation.

So the unrest is continuing, in a kind of war of attrition, with the casualties not being large enough at any one time to shock the world sufficiently for it to want to take action against the system that is the root cause of all this agony. We have warned consistently that unrest will be endemic in South Africa until its root cause is removed. And the root cause is apartheid—a vicious, immoral and totally evil, and unchristian system.

People will refer to the Nkomati accord, and we will say that we are glad for the cessation of hostilities anywhere in the world. But we will ask: Why is detente by the South African government only for export? Why is state aggression reserved for the black civilian population? The news today is that the army has cordoned off Sebokeng, a black township, near Sharpeville, and 400 or so persons have been arrested, including the immediate ex-moderator of the Presbyterian Church of Southern Africa and Father Geoff Moselane, an Anglican priest.

As blacks we often run the gauntlet of roadblocks on roads leading into our townships, and these have been manned by the army in what are actually described as routine police operations. When you use the army in this fashion, who is the enemy?

The authorities have not stopped stripping blacks of their South African citizenship. Here I am, 53 years old, a bishop in the church, some would say reasonably responsible; I travel on a document that says of my nationality that it is "undeterminable at present." The South African government is turning us into aliens in the land of our birth. It continues unabated with its vicious policy of forced population removals. It is threatening to remove the people of Kwa Ngema. It treats carelessly the women in the KTC squatter camp near Cape Town whose flimsy plastic coverings are destroyed every day by the authorities; and the heinous crime of those women is that they want to be with their husbands, with the fathers of their children.

White South Africans are not demons; they are ordinary human beings, scared human beings, many of them; who would not be, if they were outnumbered five to one? Through this lofty body I wish to appeal to my white fellow South Africans to share in building a new society, for blacks are not intent on driving whites into the sea but on claiming only their rightful place in the sun in the land of their birth.

We deplore all forms of violence, the violence of an oppressive and unjust society and the violence of those seeking to overthrow that society, for we believe that violence is not the answer to the crisis of our land.

We dream of a new society that will be truly non-racial, truly democratic, in which people count because they are created in the image of God.

We are committed to work for justice, for peace, and for reconciliation. We ask you, please help us; urge the South African authorities to go to the conference table with the ... representatives of all sections of our community. I appeal to this body to act. I appeal in the name of the ordinary, the little people of South Africa. I appeal in the name of the squatters in crossroads and in the KTC camp. I appeal on behalf of the father who has to live in a single-sex hostel as a migrant worker, separated from his family for 11 months of the year. I appeal on behalf of the students who have rejected this travesty of education made available only for blacks. I appeal on behalf of those who are banned arbitrarily, who are banished, who are detained without trial, those imprisoned because they have had a vision of this new South Africa. I appeal on behalf of those who have been exiled from their homes.

I say we will be free, and we ask you: Help us, that this freedom comes for all of us in South Africa, black and white, but that it comes with the least possible violence, that it comes peacefully, that it comes soon.

Excerpt from: Desmond Tutu, "The Question of South Africa," *Africa Report* (New York: 1985) pp. 50-52.

36. "'No!' He Said"

WOLE SOYINKA

The Nobel Prize Poet Laureate, Wole Soyinka, from Nigeria, penned this poem about Nelson Mandela and calls to mind his ordeal of decades of imprisonment in South Africa for his steadfast and unrelenting resistance to apartheid. Mandela is praised and honored for his unwillingness to make any compromise in spite of everything conceivable to get him to do so.

'No!' He Said

Shorn of landmarks, glued to a sere promontory,
The breakers sought to crush his head,
To flush the black will of his race
Back in tidal waves, to flesh-trade centuries,
Bile-slick beyond beachcombing, beyond
Salvage operations but—no, he said.

Sea urchins stung his soul. Albino eels
Searched the cortex of his heart,
His hands thrust high to exorcise
Visions of lost years, slow parade of isolation's
Ghosts. Still they came, seducers of a moment's
Slack in thought, but—no, he said.

And they saw his hands were clenched.
Blood oozed from a thousand pores. A lonely
Fisher tensed against the oilcloth of new dawns,

Hand over hand he hauled. The harvest strained.
Cords turned writhing hawsers in his hands. "Let go!"
The tempters cried, but—no, he said.

Count the passing ships. Whose argosies
Stretch like golden beads on far horizons? Those are
Their present ease, your vanished years. Castaway,
Minnows roost in the hold of that doomed ship
You launched in the eye of storms. Your mast is seaweed
On which pale plankton feed, but—no, he said.

Are you bigger than Nkomati? Blacker
Than hands that signed away a continent for ease?
Lone matador with broken paddle for a lance,
Are you the Horn? The Cape? Sequined
Constellation of the Bull for tide-tossed
Castaways on pallid sands? No, he said.

The axis of the world has shifted. Even the polar star
Loses its fixity, nudged by man-made planets.
The universe has shrunk. History reechoes as
We plant new space flags of a master race.
You are the afterburn of our crudest launch.
The stars disown you, but—no, he said.

Your tongue is salt swollen, a mute keel
Upended on the seabed of forgotten time.
The present breeds new tasks, same taskmasters.
On that star planet of our galaxy, code-named Bantustan,
They sieve rare diamonds from moon dust. In choice reserves,
Venerably pastured, you . . . but—-no, he said.

That ancient largesse on the mountaintop
Shrinks before our gift's munificence, an offer even
Christ, second-come, could not refuse. Be ebony mascot
On the flagship of our space fleet, still
Through every turbulence, spectator of our Brave New World.
Come, Ancient Mariner, but—no, he said—

No! I am no prisoner of this rock, this island,
No ash spew on Milky Ways to conquests old or new.
I am this rock, this island. I toiled,
Precedent on this soil, as in the great dark whale
Of time, Black Hole of the galaxy. Its maw
Turns steel-wrought epochs plankton—yes—and
Vomits out new worlds.

In and out of time warp, I am that rock
In the black hole of the sky.

Excerpt from: Wole Soyinka, *Mandela's Earth and Other Poems* (New York: Random House, 1988) pp. 21-23.

37. Mandela Speaks

NELSON MANDELA

Below is the address given by Nelson Mandela delivered to the rally held in Soweto, South Africa, at Soccer City Stadium on February 13, 1990. It is his first public address upon being released from prison February 11, 1990, after over a quarter of a century of confinement for his public role in resistance to apartheid and his leadership role in the Africa National Congress.

Comrades, friends and the people of Soweto at large, I greet you in the name of the heroic struggle of our people to establish justice and freedom for all in our country. I salute our President, Comrade Oliver Tambo, for his leadership of the ANC that has put our organization and the hopes of the people it represents on the political center stage in South Africa.

I salute our rank and file members and combatants of the ANC who have sacrificed all for the love of their country and their people.

I salute the South African Communist Party for its consistent and determined contribution to the struggle for a democratic government in South Africa. Our alliance is built on the unshakable foundation of our united struggle for a non-racial democracy.

I salute the United Democratic Front, the Congress of South African Trade Unions, the National Education Crisis Committee and many other formations of the MDM. The work of the UDF has ensured that none of the reformist strategies of the government has succeeded.

I salute the working class of our country. Our movement would not be where it is without your organized strength. You are an indispensable force in the struggle to end exploitation and oppression in South Africa.

We salute the victory of SWAPO, with whom we shared trenches of battle against colonialism and apartheid. You have established your right to self-determination and your victory is our victory.

I pay tribute to the many religious communities and religious leaders who carried the struggle for justice forward, and held our banner high during the most brutal periods of repression against our people.

I salute the courage and the heroism of the youth of South Africa, organized under the South African Youth Congress. At this point I wish to pay tribute to Comrade Hector Petersen who together with hundreds of young activists were mowed down by apartheid bullets in 1976. We gained inspiration by your courage and conviction during our lonely years on the island.

Today, my return to Soweto fills my heart with joy. At the same time I also return with a deep sense of sadness. Sadness to learn that you are still suffering under an inhuman system. The housing shortage, the schools crisis, unemployment and the crime rate still remain.

I am even more proud to be a member of this community because of the pioneering role it has played in the struggle for the democratization of local government. You have built democratic structures of local government in Soweto such as street committees and civic organizations that give practical import to our desire to let the people govern.

I fully support the call made by our people for democratic systems of local government that will have a single tax base. In this regard, I believe that the campaigns for open cities must receive our active support.

As proud as I am to be part of the Soweto community, I have been greatly disturbed by the statistics of crime that I have read in the newspapers. Although I understand the deprivations

our people suffer I must make it clear that the level of crime in our township is unhealthy and must be eliminated as a matter of urgency. It is through the creation of democratic and accountable structures that we can achieve this. I salute the anti-crime campaigns conducted by our organizations.

The crisis in education that exists in South Africa demand special attention. The education crisis in black schools is a political crisis. It arises out of the fact that our people have no vote and therefore cannot make the government of the day responsive to their needs. Apartheid education is inferior and a crime against humanity.

Education is an area that needs attention of all our people, students, parents, teachers, workers and all other organized sectors of our community. Let us build disciplined structures, SRCs, a united national teachers organization, parent structures and parent-teacher-student associations and the National Education Crisis Committee.

It has been the policy of the ANC that though the school and the entire eduction system is a site of struggle, the actual process of learning must take place in the schools. I want to add my voice, therefore, to the call made at the beginning of the year that all students must return to school and learn. We must continue our struggle for people's education within the school system and utilize its resources to achieve our goals. I call on the government to build more schools, to train and employ more teachers and to abandon its policy of forcing our children out of the school system by use of various measures such as the age restrictions and their refusal to admit those who fail their classes. We have consistently called for a unitary non-racial education system that develops the potential of all youth.

As I said when I stood on the dock at the Rivonia trial 27 years ago and as I said on the day of my release in Cape Town, the ANC will pursue the armed struggle against the government as long as the violence of apartheid continues.

Our armed combatants act under the political leadership of the ANC. Cadres of our People's Army are skilled, not only in military affairs, but act as the political commissars of our movement.

We are therefore disturbed that there are certain elements amongst those who claim to support the liberation struggle who use violence against our people. The hijacking and setting alight of vehicles, and the harassment of innocent people are criminal acts that have no place in our struggle. We condemn that. Our major weapon of struggle against apartheid oppression and exploitation is our people organized into mass formations of the democratic movement. This is achieved by politically organizing our people—not through the use of violence against our people.

I call in the strongest possible way for us to act with the dignity and discipline that our just struggle for freedom deserves. Our victories must be celebrated in peace and joy. In particular I call on our people in Natal to unite against the perpetrators of violence. I call on the leadership of the UDF, COSATU and Inkatha to take decisive steps to revive the peace initiative and end the scourge on our proud history. Let us act with political foresight and develop bold steps to end this mindless violence.

Joint initiatives at local, regional and national levels between the parties concerned must call for restraint. The security forces must be compelled to act with absolute impartiality and to arrest those offenders who continue with violence.

We are disturbed that attempts are being made to disrupt the unity of the oppressed by stirring tensions between African and Indian communities of Natal. Let us build on the proud tradition of unity in action as embodied by our great hero Chief Luthuli.

I am also concerned by the ongoing violence perpetrated by certain sections of the security forces against our peaceful marches and demonstrations. We condemn this.

I understand that implementing apartheid laws has made it extremely difficult for many honest policemen to fulfill their role as servants of the public. You are seen in the eyes of many of our people as an instrument of repression and injustice.

We call on the police to abandon apartheid and to serve the interests of the people. Join our march to a new South Africa where you also have a place. We note with appreciation that there are certain areas where policemen are acting with restraint

and fulfilling the real role of protecting all our people irrespective of their race.

Much debate has been sparked off by the ANC policies on the economy rotating to nationalization and the redistribution of wealth. We believe that apartheid has created a heinous system of exploitation in which a racist minority monopolizes economic wealth while the vast majority of oppressed black people are condemned to poverty.

South Africa is a wealthy country. It is the labor of black workers that has built the cities, roads and factories we see. They cannot be excluded from sharing this wealth. The ANC is just as committed to economic growth and productivity as the present employers claim to be. Yet we are also committed to ensure that a democratic government has the resources to address the inequalities caused by apartheid.

Our people need proper housing, not ghettos like Soweto. Workers need a living wage—and the right to join unions of their own choice and to participate in determining policies that affect their lives. Our history has shown that apartheid has stifled growth, created mass unemployment and led to spiralling inflation that undermined the standards of living of the majority of our people, both black and white. Only a participatory democracy involving our people in the structures of decision making at all levels of society can ensure that this is corrected. We will certainly introduce policies that address the economic problems that we face. We call on employers to recognize the fundamental rights of workers in our country. We are marching to a new future based on strong foundations of respect for each other through bona fide negotiations.

In particular we call for genuine negotiations to achieve a fair labor relations act and mechanisms to resolve conflict. Employers can play their role in shaping the new South Africa by acknowledging these rights.

We call on workers, black and white, to join industrial trade unions organized under the banner of our non-racial progressive federation, the Congress of South African Trade Unions, which has played an indispensable role in our struggle against apartheid.

A number of obstacles to the creation of a non-racial demo-cratic South Africa remain and need to be tackled. The fears of whites about their rights and place in a South Africa they do not control exclusively, are an obstacle we must understand and address.

I stated in 1964 that I and the ANC are as opposed to black domination as we are to white domination. We must accept how-ever that our statements and declarations alone, will not be suf-ficient to allay the fears of white South Africans. We must clearly demonstrate our good will to our white compatriots and con-vince them by our conduct and arguments that a South Africa without apartheid will be a better home for all. A new South Africa has to eliminate the racial hatred and suspicion caused by apartheid and offer guarantees to all its citizens of peace, secu-rity and prosperity.

We call on those who out of ignorance have collaborated with apartheid in the past, to join our liberation struggle. No man or woman who has abandoned apartheid will be excluded from our movement towards non-racial united and democratic South Africa, based on one person one vote on a common vot-ers roll.

Our primary task remains to unite our people across the length and breadth of our country. Our democratic organizations must be consolidated in all our sectors. Democratic political practice and accountable leadership must be strengthened on all fronts. Our struggle against apartheid, though seemingly uncertain, must be intensified on all fronts. Let each one of you and all of our people give the enemies of peace and liberty no space to take us back to the dark hell of apartheid. It is only dis-ciplined mass action that assures us of the victory we seek.

Go back to your schools, factories, mines and communi-ties. Build on the massive energies that recent events in our country have unleashed by strengthening disciplined mass orga-nizations.

We are going forward. The march towards freedom and justice is irreversible. I have spoken about freedom in my life-time. Your struggles, your commitment and your discipline has released me to stand here before you today. These basic principles will propel us to a free non-racial democratic united South Africa that we have struggled and died for.

Excerpt from: Nelson Mandela, 'Mandela Speaks' *African Commentary* (Amherst, MA: African Commentary Corporation, May 1990) pp. 42-44.

38. The Future of Africa

Julius K. Nyerere

The first president of Tanzania, Julius K. Nyerere, has long been known as a forthright and forceful advocate for African independence, human equality and social responsibility. Like Kwame Nkrumah, Nyerere has developed philosophical and political ideas in an African context. In this excerpt he writes about his vision for the future of Africa.

. . . But in fact the African peoples have been shaped as much by their own past, shrouded in mist though much of it still is, as they have been by their contact with the west. Therefore, as a people to a large extent determine their own future, so it can be stated quite categorically that no part of Africa will ever become a duplicate copy of any part of Europe. An African in Africa will never become simply a black European.

Sometimes Europeans talk as if we should be ashamed of our own heritage. We are not. On the other hand sometimes they talk as if we should put aside everything which is not 'traditionally African' and live forever as though the Europeans had never come into contact with us. But this too, would demand that we deny our own history; we cannot do it. We are what all our past, known and unknown, has made us. We and our grandfathers and great grandfathers, have learned and adapted from nature, from ourselves, and from the peoples of Europe, American, and Asia. This we shall continue to do, just as men and civilizations throughout the world have always done.

In determining our future out of the lessons of our present

and past, we shall be working out a new synthesis, a way of life that draws from Europe as well as Africa, from Islam as well as Christianity, from communalism and individualism. No blueprint can be drawn up, and no one can accurately foretell how all the different pressures will reveal themselves in the Africa of the year 2000. . . .

A united Africa does not mean a uniform Africa. The events which take place during the struggle for freedom, as well as economic and other factors, will affect the policies and attitudes prevalent in any one area. This means that in South Africa, for example, the people at present in power—as well as those struggling for it—are influencing the future. But their deliberate encouragement of racialism and prejudice, and their imposition of humiliation and frustration on the African people, is poisoning this future. Because whether or not Africa ever becomes united, whether or not we manage to overcome the present poverty in our continent—both of which I believe will happen—there is one thing which is quite certain. Africa will belong to Africans. I believe that this word 'Africans' can include all those who have made their home in the continent, black, brown, or white. I think this is what the majority of the people now want. Yet it can only happen if people stand as individual citizens, asking only for rights which can be accorded to all other individuals. This means forgetting color, or race, and remembering humanity. On this basis of equality I believe Africa has a good future for all her people. But the responsibility is ours. Each one of us must play our part in the struggle for the right to regard others as our brothers and sisters.

Excerpt from: Julius K. Nyerere, *Freedom and Unity* (Dar Es Salaam: Oxford University Press, 1973) pp. 116-117.

STUDY QUESTIONS:

1. How would you describe the world-wide events that contributed to the break-up of colonialism in Africa? *WW II*

2. Who was Marcus Garvey? How did he contribute to the beginning and growth of black nationalism and African nationalism?

3. What were some of the factors in Africa that contributed both to the rise of nationalist feeling and to the resistence to colonialism at the same time?

4. What is nationalism? What were some of the stages of nationalism that led up to independence in Africa?

5. Describe efforts that have been made in Africa to establish independent nations. What efforts have been made toward regional and continent-wide groupings for economic and political cooperation?

6. What are some nationalist viewpoints embraced by Africans in their fight for freedom and independence and in their efforts towards nation-building?

7. What does Kwame Nkrumah mean by the term "Conscientism"?

8. Who coined the term "Black Consciousness"? What does it mean?

9. What conditions in South Africa does Bishop Tutu describe in the speech he gave as he received the Nobel Peace Prize? What is the appeal that he made?

10. Identify the personal qualities ascribed to Nelson Mandela in Wole Soyinka's poem, "'No!' He Said."

11. What appeal does Nelson Mandela make in his 1990 speech at Soweto after his release from jail?

12. What is Julius K. Nyerere's vision for the future of Africa?

A Select Bibliography
for further reading

Africa and the international political system. Edited by Timothy M. Shaw and 'Solo Ojo. Washington, D.C.: University Press of America, 1982. Pbk

Africa and the West: intellectual responses to European culture. Edited by Philip D. Curtin. Madison: The University of Wisconsin Press, 1972.

African art studies: the state of the discipline. Washington, D.C.: National Museum of African Art, 1990.

The African child and his environment. Edited by P. O. Ohuche and B. Otaala. London, New York: Pergamon Press, 1981.

African culture: the rhythms of unity. Edited by Malefi Kete Asante and Kariamu Welsh Asante. Westport, Conn.: Greenwood Press; Trenton: Africa World Press, 1990.

The African diaspora: interpretative essays. Edited by Martin L. Kilson and Robert I. Rotberg. Cambridge, Mass.: Harvard University Press, 1976.

The African experience. Edited by John N. Paden and Edward W. Soja. Chicago: Northwestern University Press, 1970. 3 volumes.

African History and culture. Edited by Richard Olaniyan. Essex, England: Longmans, 1982.

African historical demography: proceedings of a seminar held in the Centre of African Studies, University of Edinburgh, 1977. Edinburgh: University of Edinburgh Press, 1981. 3 volumes.

African religions. Edited by Newell S. Booth: New York: Nok Publishers International, 1977.

African society, culture and politics: an introduction to African studies. Edited by Christopher Chukwuemeka Mojekwu, Victor Uchendu, and Leo F. Van Hoey. Washington, D.C.: University Press of America, 1977. Pbk

African traditional religions in contemporary society. Edited by Jacob K. Olupona. New York: Paragon House, 1991.

The African Woman in a traditional society. Edited by Daphne William Ntiri. Troy, Mich.: Bedford Publishers, 1983.

African women and the law: historical perspectives. Edited by Margaret J. Hayard and Marcia Wright. Boston: African Studies Center, Boston University, 1982. Pbk

The Africans: a reader. Edited by Ali A. Mazrui, et al. New York: Praeger, 1986.
The Africans: study guide. Edited by Toby Kleban Levine, et al. New York: Praeger, 1986.

Afro-American history: primary source. Edited by Thomas R. Frazier. Belmont, California: The Dorsey Press, 1988.

Alexandre, Pierre. *Languages and language in black Africa.* Evanston, Ill.: Northwestern University Press, 1972.

Ajaye, J.F.A., and E.A. Ayandele. "Emerging themes in Nigerian and West African religious history." *Journal of African Studies,* v. 1, no. 1 (1974): 1-39.

Akintoye, S.A. *Emergent African states: topics in twentieth century African history.* London: Longman, 1976.

Asante, Malefi Kete. *Afrocentricity.* Trenton: Africa World Press, 1989.

Baines, John and Jaromir Malek. *Atlas of Ancient Egypt.* New York: Facts on File Publications, 1986.

Bates, Robert H. *Essays on the political economy of rural Africa.* Cambridge, New York: Cambridge University Press, 1983.

Bates, Robert H. *Ethnicity in contemporary Africa.* Syracuse, N.Y.: Program of Eastern African Studies, Syracuse University, 1973. (East African studies, 14).

Biko, Steve. *I Write What I like.* San Francisco: Harper & Row, 1986.

Bennett, Norman R. *Africa and Europe.* New York: Africana, 1984.

Bohanen, Paul and Philip D. Curtin. *Africa and Africans.* Prospect Heights, Illinois: Waveland Press, 1988.

Cambridge history of Africa. Edited by John D. Fage and Roland Oliver. Cambridge, New York: Cambridge University Press, 1975 + 1986. 8 volumes.

Problems in African history. Edited by Robert W. Collins. Englewood Cliffs, N.J.: Prentice- Hall, 1968.

Chazan, Naomi, et al. *Politics and society in contemporary Africa.* Boulder: L. Rienner, 1992 second edition.

Philip Curtin, Steven Feierman, Leonard Thompson and Jan Vansina. *African history.* Boston: Little, Brown, 1978.

Curtin, Philip. *The Atlantic slave trade: a census.* Madison, Wisc.: University of Wisconsin Press, 1969. Pbk
Davidson, Basil. *The black man's burden: Africa and the curse of the nation state.* New York: Times Books, 1992.

Davidson, Basil. *Discovering Africa's past.* London, New York: Longman, 1978.

Davidson, Basil. *Let freedom come: Africa in modern history.* New York: Atlantic Monthly Press, 1978. Pbk

Davidson, Basil. *Modern Africa: a social and political history.* New York: Longman, 1989, second edition.

Davidson, Basil. "Slavery and the slave trade in the contest of African history." *Journal of African History* (10: 393-303), 1969.

Denyer, Susan. *African traditional architecture: an historical and geographical perspective.* New York: Africana Publishing Co., 1948. Pbk

Diop, Cheikh Anto. *Black Africa: economic and cultural basis for a federated state.* Westport, Connecticut: Lawrence Hill and Co.; Trenton, New Jersey: Africa World Press, joint publishers, 1987.

Diop, Chiekh Anto. *Civilization or Barbarism: an authentic anthropology.* Westport, Connecticut: Lawrence Hill, 1991.

Diop, Cheikh Anto. *The cultural unity of black Africa: the domains of patriarchy and the - matriarchy in classical antiquity.* Chicago: The Third World Press, 1987.

Diop, Chiekh Anta. *Precolonial black Africa: a comparative study of the political and social systems of Europe and black Africa, from antiquity to the formation of modern states.* Westport, Connecticut: Lawrence Hill, Trenton, New Jersey: Africa World Press, joint publishers, 1987.

Dreuvel, Henry, and Margaret Dreuvel. *Gelede masks: art and female power among the Yoruba.* Bloomington: Indiana University Press, 1983.

Esedebe, P. Olisinwuche, *Pan-Africanism; the idea and the movement, 1776-1963.* Washington, D.C: Howard University Press, 1982. Pbk

Ethnicity in modern Africa. Edited by Brian M. du Toit. Boulder, Colo.: Westview Press, 1978.

Fanon, Franz. *A dying colonialism.* New York: Grove Press, 1967. Pbk

Fagg, William and Margaret Plass. *African sculpture.* New York: E.D. Dutton, 1964.

Fortes, Meyer, and E. E. Evans-Pritchard, Eds. *African Political systems.* London: Oxford University Press, for the International African Institute, 1940. Pbk

Franklin, John Hope, and Alfred A. Moss, Jr. *From slavery to freedom: a history of negro Americans*. New York: Alfred Knopf, 1988, 6th edition.

Freed, Rita E. *Ramses II: the great pharaoh and his time*. Memphis, Tennessee: printed by Lithograph Printing Company, published by City of Memphis, 1987.

Gailey, Harry A. *History of Africa from earliest times to 1800*. New York: Holt, Rinehart and Winston, 1970.

Colonialism in Africa, 1870-1960, Edited by Lewis H. Gann and Peter Duignam. London: Cambridge University Press. 1969-1975. 5 volumes.

General history of Africa. UNESCO International Scientific Committee for the Drafting of a General History of Africa. Edited by G. Mokhtar. London: Heinemann; Berkeley: University of California Press, 1980-1990. 8 volumes. (1 & 2 published)

Global Dimensions of the African Diaspora. Edited by Joseph E. Harris. Washington, D.C.: Howard University. 1982.

Gluckman, Max. *Order and rebellion in tribal Africa*. New York: Free Press, 1963.

Greenberg, Joseph H. *The languages of Africa*. 3rd ed. Bloomington: Indiana University Research Center for Language Sciences, 1970. Pbk

Hallett, Robin. *Africa since 1875: a modern history*. Ann Arbor: University of Michigan Press, 1970.

Hallett, Robin. *Africa to 1875: a modern history*. Ann Arbor: University of Michigan Press, 1970.

Hance, William A., ed. *Population, migration and urbanization in Africa*. New York: Columbia University Press, 1970.

Harris, Joseph E. *Africans and their history*. New York: New American Library, 1972.

Hastings, Adrian. *A history of African Christianity, 1950-1975.* Cambridge, New York: Cambridge University Press, 1979. Pbk

Hiernaux, Jean. *The peoples of Africa.* New York: Scribner, 1975. Pbk

The historical study of African religion. Edited by T. O. Ranger and I. M. Kimambo. Berkeley: University of California Press, 1976.

Hontoundji, Pauline J. *African philosophy: myth and reality.* Introduction by Abiola Irele. Bloomington: Indiana University Press, 1983.

Hyden, Goran and Michael Bratton. *Governance and politics in Africa.* Boulder: L. Rienner, 1992.

Jackson, John G. *Introduction to African civilizations.* Secaucus, New Jersey: The Citadel Press, 1970.

The horizon history of Africa. Edited by Alvin M. Josephy, Jr. New York: American Heritage, 1971.

July, Robert. *A history of the African people.* Prospect Heights, Ill: Waveland Press, 1992. 4th edition.

Kenyatta, Jomo. *Facing Mount Kenya: the tribal life of the Gikuyu.* London: Secker and Warburg, 1962.

King, Noel Q. *African cosmos: an introduction to religion in Africa.* Belmont: Wadsworth, 1986.

Kpedekpo, G. M. K., and P. L. Aryd, *Social and economic indicators for Africa: their sources, collection, uses and reliability.* London, Boston: Allen & Unwin, 1981. Pbk

Lawson, E. Thomas. *Religions of Africa: traditions in transformation.* San Francisco, New York: Harper and Row, 1984.

African proverbs. Compiled by Charlotte Wolf and Leslav Wolf. Mt. Vernon, N.Y.: Peter Pauper Press, 1962.

Leuzinger, Elsy. *Africa: the art of the negro peoples.* London: Mathuen, 1960.

Lovejoy, Paul E. *Transformations in slavery: a history of slavery in Africa*. Cambridge, New York: Cambridge University Press, 1983. Pbk

The African world: a survey of social research. Edited by Robert A. Lystad. New York: Praeger, 1963.

Mbiti, John S. *African religions and philosophy*. New York: Praeger, 1969.

McCall, Daniel F. *Africa in time perspective: a discussion of historical reconstruction from unwritten sources*. London: Oxford University Press, 1969.

Marguet, Jacques. *Africanity: the cultural unity of black Africa*. New York, London: Oxford University Press, 1972.

Marguet, Jacques. *Civilizations of black Africa*. New York: Oxford University Press, 1972. Pbk

Mair, Lucy. *African societies*. New York: Cambridge University Press, 1972. Pbk

Mair, Lucy. *Primitive government*. Rev. ed. Bloomington: Indiana University Press, 1978. Pbk

The making of modern Africa. Edited by A. E. Afigbo, et al. Essex, England: Longman, 1986. 2 volumes.

No easy walk to freedom: articles and speeches and trial addresses of Nelson Mandela. Edited by Ruth Furst. Exeter, New Hampshire: Heinemann Educational, 1973. Pbk

Mannix, Daniel P., and Malcolm Cowley. *Black cargoes: a history of the Atlantic slave trade, 1518-1865*. New York: Viking Press, 1965.

Markets in Africa. Edited by Paul Bohannan and George Dalton. Evanston, Ill.: Northwestern University Press, 1962. Pbk: Garden City, N.Y.: Doubleday Anchor, 1965.

Mattaso, Katia M. *To be a slave in Brazil*. New Brunswick: Rutgers University Press, 1986.

Mazrui, Ali A. *The Africans: a triple heritage*. Boston, Toronto: Little Brown, 1986.

Mazrui, Ali A. *Africa's international relations: the diplomacy of dependency and change*. Boulder, Colo.: Westview Press, 1979.

Mitchell, Brian R., *International historical statistics: Africa and Asia*. New York: New York University Press, 1982.

Mphalele, Ezekiel. *The African Image*. New York: Praeger, 1974. Pbk

Murdock, George P. *Africa: its peoples and their culture history*. New York: McGraw Hill, 1959.

Namibia - the last colony. Edited by Reginald Green, Marja - Luisa Kiljunen and Kimmo Kiljunen. London, New York: Longman, 1982.

New religions of Africa. Edited by Benedetta Jules-Rosette. Norwood, N.J.: Ablex Publishing Corp., 1979.

Ngugi wa Thiong'o. *Decolonizing the mind: the politics of language in African culture*. Portsmouth N.H.: Heinemann, 1987.

Niane, D. T. *Sundiata: an epic of Old Mali*. Atlantic Highlands, N.J.: Humanities Press, 1963.

Nketia, J. H. Kwabena. *The music of Africa*. New York: Norton, 1974. Pbk

Nkasi, Lewis. *Tasks and masks: themes and styles in African literature*. London, New York: Longman, 1982.

Nkrumah, Kwame. *Consciencism*. New York: Monthly Review Foundation, 1970.

Nyerere, Julius K. *Freedom and development: a selection from writings and speeches, 1968- 1973.* London, New York: Oxford University Press, 1974.

Freedom and socialism: a selection from writings and speeches, 1965- 1967. London, New York: Oxford University Press, 1968.

Freedom and unity: selections from writings and speeches, 1952-65. London, New York: Oxford University Press.

Obbo, Christine. *African women: their struggle for economic independence.* London: Zed Press, 1980. Distributed by Biblio, Totowa, N.J.

O'Conner, Anthony M. *The African City.* New York: African Publishing Co., 1983. Pbk

Okigbo, Christopher. *Labyrinths.* New York: Holmes and Meier, 1971.

Okpewho, Isidore. *Myth in Africa: a study of its aesthetics and cultural relevance.* Cambridge, New York: Cambridge University press, 1983.

Oliver, Roland. *The African experience.* London: Weidenfeld & Nicolsen, 1991.

Oliver, Roland and J. D. Fage. *A short history of Africa.* Baltimore: Penguin Books, 1962.

Omari, Cuthbert K. *Strategy for rural development: the Tanzania experience.* Nairobi, Dar es Salaam: East African Literature Bureau, 1976.

Oppong, Christine. *Middle class African marriage.* London, Boston: Allen and Unwin, 1983. Bpk

Owsinde, S. H., and C. M. Ejiogu, eds. *Population growth and economic development in Africa.* London: Heinemann, in association with the Population Council, 1972.

Packenham, Thomas. *The scramble for Africa, 1876-1912*. New York: Random House, 1991.

Parrinder, Geoffrey. *Religion in Africa*. Baltimore: Penguin Books, 1969.

Peil, Margaret. *Consensus and conflict in African societies: an introduction to sociology*. London, New York: Longman, 1977. Pbk

Peil, Margaret, Peter K. Mitchell, and Douglas Rimmer. *Social science research methods: an African handbook*. London: Hodder and Stoughton, 1982.

Peoples of Africa. Edited by James L. Gibbs, Jr. abrdg. ed. New York: Irrington Pub., 1983. Pbk

Persistent principles amidst crisis. Edited by Cuthbert K. Omari. Nawabi, Uzima Press, 1989.

Pluralism in Africa. Edited by Leo Kuper and M. G. Smith. Berkeley: University of California Press, 1969. Pbk

The political economy of contemporary Africa. Edited by Peter C. W. Autkind and Immanuel Wallerstein. Beverly Hills: Sage Publications, 1976.

The politics of Africa: dependence and development. Edited by Timothy M. Shaw and Kenneth A Heard. New York: Africana Publishing Co., 1979. Pbk

Pothalm, Christian P. *The theory and practice of African politics*. Englewood Cliffs, N.J.: Prentice Hall, 1979. Pbk

Pratt, Cranford. *The critical phase in Tanzania, 1945-1968: Nyerere and the emergence of a socialist strategy*. New York: Oxford University Press, 1976.

Ray, Benjamin C. *African Religions: Symbol, Ritual and Community*. Englewood Cliffs: Prentice-Hall, 1976.

Redistribution of population in Africa. Edited by John I. Oovke and Leszek A. Kasinski, London: Heinemann, 1982.

Rhoades, John. *Linguistic diversity and language belief in Kenya: the special position of Swahili.* Syracuse, N.Y.: Maxwell School of Citizenship and Foreign Affairs, Syracuse University, 1977.

Robinson, David, and Douglas Smith. *Sources of the African past.* New York: Africana Publishing Co., 1979. Pbk

Rodney, Walter. "African slavery and other forms of social oppression on the Upper Guinea Coast in the context of the Atlantic slave trade." *Journal of African History* (7: 431-41), 1966.

How Europe underdeveloped Africa. London: Bogle-L'Ouverture Publications; Dar es Salaam: Tanzania Publishing House, 1980.

Rosberg, Carl, and Robert J. Jackson. *Personal rule in black Africa.* Berkeley: University of California Press, 1982.

Rich, Evelyn Jones and Immanuel Wallenstein. *Africa tradition and change.* New York: Random House, 1972.

Schneider, Harold K. *The Africans: an ethnographical account.* Englewood Cliffs, N.J.: Prentice Hall, 1981. Pbk

Schneider, Harold K. *Livestock and quality in East Africa: the economic basis for social structure.* Bloomington: Indiana University Press, 1980.

Senghor, Leopold. *Selected poems.* New York: Holmes and Meier, 1964.

Shorter, Aylewood. *East African societies.* London, Boston: Rautledge & Kegan Paul, 1974. Pbk

Slavery in Africa: historical and anthropological perspectives. Edited by Suzanne Miers and Igor Kopytoff. Madison: University of Wisconsin Press, 1977.

Social stratification in Africa. Edited by Arthur Tuden and Leonard Plotnicov. New York: Free Press, 1970.

Sow, Alpha I., et al. *Introduction to African culture, general aspects.* Paris, UNESCO, 1980. Pbk

Soyenke, Wole. *Mandela's Earth and other poems.* New York: Random House, 1988.

Spear, Thomas. *Kenya's past: an introduction to historical method in Africa.* London, New York: Longman, 1982. Pbl

State versus ethnic claim: African policy dilemmas. Edited by Donald Rothchild and Victor A. Olorunsola. Boulder, Colo.: Westview Press, 1982. Pbk

Sheridan, Richard B. "Africa and the Caribbean in the Atlantic slave trade." *American Historical Review* (77: 15-35), 1972.

Stamp, Laurence D. *Africa: a study in tropical development.* New York: Wiley Press, 1953.

Study Commission on U.S. Policy Toward Southern Africa. *South Africa: timing running out.* Berkeley and Los Angeles: University of California Press, 1981.

Taylor, John H. *Egypt and Nubia.* Hong Kong: The Trustees of the British Museum, 1991.

Taylor, John Vernon. *The primal vision: Christian presence amid African religion.* London: Harlow, 1968.
Theatre in Africa. Oyen Ogunba and Abida Irele, eds. Ibadan, Nigeria: Ibaden University Press, 1978.

Toward socialism in Tanzania. Edited by Bismarck U. Mwansasu and Cranford Pratt. Toronto, Buffalo: University of Toronto Press, 1981.

Traone, Bakary. *The black African theatre and its social functions.* Ibaden, Nigeria: Ibaden University Press, 1972.

Trimingham, J. Spencer. *A history of Islam in West Africa*. New York: Oxford University Press, 1962.

The influence of Islam upon Africa, London: Harlow, 1968.

Turner, Victor. *The forest of symbols: aspects of Ndembu ritual*. Ithaca: Cornell University Press, 1967.

Van Sertima, Ivan. *They came before Columbus: the African presence in ancient America*. New York: Random House, 1976.

Vansina, Jan. *Art history in Africa: an introduction to method*. London, New York: Longman, 1984.

Kingdoms of the Savanna. Madison: University of Wisconsin Press, 1966. Pbk

The oral tradition. Chicago: Aldine, 1954. Pbk: Harmondsworth: Penguin.

Wallerstein, Immanuel. *Africa: the politics of independence*. New York: Vintage, 1961. Pbk

Webster, J. B. *et al. The revolutionary years: West Africa since* 1800. London: Longman, 1980.

Willett, Frank. *African art: an introduction*. New York: Oxford University Press, 1971.

Williams, Chancellor. *The destruction of black civilization*. Chicago, Ill.: Third World Press.

Women and work in Africa. Edited by Edna Boy. Boulder, Colo.: Westview Press, 1982.

Woodson, Carter G. *The African background outlined*. Washington, D.C.: Association for the Study of Negro Life and History, 1936.

Wright, Richard A. *African philosophy: an introduction*. 2nd ed. Washington, D.C.: University Press of America, 1979. Pbk

Young, Crawford. *Ideology and development in Africa*. New Haven, Conn.: Yale University Press, 1982. Pbk

Wright, Stephen and Janice Brownfoot. *Africa in world politics: changing perspectives*. Basingstoke: Macmillan, 1987.

Understanding contemporary Africa. Edited by April Gordon and Donald L. Gordon. Boulder: L Rienner, 1992.

Young, Crawford. *Ideology and development in Africa*. New Haven: Yale University Press, 1992.

Young, Crawford. *The politics of cultural pluralism*. Madison, London: University of Wisconsin Press, 1976. Pbk

Zahan, Dominique. *The religion, spirituality and thought of traditional Africa*. Chicago, The University of Chicago Press, 1979.

INDEX

Hausa of Nigeria, 181, 183-184
Hebrew, 12
Hebrews, 47
Hegelian, 292
Herodotus, 35, 74
Hilal, Banu, 29
Hill, Barkal, 60
Hodgkin, Thomas, 281
Holy City of Napata, 48, 59, 62
Holy of Holies, 58
Hong Kong, 328
Horn of Africa, 24, 36, 74
Hottentot, 92
Houphouet-Boigny, Felix, 274
Houses of Assemblies, 250

Ibo, 93
Idiophones, 179-180, 182
Igbo of Nigeria, 169, 181
Igede of Benue State, 182
Ihlambo, 157-158
Ikenga, 161, 170-171
Ikoli, Ernest, 273
Indian Ocean, 5, 39, 55, 63, 75, 77, 94, 96-97, 99
Indonesia, 94
Initiation, 14, 131, 133, 136, 147, 189
Inkatha, 308
Inkosi, 139, 141, 143, 145, 147, 149, 151, 153, 155, 157, 159
Inner Africa, 34, 45
International African Institute, 320
Ishak, Abu, 86
Islam, 28, 40-41, 45, 74, 78, 83-84, 88, 90-91, 285, 314, 329; Islamic, 257, 280, 285; Islamic Africa, 285; Islamic Euro-Christian, 257; Islamization, 54
Isthmus of Suez, 4

Italian Somaliland, 261
Italy, 28, 260-261, 279, 281; Italian, 203, 260-261, 279
Ivory Coast, 274
Ivory, 28, 36, 56, 64, 75-77, 83, 93, 166, 169, 171, 274

Jackson, John Payne, 275
Jacques-Garvey, Amy, 267
Jallon, Futa, 23
Jesus, 54, 67, 266-267
Jews, 67
Johannesburg, 296
Jordan Valley, 5
Jose, Manoe, 233
Josephy, Alvin M., 322

Kagame, A., 18
Kalihari Desert, 95
Kamba, 77
Kamose, 47
Karamoja of Uganda, 182
Keita, Baramendana, 84
Kente of Ghana, 174
Kenya, 3, 74, 119, 131, 134, 174, 176, 201, 269, 274, 280, 322, 327-328; Kenya African National Union, 274; Kenyan, 24
Kenyatta, Jomo, 119, 131-132, 134, 274, 322
Kiluanji, Aidi, 108
Klein, Herbert, 221-222
Kongo, 93, 106-107, 111-112; Kongo, King of, 107; Kongolese, 111-112
Konjo of Uganda, 182
Koran, 89
Koyate, 197
Kpedekpo, 322
Krio of Sierra Leone, 176
KTC, 299-300